Modern Chinese

A SECOND COURSE

by the Faculty of

PEKING UNIVERSITY

With English Translations of the Illustrative Sentences and Texts
by Members of the
Department of East Asian Languages and Civilizations,
Harvard University

D0972925

Dover Publications, Inc.
New York

TRANSLATORS' NOTE

The English translation of the illustrative sentences for grammar and texts of this book has been distributed for several years as part of the classroom notes at Harvard University under the title "English Counterpart of *Modern Chinese Reader.*" It is now published with the hope that others will also find it helpful while using *Modern Chinese Reader* [*Modern Chinese: A Second Course*] as a textbook.

We have consistently attempted to make the English version as close as possible to the Chinese in meaning without resorting to unnatural English or overtranslation. In this respect, we earnestly welcome comments from users of this book.

SHOU-YING LIN   HWEI LI CHANG
LI-CHING MAIR   AI-LING CHEN
MICHAEL MAO   DORI DOMINIS

Published in Canada by General Publishing Company, Ltd., 30 Lesmill Road, Don Mills, Toronto, Ontario.

Published in the United Kingdom by Constable and Company, Ltd.

This Dover edition, first published in 1981, is a revised republication of Lessons 31 through 72, together with all the Appendixes, from the second, 1963, edition of *Modern Chinese Reader*, originally published by the "Epoch" Publishing House, Peking (first edition: 1958). The Publisher's Note and Translators' Note give further bibliographic details.

International Standard Book Number: 0-486-24155-6
Library of Congress Catalog Card Number: 80-70188

Manufactured in the United States of America
Dover Publications, Inc.
180 Varick Street
New York, N.Y. 10014

PUBLISHER'S NOTE

This book contains Lessons 31–72 and the Appendixes of *Modern Chinese Reader* (second edition, Peking, 1963), which was compiled by the instructors of the Chinese Language Special Course for Foreign Students in Peking University. Despite the original title, the book is a grammar, not a reader. It originally appeared in two volumes with a total of 72 lessons and several appendixes. In 1971 Dover published the Introduction and Lessons 1–30 with the title *Modern Chinese: A Basic Course* (ISBN 0-486-22755-3; that first volume also available in a set with three 12-inch long-playing records, ISBN 0-486-98832-5).

In the original edition, no translations were provided for any of the illustrative grammar sentences or exercise sentences ("Texts") from Lesson 13 on. All these sentences will be found translated in the present edition; the Publisher is grateful to the Harvard faculty members who permitted the use of their translation (see the Translators' Note that follows).* On the other hand, the original edition repeated all the phonetic and grammatical rules — that is, all the basic text — in Chinese, paragraph by paragraph (for the use of teachers in China). In this edition the Chinese version of this material has been omitted and only the English version is given.

The transcription system used in this book is the official pin yin of Mainland China. For those readers who are acquainted with one or both of the two most important earlier transcription systems, Yale and Wade, a comparative table has been provided.

---

*The Publisher also wishes to thank Ms. Jill Cheng of the Cheng & Tsui Co. in Boston for facilitating the use of the Harvard translation and otherwise encouraging the publication of the present volume.

COMPARATIVE TABLE OF TRANSCRIPTIONS
OF CHINESE SOUNDS

Peking (this book)	Yale	Wade
a	a	a
ai	ai	ai
ao	au	ao
b	b	p
c	ts	ts', tz'
ch	ch	ch'
d	d	t
e	e, ee	e, ê, eh
ei	ei	ei
er	er	êrh
f	f	f
g	g	k
h	h	h
i, yi	i, r, y, yi, z	i, ih, ŭ
ia, ya	ya	ia, ya
iao, yao	yau	iao, yao
ie, ye	ye	ie, ieh, ye
iou, iu, you	you	iu, yu
j	j	ch
k	k	k'
l	l	l
m	m	m
n	n	n
ng	ng	ng
o	o	o
ong	ung	ung
ʻou	ou	ou
p	p	p'
q	ch	ch'
r	r	j
s	s	s, ss
sh	sh	sh
t	t	t'
u	u	u
ü	yu, yw	ü
ua, wa	wa	ua, wa
uai, wai	wai	uai, wai
ue	we	wê
üe, yue	ywe	üe, üeh
uei, ui, wei	wei	uei, ui, wei
uo, wo	wo	uo, wo, o
x	sy	hs
z	dz	ts, tz
zh	j	ch

Contents

vi Contents

Lesson 31

生詞 Shēngcí New Words

1.	因为...所以...		yīnwèi... suǒyǐ...	because (owing to).. therefore (so).
2.	要是...就...		yàoshi...jiù...	if, (then)
3.	件	(量)	jiàn	(a measure word)
4.	事(情)	(名)	shì (qíng) [件]	matter, business
5.	虽然...但是...		suírán... dànshì...	although...(yet)..
6.	岁	(量)	suì	year (age)
7.	或者	(連)	huòzhě	or
8.	点兒	(量)	diǎnr	bit (a measure word)
9.	書店	(名)	shūdiàn	bookstore
10.	这么	(代)	zènmǒ	such, so
11.	为什么		wèishénmǒ	for what, why
12.	專业	(名)	zhuānyè	special field
13.	难	(形)	nán	difficult
14.	怎么	(代)	zěnmǒ	how
15.	玩兒	(动)	wánr	to play, to amuse one-self
16.	晚上	(名)	wǎnshǎng	night, evening

語法 Yǔfǎ Grammar

31.1 The Composite Sentence   In Chinese, there are many

kinds of composite sentences and the relations between the clauses are also of various kinds. Here in this lesson three common kinds will be introduced as follows:—

(1) 因为 … 所以 … expresses cause and effect. e. g.

1. 因为 那本 字典 太 旧, 所以 我 没 有 买.

    Because that dictionary was too old, I did not buy it.

Sometimes, we may omit 因为 or 所以. If the meaning of the context is clear enough, both 因为 and 所以 may be omitted. e. g.

2. 那本 字典 太 旧, 我 没 有 买.

    That dictionary was too old; I did not buy it.

(2) 要是… 就 … expresses a condition. e. g.

3. 要是 你 不 告诉 我 这件 事(情), 我 就 不 知道.

    If you had not told me about this matter, I would not have known.

要是 may be placed either before or after the subject in the first clause, but the word 就 must be placed before the predicate in the second clause. In general, 要是 may be omitted but 就 is always used. e. g.

4. 你 不 告诉 我 这件 事(情), 我 就 不 知道.

    If you had not told me about this matter, I would not have known.

If there is an adverbial modifier in the second clause, 就 may be omitted too. e. g.

5. (要是) 你 不 告訴 我 这件
事(情), 我 一定 不 知道.

If you had not told me about this matter, I definitely
would not have known about it.

(3) 虽然 … 但是 … shows an adversative or antithesis.

e. g.

6. 他 虽然 不 是 北京 人, 但是
北京 話 說得 很 好.

Although he is not a native of Peking, he speaks the Peking
dialect very well.

In such a sentence 虽然 is often omitted but 但是 is not.

31.2 The Substantive Sentence without Copula   We have
learned that in a sentence with a substantive predicate, the
predicate is composed of a copula and a substantive. Here, in
this lesson, we shall learn a special form of this kind of sentence in which the copula is not used. In the spoken language,
simple and short sentences take this special form. Here, we
will introduce the two most common types:

(1) When the predicate expresses time or place of birth.

e. g.

7. 今天 星期几?

What day is today?

8. 今天 星期一.

Today is Monday.

9. 你 哪兒(的) 人?

Where are you from?

10. 我 北京 人.

I'm from Peking.

(2) When the predicate contains a numeral or numerals. e. g.

11. 你　二十几岁?

How old are you? Twenty-...?

12. 我　二十二岁.

I'm twenty-two.

Note: All the examples given above are affirmative sentences, and the copula can be omitted. But in the negative sentences the copula 是 has to be used. e. g.

13. 今天　星期三,　不 是　星期四.

Today is Wednesday, not Thursday.

14. 他　十八岁,　不 是　二十岁.

He's eighteen, not twenty.

31.3 一点兒 and 有一点兒　点兒 (a bit) is a measure word showing an indefinite small quantity. The meaning of 一点兒 is similar to that of 一些. In the spoken language, we prefer to use 点兒. e. g.

15. 我　想　买　一点兒　紙.

I would like to buy some paper.

The above sentence is used more habitually than 我想买一些紙. 一点兒 is composed of a numeral and a measure word. In Chinese, if the numeral before the measure word is 一, except when it is at the beginning of a sentence, it is often omitted. e. g.

16. 我　想　买　点兒　紙.

I would like to buy some paper.

有(一)点兒 is a verb-object construction. In the spoken language, it is always used as an adverbial modifier to modify an adjective or a verb. e. g.

17. 他 今天 有 一点兒 不 高兴.

He is a little unhappy today.

18. 虽然 他 有 一点兒 想 进 城,
但是 很 忙, 不 能 去.

Although he rather wants to go into town, he is very busy and cannot go.

In example 17, 有一点兒 is used to modify the adjective 高兴, while in example 18 it is used to modify the verb 想.

31.4 或者 and 还是   These two conjunctions are different in use:

(1) 还是 is used in the interrogative sentence, while 或者 is used in the declarative sentence. e. g.

19. 您 要 借 鋼笔 还是 鉛笔?

Do you want to borrow a pen or a pencil?

20. 鋼笔 或者 鉛笔 都 可以.

Either a pen or a pencil will do.

Note: When 或者 is used to join the compound subject or the inverted objects, we must use the adverb 都 before the predicate.

(2) 还是 sometimes can also be used in a declarative sentence indicating uncertainty. e. g.

21. 他 去 圖書館 了 还是 去 書店 了?

Did he go to the library or to the bookstore?

22. 我 也 不 知道 他 去 圖書館
了, 还是 去 書店 了.

I don't know either whether he went to the library or to the bookstore.

In this case, example 22 may be briefly expressed as 我也不知道.

課文   Kèwén   Text

(a₁) 今天 星期几?

What day is today?

(b₁) 今天 星期五.

It's Friday.

(a₂) 你們 今天 上 四节 課 还是 上 三节 課?

Do you have four or three classes today?

(b₂) 我們 今天 上 四节 課.

We have four classes today.

(a₃) 你們 星期六 也 上 四节 課 嗎?

Do you have four classes on Saturdays too?

(b₃) 我們 星期六 也 上 四节 課.

We have four classes on Saturdays too.

(a₄) 你們 上 这么 多 課, 不 觉得 太 忙 嗎?

You have so many classes. Don't you feel too busy?

(b₄) 虽然 有 一点兒 忙, 但是 沒 关系.

Although we are a bit busy, it's all right.

(a₅) 为 什么?

Why?

(b₅) 要是 現在 不 上 这么 多 課、
不 快快兒地 学，我們 就 学得
太 少. 要是 中文 学得 太少，
以后 学 專业 的 时候兒，就 会
觉得 很 难. 所以 我們 現在 都
很 努力.

If we don't have so many classes now and don't learn
quickly, we will learn too little. If we learn too little
Chinese, then later on, when we specialize, we will feel it
is quite difficult. So we are all very diligent now.

(a₆) 星期日 你們 怎么 玩兒?

How do you amuse yourself on Sundays?

(b₆) 星期日 我們 常常 在 学校 看
电影，或者 进 城.

Sundays we often watch movies at school, or go into town.

(a₇) 这个 星期日，你 要 作 什么?

What do you want to do this Sunday?

(b₇) 我 想 进 城. 我 要 买 点兒
东西. 晚上 还 想 复习 語法.

I'd like to go into town. I want to do some shopping; in the
evening I'd like to review grammar.

課外練習 Kèwài liànxí Home Work

1) Copy the following sentences and fill the blanks with
the correct words given in the parentheses:

(1) 这个 同志 二十岁＿＿＿＿二十一岁?

我 也 不 知道 他 二十岁＿＿＿＿＿
二十一岁. ("还是" "或者")

(2) 因为 这个 问题＿＿＿＿难, 所以
他 回答得 不 好.
("一点兒" "有一点兒")

(3) 因为 他 説 話 説得＿＿＿＿快,
我 只 懂了＿＿＿＿.
("一点兒" "有一点兒")

(4) 我們 今天 晚上＿＿＿＿明天 晚上
一起 玩兒?
今天 晚上＿＿＿＿明天 晚上 都
可以. ("或者" "还是")

2) Make sentences with each of the following compound conjunctions:

(5) 因为... 所以...

(6) 虽然... 但是...

(7) 要是... 就...

汉字表 Hànzì biǎo Chinese Characters

1	因	冂 冈 因
2	为	ノ 为 为
3	所	户 (ノ ｲ 尸 户)
		斤
4	件	ｲ
		牛 (ノ 亠 牛)
5	事	一 口 马 马 事 事

6	情	忄
		青
7	虽	口
		虫 (口 中 虫 虫)
8	然	夕 (夕 夕)
		大 (大 犬)
		灬
9	但	亻
		旦 (旦 旦)
10	岁	山 (丨 屮 山)
		夕
11	或	一 口 匚 或 或 或
12	者	
13	店	
14	專	叀 (一 百 亩 重 叀)
		寸
15	业	丶 刂 刂刂 业 业
16	难	又
		隹
17	玩	王
		元 (二 元)

Lesson 32

生詞 Shēngcí New Words

1.	完	(动) wán	to finish
2.	着	(动) zháo	to catch, to touch, (always used as a complement)
3.	找	(动) zhǎo	to find, to seek, to look for
4.	見	(动) jiàn	to see
5.	看見	(动) kànjiàn	to see
6.	毛澤东	(名) Máozédōng	Mao Tse-tung
7.	主席	(名) zhǔxí	chairman
8.	听見	(动) tīngjiàn	to hear
9.	汉俄	hàn-è	Chinese-Russian
10.	卖	(动) mài	to sell

語法 Yǔfǎ Grammar

32.1 **The Resultative Complement** The resultative complement is used after a verb to denote the result of an action. The resultative complement may be either a verb or an adjective. e. g.

1. 他 已經 作完了 練習 了.

He has already finished the exercises.

2. 我 要 学好 中文.

I want to learn Chinese well.

In example 1 作 is a verb, and it is followed by another verb 完 as the resultative complement. In example 2 学 is a verb, and it is followed by an adjective 好 as the resultative complement.

There are two points to be noticed in using the resultative complement:

(1) In Chinese, any adjective or verb can be used as a resultative complement so long as the combination or a verb and its complement has some logical meaning. That is to say, this kind of verb-complement construction is often rather loose.

(2) But once this construction is formd, the verb and its complement become a very close unit. The complement can be put immediately after the verb without any structural particle. When there is a suffix or an object after the verb, all these elements have to be put after the verb and its complement; one must never split the verb-complement construction. This is different from the complement of degree. It is because such constructions are so closely bound that we have so many verb-complement constructions (such as 打倒 (to overthrow), 說明 (to explain) etc.) already accepted as compound verbs in common use. Such compound verbs are still increasing.

32.2 The Negative Form of the Verb Carrying Its Resultative Complement As we know, 没有 is used to negate a completed action (27.3). This rule is also applicable to the verb with a resultative complement. The reason is that when an action has already borne a certain result, it is generally completed. e. g.

3. 我 没 有 看懂 这个 問題, 所以 回答 得 不 对.

I did not understand this question, so I answered incorrectly.

4. 要是 没 有 听清楚 先生的 話, 我 就 問.

If I have not heard clearly what the teacher says, I will ask.

But, if an action denotes condition or will, we have to use 不 in the negative form (30.3). e. g.

5. 不 看懂 問題, 就 不 能 回答.

If you don't understand the question, you can't answer.

6. 你 不 寫清楚, 我們 怎么 看?

If you don't write legibly, how are we going to read (it)?

32.3 "着" Used as Resultative Complement As mentioned above, almost any adjective or verb can be used as a resultative complement, but some verbs are frequently used as resultative complements. Here, we shall introduce some of the most commonly used.

着 is a verb, but it is rarely used as predicate, and often used as resultative complement. As a complement it implies an action that has attained its expected aim or result. So it has the meaning of "attaining" or "reaching". e. g.

7. 我 借着了 一本 很好的 字典.

I borrowed (succeeded in borrowing) a very good dictionary.

8. 那枝 白 鋼笔 我 沒 有 找着.

I did not find (having tried) that old fountain pen.

借着 and 借 are different from each other in meaning, because 借 is a verb meaning "to lend or to borrow", while 借着 means that something has already been lent or borrowed. 找 and 找着 are also not the same; 找 is a verb meaning "to look for", while 找着 means "one has already got the thing one wants to find".

32.4 見 Used as Resultative Complement 見 is a verb. It is not only used as predicate, but also as resultative complement. It is often used as resultative complement to verbs expressing sensuous perception, such as: 听 and 看 etc.

看 is simply "to see", but whether the thing or object is seen or not is uncertain, but 看見 means that the object has really been seen. e. g.

9. 他 每天 都 看 报.

He reads the newspapers every day.

10. 十月 一日 我們 <u>看見</u>了 毛(澤东) 主席.

On October first we saw Chairman Mao (Tse-tung).

It is the same with 听 and 听見, and their different meanings may be observed from the following example:

11. 因为 他 沒 有 好好兒地 听, 我 說 的 問題 他 沒 有 <u>听見</u>.

Because he did not listen carefully, he did not hear the problem I talked about.

听見, 看見 and some others may be said to have already developed into words in modern Chinese.

課文　Kèwén　Text

(a₁) 你 昨天 去 書店 了 嗎?

Did you go to the bookstore yesterday?

(b₁) 去 了. 因为 我 很 想 买 一本 汉俄 字典, 上完 課 我 就 去 了.

I did. Because I wanted very much to buy that Chinese-Russian dictionary, I went right after (I finished my) class.

(a₂) 你 买着 了 嗎?

Did you get to buy it?

(b₂)   我 买着 了 我 买 的 那种
字典 很 好, 书店里的 同志 说,
买 那种 字典 的 人 很 多.

I did. The kind of dictionary I bought was very good. The man (comrade) at the bookstore said there were many people who bought that kind of dictionary.

(a₃)   你 还 买! 什么 了?

What else did you buy?

(b₃)   我 还 买了 两本 小说兒, 还 想
买 一本 旧 杂誌, 但是 没有
买着, 因为 那个 书店 不 卖 旧
杂誌.

I also bought (in addition to what I bought above) two novels; I also wished to buy an old magazine, but didn't succeed, because that bookstore did not carry old magazines.

(a₁)   北京 有 很 多 卖 旧 書 的
地方, 你 可以 去 那兒 买, 在
那兒 能 买着. 你 现在 要 用,
可以 在 圖書館 借, 一定 能
借着.

In Peking there are many places that sell old books. You can go shopping in these places. You can buy it there. (If) you want to use (it) now, you can try borrowing it from the library. You definitely can (get to) borrow it.

(b₄)   我 现在 不 用, 星期日 我 就
去 买.

I don't need (to use) it now. I will go to buy it on Sunday.

課外練習　Kèwài liànxí　Home Work

1) Answer the following questions in the affirmative:

(1) 今天 这 一课 你 都 学会 了 吗?

(2) 这 一课的 語法 你 看懂 了 沒 有?

(3) 黑板上的 句子 你 都 看清楚 了 吗?

2) Answer the following questions in the negative:

(4) 我 想 借 你的 字典, 你 用完 了 沒 有?

(5) 今天的 練習 你 翻譯好 了 沒 有?

(6) 这些 汉字 你 要是 不 写清楚, 他們 能 看懂 吗?

3) Make sentences with the following verbs and their resultative complements:

(7) 回答 对　　　　(8) 写 完

汉字表　Hànzì biǎo　Chinese Characters

1	完	宀							
		元							
2	着	丶	⌍	⌍	⌍	羊	羊	着	
3	找								
4	見								
5	毛								

6	澤	氵	
		睪	
7	主		
8	席	[illegible]	广
			廿 (一 十 廾 廿)
		巾	
9	卖	十 土 [illegible] [illegible] 壶 卖	

Lesson 33

生詞 Shēngcí New Words

1.	記	(动)	jì	to remember, to take notes to learn by heart
2.	拿	(动)	ná	to take
3.	掉	(动)	diào	to fall, to miss
4.	开	(动)	kāi	to open (a door) to drive (a car)
5.	門	(名)	mén	docr
6.	汽車	(名)	qìchē [輛 liàng]	automobile
7.	搬	(动)	bān	to move
8.	坐	(动)	zuò	to sit
9.	站	(动)	zhàn	to stand, to rise to one's feet
10.	到	(动)	dào	to reach, to arrive
11.	劳駕		láojià	excuse me, may I trouble you
12.	輛	(量)	liàng	(a measure word)
13.	錯	(形)	cuò	wrong, incorrect, mistaken
14.	热	(形)	rè	hot
15.	剛才	(副)	gāngcái	a short time ago
16.	窗戶	(名)	chuānghù	window

語法 yǔfǎ Grammar

33.1 住 Used as Resultative Complement   住 is a very common verb meaning "to live" or "to dwell", and may be used as predicate. e. g.

1. 我 朋友 在 这个 宿舍 住.

My friend lives in this dormitory.

But, when it is used as resultative complement, it has an extended meaning. e. g.

2. 我 要 记 二十个 生詞,
记住了 十八个, 两个 没 有 记住.

I want(ed) to memorize twenty new words. I memorized eighteen. There were two I didn't memorize.

3. 那枝 鉛笔 我 没 有 拿住, 掉 了.

I didn't hold on to that pencil, so I dropped it.

记住 means to have committed the words to memory through the action of 记. 沒有拿住 means that though the action of 拿 has taken place, yet one has failed to hold that pencil in hand. Therefore, the resultative complement 住 possesses the meaning of retaining or keeping the object of an action in a certain place as the result of the action.

33.2 开 Used as Resultative Complement   开 is also a common verb and may be used as predicate. e. g.

4. 图書館 七点半 开門.

The library opens at 7:30.

5. 他 会 开 汽車.

He drives (OR: can drive) a car. (OR: He drives.)

It may also be used as resultative complement:

6. 这兒的 椅子 太 多, 应該 搬开
两把.

There are too many chairs here; (we) should remove a couple.

7. 你的 朋友 来 了, 你 快 开开 门.

Your friend is here (has arrived). Go open the door quickly.

搬开椅子 means to move the chair away from its original place. 开开門 is to let the door open, that is to say, to let the door stand wide open. Hence, we may say that 开 used as resultative complement means separation or departure.

33.3 在 Used as Resultative Complement 在 is not only used as predicate, but may also be used as resultative complement after some verbs indicating existence. e. g.

8. 我們 坐在 椅子上.

We are sitting on chairs.

9. 先生 站在 黑板 旁边兒.

The teacher is standing next to the blackboard.

坐 and 站 are verbs and 在 is the resultative complement. 在 tells us the place where persons or things are as the result of a certain action (such as "putting", "packing", "sitting", "standing" etc.). Hence it is clear that the resultative complement 在 is quite different in function from the adverbial modifier 在..., which indicates the place where something has happened. Therefore, we must not say 我們学習在北京大学 or 那个同志工作在哪兒. In such cases, 在 may be used in a prepositional construction expressing, as an adverbial modifier, where an action has occurred. Therefore, we have to say 我們在北京大学学習 or 那个同志在哪兒工作.

33.4 到 Used as Resultative Complement 到 is a common verb and often used as predicate. e. g.

10. 主席 到 了 嗎?

Has the chairman arrived yet?

11. 主席 到 了.

The chairman arrived.

But 到 is also very frequently used as resultative complement, with the meaning of "attaining" or "reaching". The object following the complement indicates the place where an action has come to an end. e.g.

12. 六点 我 已經 回到 宿舍 了.

By six I had already returned to the dormitory.

13. 先生 講到 这兒 的 时候兒, 問 了 几个 問題.

When the teacher lectured to this point, he/she asked several questions.

課文 Kèwén Text

I

(a₁) 勞駕, 这輛 汽車 是 去 哪兒 的?

Excuse me, where does this car go?

(b₁) 去 北京 大学 的.

It goes to Peking University.

(a₂) 什么 时候兒 开?

When does it leave?

(b₂) 五点 一刻 开.

It leaves at 5:15.

(a₃) 什么 时候兒 可以 开到 北京 大学?

When does (can) it arrive at Peking University?

(b₃)　六点　过　五分.

6:05.

(a₄)　学完　的　語法　你　都　記住　了　嗎?

Have you memorized all the grammar we've learned?

(b₄)　都　記住　了.　但是,　我　說　話　的　时候兒,　还　常常　說錯.

Yes, but when I speak I still make mistakes all the time.

(a₅)　学了　的　詞彙　你　能　不　能　都　記住?

Can you memorize (remember) all the vocabulary you've learned?

(b₅)　不　能,　虽然　我　每天　都　練習,　但是　特別　难的　汉字　还　会　写錯.

No (I can't). Although I practice every day, I still make mistakes writing characters that are especially difficult.

III

(a₆)　桌子上的　書　是　你的　嗎?

Is the book on the table yours?

(b₆)　是　我的.　你　想　在　这張　桌子上　作　練習　嗎?

Yes, it's mine. Do you want to do your exercises at this table?

(a₇) 对了. 我的 練習 还 沒 有 作完,
我 想 在 这兒 作.

Yes. I have not yet finished my exercises; I want to do them here.

(b₇) 好, 我 拿开 我的 書.

O.K., I will move my books.

IV

(a₈) 你們 不 觉得 热 嗎?

Don't you feel hot?

(b₈) 不 觉得. 剛才 有 一点兒 热, 現
在 門 和 窗戶 都 开开 了,
不 热.

No. It was a bit hot a while ago. Now that both the door and the windows are open, it's not hot.

V

(a₉) 上 課 的 时候兒, 你 坐在
哪兒?

Where do you sit in class?

(b₉) 我 坐在 前边兒.

I sit in front.

(a₁₀) 誰 坐在 你的 旁边兒?

Who sits next to you?

(b₁₀) 我 同屋 和 一个 苏联 学生 坐在 我 旁边兒. 我 坐在 他們 中間兒.

My roommate and a Russian student sit next to me. I sit in between.

課外練習　Kèwài liànxí　Home Work

1) Notice the different Chinese characters having the same sound and fill the following blanks with the correct ones:

(1) gāng ｛ 我＿＿才 看見 他.
＿＿笔 掉 了.

(2) zuò ｛ 我＿＿錯 了 一个 句子.
誰＿＿在 汽車上?

2) Copy the following sentences, and fill the blanks with the resultative complements 开, 在, 住, and 到:

(3) 他 回＿＿宿舍, 就 作 練習.

(4) 上 課 的 时候兒, 先生 站＿＿ 黑板 旁边兒.

(5) 那张 紙 我 沒 有 拿＿＿, 掉 了.

(6) 这本 字典 要是 用完 了, 我們 就 拿＿＿.

3) Translate the following English sentences into Chinese:

(7) It is very hot, so I am standing at the window.

(8) My friend has already returned to Peking.

(9) If I had not remembered these Chinese characters, I would have written them wrong.

(10) Since the window is not open, it is a bit hot.

汉字表　Hànzì biǎo　Chinese Characters

1	記	言	
		己（乛 コ 己）	
2	拿	合	
		手（ノ 三 手）	
3	掉	扌	
		卓（ㄧ 卜 占 卓）	
4	門		
5	搬	扌	
		般	舟（ノ ʃ ⺁ 升 舟 舟）
			殳（几 殳）
6	汽	氵	
		气（ノ 乀 与 气）	
7	坐	从	
		土	
8	站	立	
		占	
9	劳	艹（一 十 艹 艹）	
		力	
10	駕	加	力
			口

		馬		
11	輛	車		
		兩(一 一 厂 丙 兩 兩 兩 兩)		
12	錯	金		
		昔		
13	热	执	扌	
			丸 (九 丸)	
		灬		
14	剛	岡		
		刂		
15	才	一 十 才		
16	窗	穴	宀	
			八	
		囱(丿 冂 甸 囱)		
17	户	丶 户		

Lesson 34

生詞 Shēngcí New Words

1. 以前 (副) yǐqián in the past, ago, before
2. 交 (动) jiāo to hand, to give
3. 忘 (动) wàng to forget
4. 带 (动) dài to bring, to carry
5. 下午 (名) xiàwǔ afternoon
6. 报告 (名、动) bàogào report, to make a report
7. 走 (动) zǒu to go, to walk
8. 台 (名) tái platform, rostrum
9. 热烈 (形) rèliè warm, enthusiastic
10. 鼓掌 (动) gǔzhǎng to applaud, to clap (one's hands)
11. 非常 (副) fēicháng uncommonly, extremely
12. 重要 (形) zhòngyào important
13. 記 (动) jì to take down (in the note-book)
14. 繼續 (动) jìxù to continue
15. 种 (量) zhǒng (a measure word)

語法 Yǔfǎ Grammar

34.1 The Simple Directional Complement The two verbs 来 and 去 are not only used as predicates, but are also frequently used as complements to other verbs. As complements, 来 and

去 are used to indicate directions of actions, and are called directional complements. If an action proceeds towards the speaker (or the thing or things under discussion), we use the directional complement 来 after the verb. We put the directional complement 去 after a verb, if the action proceeds contrariwise or away from the speaker. e. g.

1. 先生　进　教室　来　了.

The teacher is coming into the classroom.

2. 先生　进　教室　去　了.

The teacher is going into the classroom.

In the above two examples, we can see that the same action in 先生进教室 may have different complements, because the speaker's position in these two sentences is not the same. When the speaker is inside the classroom, and if the action proceeds towards the speaker, he must say 进来. On the contrary, if the action proceeds away from the speaker who is standing outside the classroom, then he must say 进去. As another example, suppose we are in the dormitory, then we must say:

3. 他　回　宿舍　来　了.

He's coming back to the dormitory.

If we are not in the dormitory or away from it, then we must say:

4. 他　回　宿舍　去　了.

He's going back to the dormitory.

34.2 The Positions of the Simple Directional Complement and the Object   Verbs with directional complements may also have objects. Such objects can be divided into two kinds. Different kinds of objects have different positions in such sentences.

(1) If the thing denoted by the object does not change its position under the influence of an action, then the object is placed before the directional complement and after the verb.

All the objects in the above examples are of this kind. We never say 先生进来敎室了 or 他囬去了宿舍.

(2) If the thing denoted by the object changes its position under the influence of an action, it should also be placed after the verb and before the complement. e. g.

5. 我 要 搬 一把 椅子 来.

I want to bring a chair here.

So in the above example, the position of the object is not different from that of the first kind. But, if the action is completed, we may say:

6. 我 剛才 搬来了 一把 椅子.

I just brought a chair here.

Here, the verb and its complement are closely knit, so that the object is placed after them. Such word order is similar to that of the resultative complement and the object.

34.3 以前   以前 may be used as an adverb, it is just the same in use as 从前. e. g.

7. 他 以前 在 这兒 工作.

He used to work here.

以前 may also be used after a word, a verbal-construction or a subject-predicate construction (clause), thus forming a construction to indicate time. e. g.

8. 十一点 以前 我 要 上 課.

I have to go to class before 11:00.

9. 来 中国 以前, 他 不 会 中文.

Before coming to China, he didn't know Chinese.

10. 上 課 以前, 你 应該 作好 練習.

Before class, you should finish your exercises.

11. 先生 來 以前, 学生 都 來 了.

Before the teacher came, all the students had come.

Note: There is a characteristic feature in such a construction, that is, the construction before 以前, whether affirmative or negative, makes no difference in meaning. Therefore, the above three examples may be re-written as follows:

12. 沒 有 來 中国 以前, 他 不 会 中文.

He didn't know Chinese until he came to China.

13. 沒 有 上 課 以前, 你 应該 作好 練習.

Before class, you should finish your exercises.

14. 先生 沒 有 來 以前, 学生 都 來 了.

Before the teacher came, all the students had come.

34.4 以后　Just like 以前, 以后 may be used as an adverb, and may also be placed after a word, a verbal construction, or a subject-predicate construction, thus forming a construction indicating time. e. g.

15. 十五号 以后, 他們 要 开始 一个 新的 工作

After the 15th, they're going to begin a new project.

16. 工作 以后, 你 应該 休息.

After work you should rest.

17. 这个 同志 来了 以后, 很 积極地
作了 很 多 工作.

After this comrade came he enthusiastically did a lot of work.

18. 听 清楚 問題 以后, 他 就 回答.

After listening carefully to the question, he answers (answered).

Note: The elements before 以后 can never be negative in form.

課文 Kèwén Text

I

(a₁) 張友文 到 哪兒 去 了?

Where did Zhang You-wen go?

(b₁) 回 宿舍 去 了.

He went back to the dormitory.

(a₂) 他 为 什么 現在 回去?

Why has he gone back now?

(b₂) 我們 今天 要 交 練習, 他的 本子
忘在 宿舍里 了.

We have to hand in our exercises today. He left his notebook in the dormitory.

(a₃) 你的 本子 带来 了 嗎?

Have you brought your notebook?

(b₃) 帶來 了. 我 沒 有 忘. 我 每天
都 帶 本子 來.

Yes, I have. I didn't forget. I bring my notebook every day.

(a₄) 今天 要 用 字典, 你 也 帶來
了 嗎?

We're going to use the dictionary today. Have you brought
(that) too?

(b₄) 帶來 了. 你 看, 這本 漢俄 字典
是 我 昨天 從 城裡 買來 的.

Yes, I did. Look, this is the Chinese-Russian dictionary
that I bought yesterday in town.

II

今天 星期六. 我們 下午 在 礼堂
听 报告. 两点半 报告 开始, 我 两点
过 十分 就 到 礼堂 去 了. 那时候兒
到 的 人 还 不 多, 我 就坐在 前
边兒. 十分鐘 以后, 听 报告 的 都
进 礼堂 来 了.

Today is Saturday. In the afternoon we listened to a
report in the auditorium. The report started at 2:30. I
went to the auditorium as early as 2:10. There weren't too
many who had arrived then. I sat in the front. Ten
minutes later, all the people who wanted to listen to the
report came into the auditorium.

两点半, 作 报告 的 同志 从 外边兒
进来 了. 他 走到 主席 台上 去 的
时候兒, 我們 都 热烈地 鼓掌. 他的 报
告 非常 重要, 很 多 应該 记住 的
地方, 我 都 记在 本子里 了. 講到 四
点 一刻, 我們 有 五分鐘的 休息. 休
息 以后, 他 繼續 講, 講到 五点 二
十. 我 回到 宿舍 来 的 时候兒. 已
經 五点 三刻 了.

At 2:30 the comrade who was making the report came in (from the outside). When he walked up to the podium we all applauded enthusiastically. His report was very important. There were many points that should be memorized, all of which I jotted down in my notebook. He lectured till 4:15, then we had a five-minute recess. After the recess, he continued his talk until 5:20. When I returned to the dormitory, it was already 5:45.

这个 报告 虽然 有 一点兒 長, 但
是 給 我的 帮助 很 大. 我 非常 喜
欢 听 这种 报告.

Although the report was a bit long, it gave me a great deal of help. I like very much listening to this kind of report.

課外練習 Kèwài liànxí Home Work

1) Fill each of the following blanks with a proper directional complement 来 or 去:

(1) 因为 想 借書, 我 要 到 圖書館＿＿.

(2) 我 从 朋友 那兒 拿＿＿了 两本 画报.

(3) 今天 城里 有 一个 报告, 我 必須 进 城＿＿. (説話人在城外)

(4) 我 同屋 从 外边兒 搬＿＿了 一張 桌子. (説話人在里边)

2) Make sentences with each group of words (a verb and its object), and use a proper directional complement 来 or 去 in each of your sentences:

(5) 进 書店

(6) 买 东西

(7) 回 学校

(8) 借 鉛笔

3) Copy the five groups of Chinese characters in the following, and make a " ＝ " mark between characters of the same sound, and " ≠ " between those that are different:

(9) 带 太

(10) 午 五

(11) 張 掌

(12) 記 繼

(13) 重 鐘

汉字表 Hànzì biǎo Chinese Characters

1	交	
2	忘	亡
		心

3	帶	一	十	卅	卅	洪	帶	
4	午	丿	仁	午				
5	走							
6	台							
7	烈	列	歹（一歹）					
			刂					
		灬						
8	鼓	壹（士吉吉吉壹）						
		支						
9	掌	尚						
		手						
10	非	丿	╛	╛	╡	非	非	非
11	重							
12	繼	糸						
		㡭（ㄥㄠㄠ丝丝絲㡭）						
13	續	糸						
		賣	士					
			買	四				
				貝	目			
					八			
14	种	禾						
		甲						

Lesson 35

生詞 Shēngcí New Words

1.	前天	(名)	qiántiān	day before yesterday
2.	話劇	(名)	huàjù	drama, stage-play
3.	首都	(名)	shǒudū	capital
4.	劇場	(名)	jùchǎng	theatre
5.	班	(名)	bān	class
6.	同学	(名)	tóngxué	school-mate
7.	出發	(动)	chūfā	to start, to set out
8.	开演	(动)	kāiyǎn	to perform, to give a performance
9.	吃	(动)	chī	to eat
10.	晚飯	(名)	wǎnfàn	evening meal, supper
11.	大家	(代)	dàjiā	all
12.	演員	(名)	yǎnyuán	actor, actress
13.	演	(动)	yǎn	to perform, to play the role of...
14.	差不多	(副)	chàbùduō	more or less, almost
15.	了解	(动)	liǎojiě	to understand
16.	情况	(名)	qíngkuàng	state, situation, case

語法 Yǔfǎ Grammar

35.1 The Verbal Sentence with (是)…的   When we wish to stress a completed action, we add the suffix 了 after the verb (27.1). But when it is understood that the action has already happened, and we wish especially to emphasize the time, place or manner of its happening etc., then we use the construction (是)……的. e. g.

1. 他 (是) 昨天 来 的.

> He came *yesterday*. (It was yesterday that he came.)

Here, it is quite clear that the action in 他来 is completed, and the emphasis is laid on the adverbial modifier 昨天. Another example is:

2. 我 (是) 在 圖書館里 复習 的.

> I reviewed (this) *in the library*. (It was in the library that I reviewed this.)

There is no doubt about the completion of the action 复習. What is stressed here is the prepositional construction 在圖書館里, used as an adverbial modifier of place. Another example is:

3. 她 (是) 跟 我 一起 去 的.

> She went with *me*.

What is emphasized here is the prepositional construction 跟我一起, an adverbial modifier expressing the manner of the action. Therefore, it is clear that in such kind of sentence with a verbal predicate there must be an adverbial modifier indicating the time, place or manner of the action expressed by the verb. Notice the suffix 了 is no longer required after the verb, though the action is completed.

35.2 The Negative Form of the Verbal Sentence with (是) ……的 When we are certain that an action is completed, but wish to emphasize that the action was not completed at a certain time or place or in a certain manner etc., we use the negative form of 是……的, that is to say, the construction 不是…的. e. g.

4. 她 不 是 昨天 来 的, 是 前天 晚上 来 的.

She didn't come yesterday. She came the night before.

5. 我 不 是 在 圖書館里 复習 的,
   是 在 宿舍里 复習 的.

I didn't review this in the library. I reviewed it in the
dormitory.

6. 她 不 是 跟 我 一起 去 的,
   她 是 跟 謝 同志 一起 去 的.

She didn't go with me. She went with Comrade Xie
(Hsieh).

What is to be noticed is that in the affirmative sentence
the word 是 can be omitted; while in the negative sentence
the word 是 in 不是……的 can never be omitted.

35.3 The Object in the Verbal Sentence with (是)...的
When there is an object in such kind of sentence we often
place it at the end of the sentence. e. g.

7. 我 (是) 前天 进 的 城.

I went into town day before yesterday.

8. 他 不 是 在 这兒 买 的 字典.

He didn't buy his dictionary here.

But we may also place the object after the verb and before the word 的, especially when the object is a personal pronoun or the predicate consists of a verb-object construction
followed by a directional complement. e. g.

9. 我 (是) 前天 进 城 的.

I went into town day before yesterday.

10. 我 (是) 昨天 看見 他 的.

I saw him yesterday. (It was yesterday that I saw him.)

11. 他（是）上星期 到 北京 来 的.

He came to Peking last week.

35.4 The Interrogative Sentence (5)   The fifth kind of interrogative sentence is formed by placing the interrogative construction 是不是 in a declarative sentence. As to its position, there are three possibilities:—

(1) 是不是 placed at the beginning of a sentence. e. g.

12. 是 不 是 你們 都 住在 学校里?

Is it true that you all live at school?

13. 是 不 是 这本 小説兒 很 有意思?

Is it true that this novel is very interesting?

(2) 是不是 placed at the end of a sentence. e. g.

14. 你們 都 住在 学校里, 是 不 是?

You all live at school, right?

15. 这本 小説兒 很 有意思, 是 不 是?

This novel is very interesting, don't you think so?

(3) 是不是 placed before the question concerned (in the predicate). e. g.

16. 你們 是 不 是 都 住在 学校 里?

Is it true that you all live at school?

17. 这本 小説兒 是 不 是 很 有意思?

Is this novel very interesting?

課文 Kèwén Text

(a₁) 上星期六 你 （是） 怎么 玩兒 的?

How did you spend last Saturday?

(b₁) 我 晚上 看了 一个 話剧.

I went to a play in the evening.

(a₂) 你 (是) 在 哪兒 看 的 話剧?

Where did you see it?

(b₂) 在 城 里边兒——首都 剧場.

In town (inside)—the Capital Theatre.

(a₃) 你 (是) 跟 誰 一起 去 的?

Whom did you go with?

(b₃) 跟 我們 班上的 先生 和 同学 一起 去 的.

I went with my teacher and students in the class.

(a₄) 你們 (是) 什么 时候兒 出發 的?

When did you leave (i.e., set out to go)?

(b₄) 七点 一刻 开演, 我們 (是) 吃了 晚飯 以后 六点半 出發 的.

The play began at 7:15. We left after supper, at 6:30.

(a₅) 这个 話剧 怎么样?

How was the play?

(b₅) 很 好, 大家 都 很 喜欢 看 这个 話剧.

Very good. Everyone liked it.

(a₆) 你 現在 看 中国 話剧 是 不 是 都 能 懂?

Can you now understand everything when you watch a Chinese play?

(b₆) 还 不 能 都 懂. 但是 因为 演員 演得 好, 說 話 說得 清楚, 我 差不多 都 懂 了.

I still can't understand everything. But since the performers performed well, and spoke clearly, I understood almost everything.

(a₇) 是 不 是 你 常常 看 話剧?

Do you go to plays often?

(b₇) 对 了. 我 非常 喜欢 看. 因为 看 話剧 可以 多 了解 中国的 情况.

Yes. I like watching plays a lot. Because watching plays can further my understanding of the Chinese scene (conditions).

(a₈) 这个 話剧 長 不 長? 你們 (是) 几 点 回 学校 来 的?

Was the play long? When did you get back to school?

(b₈) 話剧 不 太 長, 我們 (是) 差不多 十一点半 回到 宿舍 的.

The play wasn't too long. We got back to the dormitory at about 11:30.

課外練習　Kèwài liànxí　Home Work

(1) Change the following into sentences using (是) ... 的, emphasizing the adverbial modifiers:

(1) 我的 朋友 从上月起 翻譯 这本 書.

(2) 他 跟 那个 同学 一起 去 了.

(3) 昨天 那个 演員 在 北京 剧場 演 話剧.

(2) Answer the following questions in the negative:

(4) 你 是 不 是 一九五六年 到 这个 班上 来 的?

(5) 你 是 不 是 在 同学 那兒 借 的 小説兒?

(3) Re-write the following sentences using 是不是:

(6) 这个 問題 非常 重要 嗎?

(7) 先生 已經 了解了 他的 学習 情况 了 嗎?

汉字表　Hànzì biǎo　Chinese Characters

1	剧	居	尸
			古（一 十 古）
		刂	
2	首		
3	場	土	
		昜（日 旦 旯 昮 昜 昜）	
4	班	王	
		丿（丿 丿）	

		王 （一 二 千 王）		
5	出	一 凵 凵 屮 出 出		
6	發	癶 （フ ㇇ ㇀ ㇒ ㇒ 癶）		
		弓		
		殳		
7	演	氵		
		寅 （宀 宀 富 寅）		
8	吃	口		
		乞 （丿 ㇀ 乞）		
9	飯			
10	家	宀		
		豕 （一 ㇇ 万 豕 豕 豕 豕）		
11	員	口		
		貝		
12	解	角 （丿 ㇄ ㇆ 角 角 角）		
		爭 （㇆ ㇕ ㇜ 至 爭）		
13	況	冫		
		兄	口	
			儿	

Lesson 36

語法复習　Yǔfǎ fùxí　Review

36.1 The Five Kinds of Interrogative Sentences　We have learned five kinds of interrogative sentences (13.3, 15.3, 19.1, 29.2, 35.4) covering almost all the chief methods of asking questions in Chinese. In this lesson, let us review their different uses.

(1) The Interrogative Sentence with the Particle 嗎 and the Alternative Interrogative Sentence　These two kinds of interrogative sentences are very common in use. When we are very objective in inquring about a matter or thing, and when we have not taken into consideration whether the expected answer be in the affirmative or in the negative, we prefer to use these two kinds of interrogative sentences. e. g.

1. 那些 汉字 他 都 念得 对 嗎?

   Did he pronounce all those characters correctly?

2. 那些 汉字 他 都 念得 对 不 对?

   Did he pronounce all those characters correctly (or not)?

3. 汽車 开来 了 嗎?

   Is the automobile here? (Has the automobile been driven here?)

4. 汽車 开来 了 沒 有?

   Is the automobile here (or not)?

(2) The Interrogative Sentence with An Interrogative **Word**
When we wish especially to know who, what, where, when, how, how much etc., we must use interrogative words **in** asking these questions. e. g.

5. 你 今年 二十几岁?

How old are you? (LIT.: How many years past twenty are you this year?)

6. 先生 講到 什么 地方 了?

How far (LIT.: to what point) has the teacher lectured?

We cannot use the particle 嗎 in an interrogative sentence in which there is an interrogative word. In answering such a question, one must aim at what is asked by the interrogative word, and the position of the answer in the sentence should be the same as that of the interrogative word. e. g.

7. 我 今年 二十五岁.

I'm twenty-five (this year).

8. 先生 講到 这个 地方 了.

The teacher has lectured up to this part.

(3) The Interrogative Sentence with (还是)...还是   When the person asking the question thinks that the answer may be given in two or more ways, he may use this kind of inter-rogative sentence. e. g.

9. 你們 复習得 怎么样? 有 問題 还是 沒 問題?

How are you coming along in your review? Do you have problems (or not)?

10. 你 現在 还是 到 圖書館 去 还是 回 宿舍 去?

Are you going to the library now or are you returning to the dormitory?

(4) The Interrogative Sentence with 是不是 When the person asking the question wishes to make sure whether a certain fact or matter is real or not, whether it is right or wrong, he may use this kind of interrogative sentence. e. g.

11. 那个 話剧 很 短, 是 不 是?

That play was very short, right?

12. 是 不 是 那个 話剧 很 短?

Was that play very short?

13. 那个 話剧 是 不 是 很 短?

Was that play very short?

36.2 The Verbal Sentence with (是)...的 and the Sentence with a Substantive Predicate (2) When we wish to emphasize when, where, or how an action was completed, we use the verbal construction of (是) ... 的. e. g.

14. 我 (是) 九月 一号 来 的.

I came on September first.

15. 他 (是) 在 北京 大学 学 的 中文.

He studied Chinese at Peking University.

16. 他 (是) 在 北京 大学 学 中文 的.

He studied Chinese at Peking University.

The sentence structure of such kind of sentence is similar to that of the sentence with a substantive predicate (2), because the construction 是 ... 的 is also found in the latter. e. g.

17. 这本 杂誌 是 九月 一号 来 的.

This magazine is the one that came on September first.

18. 他 是 在 北京 大学 学 中文 的.

He is the one who studied Chinese at Peking University.

But there is a difference between these two kinds of sentences:

(1) So far as the sentence structure is concerned, the copula 是 is absolutely necessary in the sentence with a substantive predicate, but it is often omitted in the sentence with a verbal predicate. In the former, the adjective modifier composed of a verb-object construction (such as 学中文) should be used before the particle 的; while in the latter, if there is an object, it is often put after 的, though it may also be put before it.

(2) So far as the sentence meaning is concerned, the sentence with a verbal predicate is used in describing an action, but the verbal sentence with the construction (是) ... 的 is used to tell about the time, place or manner of an action. The sentence with a substantive predicate is used to form a judgement on the subject, for example, the sentence 他 (是) 在北京大学学的中文 chiefly tells where he learned Chinese, but the sentence 他是在北京大学学中文的 is used to describe what kind of a person he is.

36.3 A Summary on the Resultative Complement Since we first learned about the resultative complement (32.1), we have now come across many more such complements. Here all the resultative complements are summarized as follows:

Resultative comple-ments	The extended meanings	Constructions we have already learned	
着	to gain to reach	买着 to have bought 借着 to have lent or borrowed 找着 to have found	
见	to receive something through one's sense perception	看见 to have seen 听见 to have heard	
住	to keep the object of an action	拿住 to hold 記住 to bear in mind	
开	to leave, to depart, to separate	搬开 to move away 拿开 to take away 开开 to open	

在	to be at a certain place as the result of an action	坐在 to sit on 站在 to stand on 住在 to live in 記在 to keep in mind 忘在 to forget
到	the goal of an action	回到 to go back 講到 to explain to (汽車)开到 to drive to 走到 to walk to
会		学会 to have learned to do
完		作完 to have done 卖完 to sell out 用完 to use up 写完 to have written
懂		看懂 to understand by reading 听懂 to understand by listening
对		回答对 to answer correctly (right) 念对 to read correctly (right)
错		說错 to speak wrongly 写错 to write wrongly
好	to attain or achieve the ideal result or effect	作好 to make well 学好 to study well 翻譯好 to translate well
清楚		听清楚 to hear clearly 看清楚 to see clearly 写清楚 to write clearly

Of all the resultative complements mentioned above, some are verbs and some are adjectives. But any verb or adjective may be used after another verb to form a verb-complement construction, if only there is some logical meaning in such a combination.

Special attention should be paid to the following three points:

(1) Verbs and their complements are so closely knit together that some of them have even become compound verbs. So all the verb suffixes and objects have to be placed after complements, and not between verbs and their complements. e. g.

19. 他　翻譯完了　兩本　小説兒.

He finished translating two novels.

20. 你　应該　写清楚　你的　名字.

You should write your name legibly.

(2) Many resultative complements, as shown in the above list, possess extended meanings. e. g.

21. 上課的時候兒，大家要坐好.

Everyone should sit nicely during class.

The word 好 in 坐好 here means "sitting in one's place without stirring", while in the following example:

22. 他　作好　練習　了.

He finished his exercises.

the complement 好 means "finished".

(3) In Chinese, the resultative complement is very extensively used. Although a verb is sometimes enough to express an idea without complement, it is better idiomatically to use a verb-complement construction. For example, if we say 我懂了今天的語法 it is of course grammatically correct, but it will be much better if we add a complement. Therefore, we prefer to say:

23. 今天的　語法　我　听懂　了.

I understood today's grammar (after listening).

24. 今天的　語法　我　看懂　了.

I understood today's grammar (after reading).

課文　Kèwén　Text

I

(a₁) 你　看，走到　台上　去　的　那个

同志 是 誰? 是 作 报告 的 嗎?

Look, who's the comrade who's walking onto the stage? Is he the one who's making the report?

(b₁) 不 是, 作 报告 的 同志 还 没 有 来 呢. 这 是 今天的 主席 方明 同志.

No, the comrade who is making the report has not come yet. This is the chairman for today, Comrade Fang Ming.

(a₂) 方明 同志? 我 常常 听見 这个 名字.

Comrade Fang Ming? I've heard the name often.

(b₂) 对, 他 从 一九五二年 起 在 这兒 工作, 所以 很 多 人 都 知道 他. 你 看, 作 报告 的 同志 来 了.

Right. He's been working here since 1952, so a lot of people know him. Look, the comrade who's making the report is here.

II

(a₃) 剛才的 問題 你 都 回答 了 嗎?

Have you answered all the questions raised just now?

(b₃) 都 回答 了. 只 有 八个 問題, 是 不 是?

All of them. There were only eight, right?

(a₄) 是, 但是 我 只 回答对了 七个,
后边兒的 那个 我 不 太 会,
虽然 写了 一点兒, 但是 一定
写错 了. 你 是 怎么 回答 的?

Yes, but I answered only seven correctly. It didn't know
the last one too well. Although I wrote a little on it, I'm
sure I was wrong. How did you answer?

(b₄) 我 是 这么 回答 的, 你 看.

Look, this is the way I answered.

III

(a₅) 你 到 哪兒 去 了?

Where did you go?

(b₅) 我 到 先生 那兒 去 了.

I went to the teacher's.

(a₆) 先生 住在 什么 地方?

Where does the teacher live?

(b₆) 他 住在 学校 旁边兒的 宿舍里.

He lives in the dormitory next to the school.

(a₇) 从前 他 住在 城里, 是 什么
时候兒 搬来 的?

He used to live in the city. When did he move (here)?

(b₇) 他 是 上月 搬到 城外 来 的.
你 不 知道 吗?

He moved (here) to the suburbs last month. Didn't you know that?

(a₈) 不 知道. 要是 知道, 我 早
去 他 那兒 了.

No, I didn't. If I had known I would have gone to his place a long time ago.

Lesson 37

生詞　Shēngcí　New Words

1.	第	(头) dì	(a prefix)
2.	年級	(名) niánjí	(year) class
3.	哥(哥)	(名) gē(ge)	elder brother
4.	元	(量) yuán	dollar (a measure word)
5.	角	(量) jiǎo	ten cents (a measure word)
6.	分	(量) fēn	cent (a measure word)
7.	塊	(量) kuài	(a measure word)
8.	毛	(量) máo	(a measure word)
9.	錢	(名) qián	money
10.	上午	(名) shàngwǔ	morning, the forenoon
11.	合作社	(名) hézuòshè	co-operative store
12.	遇見	(动) yùjiàn	to meet
13.	樣兒	(名) yàngr	shape, sort, style
14.	又	(副) yòu	again, too
15.	一共	(副) yígòng	totally, all together
16.	找	(动) zhǎo	to return (change), to look for
17.	糖	(名) táng [塊; 斤 jīn]	sugar, candy
18.	水菓	(名) shuǐguǒ [斤]	fruit
19.	出	(动) chū	to go (come) out

語法 Yŭfǎ Grammar

37.1 Ordinal Numerals In Chinese, the word 第 is the prefix used to indicate the order of numbers. Ordinal numerals are formed by placing the prefix 第 before the cardinal numerals. e. g.

1. 我 坐在 第二輛 汽車上.

I sat in the second automobile.

2. 每年的 第一个 月 叫 一月.

The first month of each year is called January.

In the above sentences, 第一 and 第二 are ordinal numerals. The following two points must be observed in using ordinal numerals:

(1) Just like cardinal numerals, ordinal numerals in general require measure words when they are joined with nouns, such as the measure words 輛 in example 1 and 个 in example 2.

(2) 第二 cannot be 第兩.

Besides the general ordinal numerals, there are some exceptions. That is to say, sometimes no prefix is used before certain numerals, yet they are ordinal numerals. Some of the exceptional ordinal numerals in common use are as follows:

a) None of the numerals indicating the year, the month, the day and the hour take a prefix, nevertheless, they imply the order of time. e. g.

3. 二月 二日

February 2nd.

The above example means the second day of the second month in a year. Hence it is clear that 二 must be used instead of 兩 in expressing an ordinal number, whether there is the prefix 第 or not.

b) We do not use the prefix in expressing different classes of things. e. g.

4. 一年級 学生

First-year student.

c) In general, the prefix is not used in calling members of the family and relatives. e. g.

5. 三哥(哥)

Third (elder) brother.

Although from the above exceptions we know that there are some ordinal numerals actually used without the prefix, this does not mean that ordinal numerals without the prefix may be confused with the general cardinal numerals. We must notice that cardinal numerals carry measure words when they are used before nouns, but ordinal numerals without the prefix do not require any measure word when they are used before nouns, e. g., the numerals in 二月 and 三哥 are ordinal numerals without the prefix 第, so we do not use any measure word. If we say "two months" and three elder brothers", they should be translated as 两个月 and 三个哥哥.

37.2 Approximate Numbers   In Chinese, there are many ways of indicating approximate numbers. Here, we shall introduce only the most common ones:

(1) The use of two neighbouring numerals. e. g.

6. 他 写错了 三四个 汉字.

He wrote three or four characters incorrectly.

7. 我 朋友 这个 月 十七八号 到 北京 来.

My friend is coming to Peking on the 17th or the 18th of this month.

8. 这个 教室 有 二三十把 椅子

There are 20 to 30 chairs in this classroom.

(2) The use of the word 几 (several) to indicate an indefinite number. e. g.

9. 教室里 那 几个 窗户 都 开开 了.

Those (several) windows in the classroom are all open.

10. 我們 每天 学 十几个 生詞.

We learn 10 to 20 new words every day.

11. 这 几十个 学生 都 要 学習
这个 專业.

These (scores of) students all want to specialize in this.

(3) The use of the word 多 after a numeral indicates more than the number shown by that numeral. The positions of the measure word and the word 多 are shown in the following:

a) If the approximate number is a part of a large number, 多 is used before the measure word or before a noun not requiring a measure word. e. g.

12. 我們 学了 二十多課 語法 了.

We've learned 20-odd lessons of grammar.

13. 三十多年 以前, 他 也 是 北京
大学的 学生.

More than 30 years ago, he was also a student of Peking University.

b) If the approximate number is a fraction of the whole, 多 is used after the measure word or a noun not requiring a measure word. e. g.

14. 他 昨天 复習了 两課多 語法.

He reviewed a little more than two lessons of grammar yesterday.

15. 他 (是) 三年多 以前 到 中国
来 的.

He came to China more than three years ago.

37.3 The Counting of Money   In Chinese, the units of currency are 元, 角 and 分, while in the spoken language they are called 塊, 毛 and 分 respectively. After the last unit we often use the word 錢. e. g.

16. 3.00元＿＿三元＿＿三塊(錢)

$3.00 — — three dollars — — three dollars

17. 0.50元＿＿五角＿＿五毛(錢)

$0.50 — — fifty cents — — five dimes

18. 0.08元＿＿八分＿＿八分(錢)

$0.08 — — eight cents — — eight pennies

19. 1.45元＿＿一元　四角　五分＿＿

一塊　四毛　五(分錢)

$1.45 — — one dollar and forty-five cents — — one dollar, four dimes, five pennies

20. 25.20元＿＿二十五元　二角＿＿

二十五塊　二(毛錢)

$25.20 — — twenty-five dollars and twenty cents — — twenty-five dollars, two (dimes)

The rules of the use of 多, stated above, are also suitable for money expressions. e. g.

21. 他　有　三十多塊　錢.

He has thirty-odd dollars.

22. 他　有　五塊多　錢.

He has a little more than five dollars.

課文　Kèwén　Text

上午　十二点　四十(分)，我們　上完了
第四节　課. 回　宿舍　的　时候兒，在　圖
書館　前边兒，我　遇見了　一个　二年級的
学生. 他　要　到　合作社　去. 我的　練
習　本子　用完　了，必須　买　几本　新
的. 所以　我　就　帶了　两三塊錢　跟　他
一起　去　了.

At 11:40 in the morning, we were returning to the dormitory after having attended the fourth period. I ran into a second-year student in front of the library. He wanted to go to the cooperative store. I had used up my exercise notebooks and had to buy a few new ones. So I brought two or three dollars with me and went with him.

合作社　在　学生　宿舍的　旁边兒. 我
进去　就　問："同志，有　練習　本子　沒
有?" 卖　东西　的　同志　回答："有，您
要　什么　样兒的? 都　在　这兒·"

The co-op is next to the student dormitory. As soon as I entered, I asked, "Comrade, do you have exercise notebooks?" The salesperson answered, "Yes, we do. Which kind do you want? They are all here."

我　看見了　一种　我　喜欢　的，就
問　他："那种　本子　多少錢?" 他　说:

"两毛 二 一本". 我 告訴 他:"我 要
六本", 就 給了 他 两塊錢. 他 給 我
本子 以后, 又說:"一共 一塊 三毛 二,
找 您 六毛 八".

When I saw a kind I liked, I asked him, "How much is
that kind of notebook?" He said, "Twenty-two cents each."
I told him, "I would like six," and give him two dollars.
After he gave me the notebooks, he said, "Altogether one
thirty-two; here's the change: sixty-eight cents."

这时候兒, 我的 朋友 已經 买好了
糖 和 水菓. 我 拿了 找来 的 錢
和 本子 就 跟 他 一起 出来 了.

At this point my friend had already bought some candies
and fruit. After I took my change and notebooks, I came
out (of the store) together with him.

課外練習　Kèwài liànxí　Home Work

1) Copy and answer the following questions:

(1) 今天 几月 几号?

(2) 你 是 几年級 学生?

(3) 一年級 一共 有 多少 学生?

2) Write out the following approximate numbers in Chinese:

(4) thirty or forty
(5) twenty five or six
(6) more than fifty　(use 几)
(7) more than eighty　(use 多)

3) Write out the following sums of money in Chinese (both
the oral and written forms):

(8) 0.27元　　　(9) 8.95元　　　(10) 36.00元
(11) 2.17元　　　(12) 0.04元　　　(13) 13.50元

汉字表　Hànzì biǎo　Chinese Characters

#	字	部件	练习
1	第	竹	竹 (practice strokes)
		弔 (一 ⁇ 弓 弔 弔)	
2	級	糸	
		及 (丿 ⼅ 乃 及)	
3	哥	哥	
4	元	元	
5	角	角	
6	塊	土	
		鬼 (丿 田 鬼 鬼)	
7	錢	金	
		戔	戈
			戈
8	合	合	
9	社	社	
10	遇	禺 (日 ⼞ 马 禺 禺 禺)	
		辶	
11	又	又	
12	共	一 十 廿 共 共	
13	糖	米 (丶 丷 ⼂ 半 米 米)	
		唐 (广 广 庐 庐 庸 唐)	
14	水	丨 ⼅ 水 水	
15	菓	艹	
		果	

(marginal pinyin notes: dì (practice); niányí year/class; gē (gē); yuán (dollar); jiǎo (China); kuài (dollar); qián (money); hézuòshè; xiāngyùn (meet); yòu; yìgòng; táng (sugar); shuǐguǒ)

Lesson 38

生詞 Shēngcí New Words

1. 請 (动) qǐng — please, to invite, to ask
2. 讓→让 (动) ràng — to let, to cause
3. 討論 (动、名) tǎolùn — to discuss, discussion
4. 又...又... yòu...yòu... — (compound connective)
5. 也...也... yě...yě... — (compound connective)
6. 开(会) (动) kāi (huì) — to hold (a meeting)
7. 会 (名) huì — meeting
8. 叫 (动) jiào — to call, to shout, to let
9. 通知 (动、名) tōngzhī — to inform, information
10. 談 (动) tán — to talk, to tell
11. 介紹 (动、名) jièshào — to introduce, introduction
12. 自己 (代) zìjǐ — oneself, self
13. 經驗 (名) jīngyàn — experience
14. 方面 (名) fāngmiàn — respect, side
15. 意見 (名) yìjiàn — opinion
16. 提 (动) tí — to raise, to express
17. 欢迎 (动、名) huānyíng — to welcome, welcome
18. 准备 (动、名) zhǔnbèi — to prepare, preparation

語法　Yǔfǎ　Grammar

38.1 The Telescopic Form There is a kind of sentence with a verbal predicate that is rather complicated in construction ——the telescopic form. In the predicate of such a sentence, there is some other element following the object, besides the verb and its object. Such an element describes the action or state of the object, so that the relation between the object and such an element becomes one of subject and predicate. Since the object has at the same time the function of being the subject of the other element following it, it is called the double-function word. Moreover, since there exists between the object and the other element the relation of subject and predicate, such an element is also the predicate of the double-function word. This is why we call it a sentence in the telescopic form. e. g.

1. 我 請 你 来.

I ask you to come. (Please come.)

2. 这件 事情 讓 我 很 高兴.

This matter makes me very happy.

我 and 这件事 are subjects, 請 and 讓 are verbs, 你 and 我 are double-function words, and 来 and 很高兴 are the predicates of the double-function words. We can see that there exists between 你 and 来, 我 and 很高兴 the relation of subject and predicate. Therefore, all the sentences of the telescopic form have the following sentence pattern:

Subject — verb — the double-function word — the predicate of the double-function word — predicate

The verbs used in such sentences are always 請, 讓, 叫 etc. The predicate of the double-function word, as in other sentences, may be a substantive, an adjective, a verb or a subject-predicate construction which we shall learn later.

38.2 The Reduplication of Verbs We have learned that adjectives can be used reduplicatively (20.2). Here we shall

learn the reduplication of verbs. In Chinese, the reduplication
of verb implies a short and quick action. e. g.

3. 我 想 <u>看看</u> 小說兒.

I want to read some novels.

4. 他 請 他 朋友 在 宿舍里 <u>坐坐</u>.

He asked his friend to visit a while (LIT.: sit a while) in the
dormitory.

In such cases, the speaker has the feeling that the action
is short and quick; so the reduplication of a verb may in some
cases also express some informal or random action. e. g.

5. 这个 星期日 上午, 我 <u>复習复習</u>
生詞、<u>看看</u> 报, 就 已經 十二点 了.

This Sunday morning, I reviewed my vocabulary a little,
read some newspapers, and it was already twelve.

Sometimes it may also express an attempt or trial.

6. 我 覺得 这本 小說兒 很 有意
思, 你 <u>看看</u>.

I think that this novel is very interesting. Take a look. (Try
reading it.)

7. 你們 应該 <u>討論討論</u> 这个 問題.

You should discuss this problem a little.

Special attention should be paid to the following three
points:

(1) When the monosyllabic verb is used reduplicatively, we
may insert the word 一. e. g.

8. 他 想 看一看 小說兒.

He wants to read some novels.

9. 他 請 他 朋友 在 宿舍里 坐
一坐.

He asked his friend to visit a while in the dormitory.

The suffix 了 is **also** placed between the two forms of the verb, and in **such a** case the numeral 一 may be omitted. e.g.

10. 我 看了(一)看 那本 小說兒.

I took a look at (skimmed through) that novel.

11. 他 朋友 在 他 宿舍里 坐了(一)坐
就 走 了.

After visiting a little while in his dorm, his friend left.

(2) The dissyllabic verb repeats its bound-form. e. g.

12. 你 应該 休息休息.

You should take a little rest.

13. 这个 方法 很 好, 我 要 学習
学習.

This method is very good. I like to learn it (a little).

The reduplication of the dissyllabic verb should be clearly **distinguished** from that of the dissyllabic adjective. At the **same** time, notice that the word 一 is never **inserted** when a dissyllabic verb is reduplicated.

(3) As to a verb-object construction, we only reduplicate the verb and not the object. e. g.

14. 現在 你們 可以 唱唱 歌兒.

You can sing some songs now.

Of course, we can insert the word — when monosyllabic verbs are reduplicated. e. g.

15. 現在　你們　可以　唱一唱　歌兒.

You can sing some songs now.

38.3 又……又…… In Chinese, we often use this construction (compound connective) to connect two parallel elements and to stress that the two states or characteristics exist at the same time. e. g.

16. 他　又　是　我的　先生, 又　是　我的　朋友.

He is both my teacher and my friend.

17. 这張　桌子　又　新、又　大.

This table is both new and big.

18. 这个　同志　又　会　中文、又　会　俄文.

This comrade knows Chinese as well as Russian.

19. 他　說　中文　說得　又　快、又　清楚.

He speaks Chinese both fast and clearly.

There are two points to be observed in using this construction:

(1) 又 has to be placed before the predicate or before the complement of degree.

(2) When there are more than two parallel elements, we have to use 又 before each of the elements. e. g.

20. 他 写 汉字 写得 又 快、又 清楚、又 好看.

He writes characters fast, legibly and beautifully.

38.4 也…也… This construction is also used to connect two parallel elements. In general, it is always used to connect two parallel elements composed of verbs. e. g.

21. 他 会 中文——也 能 说, 也 能 写.

He knows Chinese—he can speak it and also write it.

22. 昨天 星期日, 我 也 玩兒 了, 也 学習 了.

Yesterday was Sunday; I played, and also studied.

課文 Kèwén Text

(a₁) 今天 开 会, 你 知道 了 嗎? 先生 叫 我 通知 你.

There's a meeting today. Do you know about it? The teacher asked me to notify you.

(b₁) 謝謝. 我 已經 看見 那个 通知 了. 下午 三点 开, 是 不 是?

Thanks. I have already seen the notice. It starts at three P.M., right?

(a₂) 是 三点. 你 能 不 能 来?

Yes, at three. Can you come?

(b₂) 能 来. 但是 为 什么 开 这个
会, 我 还 不 太 清楚.

Yes, I can come. But I'm not too clear yet about why this
meeting was called.

(a₃) 先生 要 和 大家 一起 討論討論
学習 問題. 他 想 讓 大家 学
得 又 多、又 快、又 好, 所以
他 要 和 大家 談一談. 他 还
要 請 張友文 同学 介紹介紹
自己的 經驗.

The teacher wants to discuss (a little) the problems of
learning with everyone. He wants everyone to learn a lot,
fast and well. So he wants to have a talk with everyone.
He's also going to ask our schoolmate Zhang You-wen to
talk about (introduce) his own experience.

(b₃) 張友文的 学習 方法 一定 很
好. 他 学習得 特別 好, 但是
他 不 覺得 忙, 他 每天 也
学習 了, 也 休息 了.

Zhang You-wen's method of learning must be very good.
He learns especially well, yet he doesn't feel busy. Every
day he can learn things as well as rest.

(a₄) 所以 这 是 一个 很 重要的 会,
大家 应該 好好兒地 听听 他的
經驗. 学習 方面的 意見, 你們
也 可以 提一提.

Therefore this is a very important meeting. Everyone should listen carefully to his experience. You can also bring up your ideas regarding learning.

(b₄) 还 要 提 意見 嗎?

Do we also have to bring up our ideas?

(a₅) 对 了, 先生 非常 欢迎 大家的 意見, 他 叫 你們 准备 意見, 你 可 以 好好兒地 想一想.

Right. The teacher really welcomes everyone's ideas. He asked all of you to seriously think of ideas (LIT.: prepare your ideas). You can think about it carefully.

(b₅) 好, 我 准备准备.

O.K., I'll do so (do a little preparation).

課外練習 Kèwài liànxí Home Work

1) Make sentences with each of the following verbs and repeat the verbs in your sentences:

(1) 討論
(2) 問

2) Complete the following telescopic sentences:

(3) 我們 請 新 同学＿＿＿＿＿.
(4) 先生 叫 我＿＿＿＿＿＿＿.
(5) 他 說 的 話 讓 我＿＿＿.

3) Translate the following sentences into Chinese, using 也 … 也 … or 又 … 又 … :

(6) The Capital Theatre is big and good.
(7) The elder brother has bought sweets and fruits from the co-operative store.

汉字表   Hànzì biǎo   Chinese Characters

1	請		
2	讓	言	
		襄（丶 亠 亣 亩 宣 审 韩 童 寧 裏 襄 襄）	
3	討	言	
		寸	
4	論	言	
		侖（人 亼 个 伶 侖 侖）	
5	通	甬（マ マ 甬）	
		辶	
6	談	言	
		炎	火
			火
7	介	人 个 介	
8	紹	糹	
		召	刀
			口
9	自		
10	己		
11	驗	馬	

		僉（人 厶 僉 僉）
12	面	一 丅 丙 丙 而 而 面 面
13	提	扌
		是
14	迎	丿 ㇄ 卬 迎
15	准	冫
		隹
16	备	夂
		田

Lesson 39

生詞 Shēngcí New Words

1.	身体	(名)	shēntǐ	body, health
2.	头	(名)	tóu	head
3.	疼	(动)	téng	to ache, to feel pain
4.	希望	(动、名)	xīwàng	to hope, hope
5.	有的		yǒudě	some
6.	全面	(形)	quánmiàn	over-all, whole
7.	發展	(动、名)	fāzhǎn	to develop, development
8.	極了		jílě	very, extremely
9.	病	(名、动)	bìng	disease, illness, to fall ill
10.	医院	(名)	yīyuàn	hospital
11.	大夫	(名)	dàifū	doctor, physician
12.	藥	(名)	yào	medicine
13.	也許	(副)	yěxǔ	perhaps, probably
14.	好	(动)	hǎo	to recover
15.	成	(动)	chéng	to become

語法 Yǔfǎ Grammar

39.1 **The Sentence with a Clause Predicate** In Chinese, besides the sentence with a substantive predicate, the sentence with an adjectival predicate and the sentence with a verbal

predicate, there is another kind of sentence that is composed
of a clause predicate, that is to say, there is a subject-predicate
construction (clause) in the predicate. e. g.

1. 他 身体 好.

He's healthy. (His health is good.)

2. 我 头 疼.

I have a headache. (My head aches.)

The subjects of these two sentences are 他 and 我, and the
subject-predicate construction 身体好 and 头疼 are the predicates
of 他 and 我. Since the predicates contain subject-predicate
constructions, such sentences are called sentences with clause
predicates.

The characteristic feature of the sentence with a clause
predicate is that there is a relation between the person or thing
denoted by the subject of the subject-predicate construction
and the person or thing denoted by the subject of the whole
sentence, that is to say, what is denoted by the subject of the
predicate is always part of the person or thing denoted by the
subject of the whole sentence. For instance, in example 1 身
体 belongs to 他 and in example 2 头 belongs to 我. So far as
the sentence function is concerned, the clause-predicate sentence
is descriptive in nature.

39.2 The Subject Predicate Construction Used as Subject
The subject-predicate construction may be used as subject in
a sentence. e. g.

3. 身体 好 很 重要.

It's important to have good health.

4. 他 不 努力 学习 是 不 对 的.

It's not right that he does not study diligently (i.e.: He
should be diligent).

身体好 and 他不努力学习 in the above two examples are
independent sentences when they stand alone. Here, they are
used as subjects only.

39.3   The Subject-Predicate Construction Used as Object
The subject-predicate construction is also very often used as object in a sentence. e. g.

5. 我 希望 你 能 来.

I hope you can come.

6. 大家 都 知道 他 要 到 苏联 去.

Everyone knows that he wants to go to the Soviet Union.

The subject-predicate constructions, 你能来 and 他要到苏联去 are used as objects in these two sentences.

Note: The sentence in which the object is a subject-predicate construction seems similar to the sentence of the telescopic form, but actually they are different.

(1) Verbs used in the telescopic sentence are always causative verbs, such as 使, 讓, 叫 etc.; the subject-predicate construction is generally used as the object of such verbs as 看見, 听見 知道 etc., which are not causative in meaning.

(2) The object of the verb in the telescopic sentence is the double-function word. There is some connection in meaning between the verb and the predicate of the double-function word. But in a sentence in which the object is a subject-predicate construction, the object of the verb is the whole construction, and there is no connection whatever between the verb and the predicate of the construction.

(3) The double-function word of the telescopic sentence is so closely knit together with the main verb before it that there should be no other element between them, and no pause when spoken. But, when a subject-predicate construction is used as the object in a sentence, the subject in the construction and the main verb of the sentence are not so closely knit. There is generally a pause between them especially when the subject-predicate construction is comparatively long.

39.4 有的 We often use the word 有的 to modify nouns, expressing indefinite designation. e. g.

7. <u>有的</u> 班 学生 多, <u>有的</u> 班 学生 少.

Some classes have a lot of students; some classes have very few students.

8. <u>有的</u> 同学 已經 出發 了.

Some of the schoolmates have already set out.

When the central word is clearly indicated by context, it can be omitted. e. g.

9. 他 有 不 少 經驗, <u>有的</u> 非常 好.

He has quite a bit of experience, some of which is very good.

10. 他 提了 很 多 意見, <u>有的</u> 对, <u>有的</u> 不 一定 对.

He made many suggestions, some of which are right, some not necessarily right.

The word 有的 and some central words have become bound-forms, and the word 的 may be omitted. Instead of saying 有的 人 and 有的时候兒 we often say 有人 and 有时候 without the word 的.

11. <u>有人</u> 带 字典 来 了, <u>有人</u> 沒 带.

Some have brought (along) dictionaries; some have not.

12. 有时候兒　中国　同学　帮助　我.
　　有时候兒　我　自己　学習.

Sometimes Chinese schoolmates help me, sometimes I study by myself.

課文　Kèwén　Text

I

1. 他　身体　好, 学習　好, 工作　好,
　是　一个　全面　发展　的　学生.

His health is good, his work is good, and his studies are good. He's a well-rounded student.

2. 这个　先生　經驗　多, 方法　好.

This teacher has a lot of experience, and his methods are good.

3. 先生　了解　学生的　学習　情况　是
　非常　重要　的.

It's extremely important that the teacher understands the students' learning situations.

4. 他　来　很　好, 他　不　来　也　沒
　关系.

If he comes, great. If he doesn't, it doesn't matter.

5. 我　听見　你們　討論得　热烈　極了.

I heard you discussing (debating) extremely enthusiastically.

6. 先生 知道 有人 要 听 报告, 所以 今天 不 开会.

The teacher knew that there are people who want to listen to reports, so there is no meeting today.

7. 昨天的 話劇, 有的 演員 演得 好, 有的 演得 不 很 好.

In the play yesterday, some actors were good, some were not so good.

8. 有的 同学 以后 还要 繼續 学習 中文.

Some students will continue learning Chinese in the future.

II

(a₁) 張友文 为 什么 沒 有 来?

Why didn't Zhang You-wen come?

(b₁) 他 病 了.

He's ill.

(a₂) 什么 病?

What (is his) illness?

(b₂) 他 头 疼. 他 說 他 今天 不 上 課, 要 在 宿舍 休息休息.

He has a headache. He said he's not attending class today. He was to rest a little in the dormitory.

(a₃) 为 什么 他 不 到 医院 去? 他 要是 现在 找 大夫 看看, 吃 一点兒 藥, 也許 明天 就 能 好.

Why doesn't he go to the hospital? If he goes to a doctor, and takes some medicine, maybe he'll get well by tomorrow.

(b₃) 我 告訴 他 了. 他 說 头 疼 沒 关系, 不 一定 要 找 大夫.

I told him (that). He said a headache is nothing. He doesn't need to get a doctor.

(a₄) 他 这么 想, 有 点兒 不 对. 有 时候兒 头 疼 也 能 發展成 大 病. 我 希望 你 下 課 以后 跟 他 說一說, 一定 叫 他 到 医 院 去.

It's not right to think this way. Sometime a headache can develop into a major illness. I hope after class you'll have a talk with him, and insist that he goes to the hospital.

課外練習　Kèwài liànxí　Home Work

1) Copy the following sentences, and underline the <u>subjects</u> or <u>objects</u> in the subject-predicate (clause) constructions:

(1) 他 知道 他 要 作好 工作 就 必须 了解 全面 情况.

(2) 大家 一起 讨论 *[discuss]* 给 我 很 大的 *[some]*
帮助.

(3) 他 很 希望 *[wishes/hope]* 他 能 在 这兒
继續 学習.

2) Translate the following sentences into Chinese.

(4) I hope I can find that doctor.

(5) He knows that the doctor in that hospital has more experience.

(6) On Saturday evening some (people) attended a meeting (literally hold a meeting), and some (people) danced.

(7) Some school-mates are well-prepared but some are not well-prepared.

3) Copy the following Chinese characters, word groups and sentences, fill the blanks with proper phonetic spellings, but notice that one Chinese character may be pronounced differently in different context:

(8) 大 *[dà]*
{ 北京 __da__ 学 *[beijing da]*
  医院里的 __dài__ 夫 }

(9) 都 *[dōu]*
{ 首 __dū__ 剧場
  我 __dōu__ 懂 了. }

(10) 了 *[le]*
{ 他 __liǎo__ 解 情况.
  朋友 来 __le__. }

(11) 还 *[hái]*
[(still)]
{ 我 也 借 書, 也 ___ 書.
  报 ___ 没 有 来 呢! }

[other sound → huán]

汉字表 Hànzì biǎo Chinese Characters

1	身	
2	体	亻

		本
3	头	、 ` ミ 头 头
4	疼	
5	希	ノ メ 兰 圣 希
6	望	、 亠 亡 坣 坣 望
7	全	入 (ノ 入)
		王
8	展	尸 尸 尼 屈 屈 展 展 展
9	病	疒
		丙 (一 冖 冇 丙)
10	医	一 医 医
11	院	阝
		完
12	夫	二 夫 夫
13	藥	业
		樂	白
			幺 (乙 幺 幺)
			幺
			木
14	許	言
		午
15	成	

Lesson 40

生詞　Shēngcí　New Words

1.	过	(尾) guò *lè*	(a suffix) *(another suffix for things that already happened.)*
2.	治	(动) zhì	to cure, to heal
3.	次	(量) cì	(a measure word)
4.	下兒	(量) xiàr	(a measure word)
5.	鐘 钟	(名) zhōng	clock, bell
6.	敲	(动) qiāo	to knock
7.	对不起	duìbuqǐ	Excuse me, I'm sorry, I beg your pardon.
8.	表	(名) biǎo	watch
9.	停	(动) tíng	to stop
10.	带	(动) dài	to wear, to put on *(for objects like a string or watch ties) strings like things*
11.	有名	(形) yǒumíng	famous, noted
12.	参加	(动) cānjiā	to take part, to join
13.	晚会	(名) wǎnhuì	evening party
14.	座位	(名) zuòwèi	seat
15.	舒服	(形) shūfú	comfortable
16.	意思	(名) yìsi	meaning
17.	查	(动) chá	to look up (word in dictionary)

穿 chwan yifou (wear clothes)

語法　Yǔfǎ　Grammar

40.1 The Suffix 过 Emphasizing Past Experience   In a sentence with a verbal predicate, when we wish to stress an action in the past (that happened once or several times), we add the suffix 过 after the verb. e. g.

1. 他　从前　来过.

He came before. (He has been here before.)

2. 我　去过　那个　書店.

I've been to that bookstore.

In the above two examples, we emphasize 来 and 去 as past experiences. If there is a resultative complement or a complement of direction, the suffix 过 should be placed after them. e. g.

3. 那个　大夫　治好过　这种　病.

The doctor has cured this kind of illness before.

4. 我的　朋友　到　苏联　去过.

My friend has been to the Soviet Union.

As we know the suffix 了 is used to indicate the perfective aspect, so 过 and 了 can be used together when stress is laid on the completion of an action as a past experience. Generally speaking, the suffix 过 precedes the suffix 了. e. g.

5. 他　前天　来过　了.

He was here day before yesterday. (He came, but has left.)

6. 那本　小說兒　我　已經　看过　了.

I've already read that novel.

In the negative sentence, we put the negative adverb 没有 immediately before the verb carrying the suffix 过. It differs from the perfective aspect in that the suffix 过 has to be retained in the negative sentence, but the suffix 了 must be dropped. e. g.

If you were using (le)"了", then you would just drop it.
use "mei you" to negate guo

7. 他 沒 有 来过.

He hasn't come (before). (He has never been here before.)

8. 我 沒 有 看过 那本 小說兒.

I have never read that novel.

In turning such sentences into alternative interrogative sentences, we do the following:

9. 他 来过 沒 有?

Has he been here?

10. 你 看过 这本 小說兒 沒 有?

Have you ever read this novel?

When there is an object, it is often placed at the beginning of the sentence. e. g.

11. 这本 小說兒 你 看过 沒 有?

Have you ever read this novel?

12. 那个 演員 你 看見过 沒 有?

Have you ever seen that actor before?

40.2 The Verbal Measure Word 次 In Chinese, besides nominal measure words (14.1), there are also verbal measure words. But they are not the same in use: the nominal measure words and numerals are used together as adjective modifiers before nouns, while the verbal measure words and numerals are used together as complements after verbs. 次 is one of the common verbal measure words. e. g.

13. 上星期 他 来了 两次.

He came twice last week.

verb

14. 我　看过　一次　中国　話劇.

I have been to the Chinese play once.

40.3　下兒　It is also a verbal measure word, but sometimes it has a concrete meaning——the frequency of the action. e. g.

15. 鐘　敲了　三下兒.

The clock struck three times.

But it is more often used together with 一 showing that an action has lasted only for a very short time. e. g.

16. 我　要　想　一下兒　这个　問題.

I want to think about this problem.

17. 我　必須　准备　一下兒　那个　报告.

I must prepare (do a little preparation) for that report.

When 下兒 is used to indicate the frequency of an action, we may use any numeral before it; but when it is used to indicate that an action has lasted for only a short time, we can only use 一 before it. We know that when a verb is used reduplicatively, it always indicates that the action has lasted for only a little while (38.2). 一下兒 used after a verb plays the same role as the reduplication of the verb. Therefore, examples 16 and 17 can be expressed equally well by reduplicating the verbs:

18. 我　要　想(一)想　这个　問題.

I want to think about this problem.

19. 我　必須　准备准备　那个　报告.

I have to do some preparations for that report.

40.4　The Positions of the Object and the Verbal Measure

Word   When there is an object in a sentence, we have to pay attention to the position of the verbal measure word.

(1) If the object is a noun, the measure word, in general, must be placed before the object. e. g.

20. 他 哥哥 去了 一次 北京 医院.

His brother went to the Peking Hospital once.

21. 我 在 这个 合作社 买过 五六次 东西.

I've shopped five or six times in this co-op.

22. 先生 想 了解 一下兒 他的 学习 情况.

The teacher wants to understand his learning situation.

(2) When the object is a pronoun, the measure word should be placed after the object. e. g.

23. 他 住在 医院 的 时候兒, 我 看过 他 三次.

I visited him three times when he was staying at the hospital.

24. 我 到 这兒 来过 两次.

I have been (to) here twice.

25. 先生 叫 我 帮助 他 一下兒.

The teacher asked me to give him a little help.

課文 Kèwén   Text

I

(a₁) 对不起, 我的 表 停 了. 我

想 問 一下兒: 現在 几点 几分?

Excuse me, my watch has stopped. I'd like to ask you: "What time is it now?"

(b₁) 我 今天 沒 有 帶 表. 但是,
剛才 我 听見 鐘 敲了 两下兒.
我 想 現在 差不多 是 两点
过 四五分鐘.

I'm not wearing a watch today. But I heard the clock strike twice just now. I think it's probably four or five minutes after two.

II

(a₂) 星期六 晚上 你 去 首都 劇場
了 嗎?

Did you go the Capital Theatre Saturday evening?

(b₂) 沒 有.

No, I didn't.

(a₃) 为 什么 沒 有 去? 你 不
知道 那个 話劇 非常 有名 嗎?

Why not? Didn't you know that play was very famous?

(b₃) 知道. 但是, 我 已經 看过 两次
了, 所以 沒 有 去.

I did. But I had already seen it twice, so I didn't go.

(a₄) 首都 劇場 你 也 去过 嗎?

Have you also been to the Capital Theatre?

(b₄) 对了, 也 去过. 我 在 那兒
参加过 一次 晚会. 那个 劇場
又 新 又 大, 座位 很 舒服.

Yes, I have. I once attended an evening party there. That theatre is new and big. The seats are very comfortable.

III

(a₅) 劳駕! 这个 字 念 什么? 是 什么
意思? 你 告訴 我 一下兒.

Excuse me. How do you pronounce this word? What does it mean? Please tell me.

(b₅) 对不起, 我 沒 学过 这个 字, 我
也 不 知道.

I'm sorry. I haven't learned that word. I don't know it either.

(a₆) 你 有 字典 嗎?

Do you have a dictionary?

(b₆) 我 有, 你 查 一下兒.

I do. You may look it up.

(a₇) 你 看 这个 字 在 这兒, 講得
很 清楚.

Look, here's the word; it's explained clearly.

(b₇)   对了，我們 以后 要是 遇見 不
認識 的 字，就 应該 查 字典.

Right. From now on if we come across a word we don't
know (recognize), we should look it up in the dictionary.

課外練習 Kèwài liànxí Home Work

1) Write interrogative sentences for the following declarative sentences:

(1) 那个 大夫 治过 这种 病.

(2) 到 北京 大学 以后, 他 参加过
晚会.

2) Re-write the following sentences using 一下兒: xiàr

(3) 这个 意見 很 重要, 大家 应該
討論討論.

(4) 你 听听, 这个 表 停 了 沒 有？

3) Put the words 两次 into the following sentences:

(5) 他 在 合作社 买过 水菓.

(6) 我 在 晚会上 遇見过 他.

4) Fill the following blanks with 过 or 了:

昨天 我 参加＿＿一个 会. 在 会上
听＿＿一个 报告. 这个 作 报告 的
同志 是 一个 很 有名的 人. 从前
我 听＿＿他的 报告. 这 两次 他 都
講得 很 好.

汉字表 Hànzì biǎo Chinese Characters

１	治	氵

	治	治 治 治 治 治 治 治 治 治 治
2	次	次 次 次 次 次 次 次 次 次
3	敲	高攵 高攵 高攵 高攵 高攵 高攵 高攵
		攵 (丿 乁 攵) 高攵 高攵 高攵 高攵
4	表	表 表 表 表 表 表 表 表 表 表 表 表
5	停	亻 停 停 停 停 停 停 停
		亭 (亭 停 停 停 停 停) 停 停 停
6	参	厶 参
		大
		彡 参 参 参 参 参 参 参 参
7	加	加口 加口 加口 加口 加口 加口 加口 加口
8	座	座位 座位 座位 座位 座位
		座位 座位 座位 座位 座位
9	位	亻
		立
10	舒	舍 舒服 舒服 舒服 舒服
		予 (予 予 予 予) 舒服 舒服
11	服	月
		艮
12	查	木 查 查 查 查 查 查 查 查 查
		旦 查 查 查 查 查 查 查 查 查

Lesson 41

生詞 Shēngcí New Words

1. 为 （介）wèi — for
2. 建設 （动、名）jiànshè — to construct, construction
3. 社会主义 （名）shèhuìzhǔyì — Socialism
4. 进步 （名、形、动）jìnbù — progress, progressive, to progress
5. 服务 （动）fúwù — to serve
6. 替 （动、介）tì — to replace, to substitute, instead of, for...
7. 給 （介）gěi — for
8. 先...再... xiān...zài... — first... then...
9. 組織 （动、名）zǔzhǐ — to organize, organization
10. 联欢 （动）liánhuān — to hold a party, to hold a reunion
11. 封 （量）fēng — (a measure word)
12. 信 （名）xìn [封] — letter
13. 寄 （动）jì — to post, to mail
14. 早上 （名）zǎoshǎng — morning
15. 接到 （动）jiēdào — to receive
16. 国家 （名）guójiā — country

語法　Yŭfǎ　Grammar

41.1 The Preposition 为　为 is one of the commonly used prepositions.　We have learned that 为什么 is a prepositional construction.　Its object is always a noun denoting persons or things. Such a prepositional construction may describe the purpose of an action, the reason of the existence of a certain state, or the object of service. e. g.

1. 中国 人民 为 建设 社会主义 努力
工作.
　　people

   The Chinese people work hard in order to build (OR: for the purpose of building) socialism.

2. 大家 都 为 你的 进步 高兴.

   Everyone is happy over your progress.

3. 我們 要 为 人民 服务.
　　　　　　people

   We have to (OR: want to) serve the people.

In example 1 建设社会主义 is the object or purpose of 努力工作; in example 2 你的进步 is the reason for 高兴; and in example 3 人民 is the object of 服务. Sentences with such constructions are frequently used in a rather formal situation.　Moreover, such constructions have to be put where adverbal modifiers usually stand, and are never allowed at the end of a sentence. We must not say: 中国人民努力工作为建设社会主义.

41.2 The Preposition 替　替 may be used as a verb and suggests the meaning of "to be in the place of". e. g.

4. 張 先生 今天 有 事 不 能 上
課, 謝 先生 替 他.

   Mr. (OR: teacher) Zhang cannot attend the class (because) he is busy (has something to do) today. Mr. Xie is substituting for him.

But 替 is often used as a preposition. e. g.

5. 謝　先生　替　張　先生　上　課.

Mr. Xie is giving class in place of Mr. Zhang.

6. 哥哥　替　我　买了　一本　小説兒.

My (elder) brother bought me a novel (a novel for me).

7. 我　替　他　找着了　他的　表.

I found his watch for him.

In the above examples, 替張先生，替我 and 替他 are all pre-positional constructions used as adverbial modifiers.

41.3　The Preposition 給　We have already learned that 給 is used as a verb. But it is also often used as a preposition and serves as an adverbial modifier together with its object. e. g.

8. 我　給　朋友　开　門.

I opened the door for my friend.

9 先生　給　我們　講　語法.

The teacher explained grammar to us.

Here, 給朋友 and 給我們 are adverbial modifiers, therefore such prepositional constructions have to be placed before verbs. We cannot say: 我开朋友門 or 先生講我們語法. Neither can we say: 我开門給朋友, or 先生講語法給我們.

給 and 为 can be both translated into "for" in English, and may both introduce an object of service; but 为 can also indicate the aim or reason of an action, while 給 can only indicate the object of service. Therefore 給 can never be used to express the aim or reason of action in any sentence.

給 sometimes may be used instead of 替. e. g.

10. 他　从　城里　給　我　买　来了　一本　書.

He bought a book for me from the city.

Under certain circumstances 給我 may have the meaning of 替我.

41.4 先...再...   The construction 先...再... is used to lay stress on the order of two actions; the first verb should be placed after the word 先 (first) and the second verb should be placed after the word 再 (then). e. g.

11. 我們 应該 先 复習 語法 再 作 練習.

We should review grammar first, and then do the exercises.

12. 我們 現在 先 学 中文，以后 再 学 專业.

We learn Chinese first now and specialize later on.

課文 Kèwén Text

I

1. 他 为 参加 討論 会 准备了 不 少 意見.

He prepared a lot of opinions/suggestions in order to join in the discussion.

2. 我們 为 欢迎 新 来 的 同学 組織了 一个 联欢 会.

We organized a welcoming party so as to welcome the new (newly arrived) schoolmates.

3. 我 替 他 买了 一些 水菓 来.

I bought some fruit for him.

4. 張　先生　有　病　的　时候兒，这个
先生　替　他　上过　一次　課.

When Mr. Zhang was ill this instructor substituted for him
once before.

5. 要是　您　認識　他，我　想　請
您　給　我們　介紹介紹.

If you know him, I'd like to have you introduce us.

6. 这个　很　有　經驗　的　大夫　給
他　治好了　病.

This very experienced physician cured him (his illness).

7. 到　朋友　那兒　的　时候兒，你
应該　先　敲　門，再　进去.

When you go to your friend's, you should first knock and
then enter.

II

我　哥哥　給　我　寫了　一封　信.
这封　信　是　两个　星期　以前　寄　的.
今天　早上　寄到　了. 我　同屋　知道
我　希望　接到　信　所以　就　替　我
拿来　了. 我　哥哥　在　信里　寫了　很
多　我們　国家的　情况，也　談到了　自己的
工作. 他　叫　我　先　学好　中文，再　学習

專业. 学好 專业 就 可以 好好兒地 为
人民 服务. 我 看了 信, 非常 高兴, 我
同屋 也 为 我 高兴.

My brother wrote me a letter. The letter was mailed two weeks ago. It arrived this morning. My roommate knew that I was hoping to receive (the) letter(s), so he brought it to me. In his letter my brother wrote a lot about the condition of our country, and also talked about his own work. He told me to learn Chinese well first, and then specialize. After specializing I would be able to serve the people well. After reading the letter I was very happy. My roommate was also happy for me.

課外練習　Kèwài liànxí　Home Work

1) Fill the blanks with proper prepositions:

(1) 我 想 請 您 给 我 講講 这个 生
詞的 意思. *I want you to explain the meaning of the word for me*

(2) 他的 报告 很 好, 我們 听完了
都 为 他 鼓掌.

(3) 我 今天 不 能 到 你們 宿舍
去, 希望 你 能 替 我 通知
一下兒 你的 同屋.

(4) 他 为 写 这封 信, 今天 没 有
休息.

2) Translate the following sentences into Chinese:—

(5) The teacher has already explained for me the meaning ot this word.

(6) My elder brother has borrowed a Chinese-English dictionary for me from the university library.

(7) The teacher has talked several times with me in order to see my point of view.

3) Copy the following words and word groups, transcribe the underlined Chinese characters, and compare their different ways of writing:

(8) { 身<u>体</u> / <u>本</u>子 }

(9) { 我們 / <u>找</u>   大夫 }

(10) { <u>从</u>前 / <u>以</u>前 }

(11) { <u>大</u>   汽車 / <u>太</u>   慢 }

(12) { <u>自己</u> / <u>己</u>經 }

(13) { 一<u>張</u>   紙 / <u>長</u>   桌子 }

汉字表   Hànzì ьiǎo   Chinese Characters

1	义	ノ 乂 义	
2	步	丨 卜 𣥂 止 牛 歩 步	
3	务	夂	
		力	
4	建	聿 (⁊ ⁊ 聿 聿 聿 聿)	
		廴 (𠂆 廴)	
5	設	言	
		殳	
6	替	夫夫	夫
			夫
		日	
7	再	一 丅 再 再	

8	組	糸	
		且	
9	織	糸	
		戠	
10	封	圭	土
			土
		寸	
11	信	亻	
		言	
12	寄	宀	
		奇	
13	接	扌	
		妾	立
			女

Lesson 42

語法复習 Yǔfǎ fùxí Review

42.1 Four Kinds of Sentences In Chinese, sentences may be divided into four kinds according to their construction.

(1) The Sentence with a Substantive Predicate This kind of sentence is used to describe or judge of the subject "what it is", "to what it is equivalent", "of what quality" and "of what kind". In the predicate there must be a substantive or a substantive construction. The copula 是 is most frequently used in the sentence (13.1). e. g.

1. 他 是 一年級 那班的 先生.

He is the instructor for that first-year class.

2. 今天的 晚会 是 欢迎 会.

The party that evening is a welcoming party.

叫 may be used instead of 是 (19.2). e. g.

3. 那个 剧場 叫 首都 剧場.

That theatre is called the Capital Theatre.

4. 那个 話剧 叫 什么 名字?

What is that play called? (What is the name of that play?)

Yet, there are a number of sentences of this kind, where a substantive construction in the form of ...的 is used after the copula 是 instead of a simple substantive (17.1). e. g.

5. 这个 意見 是 張 同志 的.

This idea is Comrade Zhang's.

6. 桌子上的 表 是 他的.

The watch on the table is his.

7. 那封 信 是 一个 朋友 寄来 的.

That letter was sent (here) by a friend.

8. 他 談 的 經驗 是 很 重要的.

The experiences he talked about are very important.

Besides the above-mentioned sentences, there are still some other sentences in which the copula is not used (31.2). e. g.

9. 这个 同志 五十多岁.

This comrade is fifty-odd years old.

10. 明天 十月 三十.

Tomorrow is the 30th of October.

11. 那个 鐘 十五塊 錢.

That clock is (costs) fifteen dollars.

But all the above sentences in the negative form must use the copula.

(2) The Sentence with an Adjectival Predicate (14.3) In this kind of sentence the predicate is an adjective, describing the subject. e. g.

12. 他 新 买 的 表 非常 好看.

His newly bought watch is very good-looking.

13. 從 上月 起, 他 学習 方面的
进步 很 大.

Since last month, his progress in studies has been great.

14. 这次 他 写 的 信 特别 長.

The letter he wrote this time is exceptionally long.

(3) The Sentence with a Verbal Predicate (16.1)   In this kind of sentence the predicate is a verb and is used to describe an action. e. g.

15. 誰 在 外边兒 敲 門?

Who's knocking on the door outside?

16. 新 中国 建設得 很 快.

The new China has been constructed very swiftly.

17. 她 (是) 在 合作社 买 的 水菓.

She bought her fruit at the co-op.

18. 我 請 他 替 我 拿 一点兒 藥 来.

I asked (requested) him to bring me some medicine.

19. 我 希望 我 能 很 快地 学好
中文.

I hope I can master Chinese very quickly.

(4) The Sentence with a Clause Predicate (39.1)   The predicate of this kind of sentence is made up of a subject-predicate construction. e. g.

20. 首都 劇場 座位 舒服.

The Capital Theatre has (more) comfortable seats. (As for the Capital Theatre, the seats are [more] comfortable.)

21. 这个 医院 大夫 多.

There are many (OR: more) doctors in this hospital.

42.2 Nominal **Measure Words** and **Verbal Measure Words**
We know that there is a special part of speech in Chinese——
the measure word. When a demonstrative pronoun or numeral
is used before a noun, there must be a measure word to connect them (14.1). e. g.

22. 我 刚才 接到 一个 开会 的 通知.

I just received a notice for a meeting.

23. 这辆 汽车 是 谁 叫 来 的?

Who called for this car?

We have also learned the verbal measure words (40.2), and
know that they are used together with verbs. But there is one
point to be noticed, the nominal measure words are used before
nouns and the verbal measure words are used after verbs. e. g.

24. 他 去过 两次 北京 剧场.

He's been to the Peking Theatre twice.

25. 我 忘了 表 在 哪儿, 要 找 一下儿.

I've forgotten where the watch is—have to look for it.

Besides, there is one more difference: when the numeral
before the nominal measure word is 一, it is always omitted
except at the beginning of a sentence. e. g.

26. 我 想 给 您 提 个 意见.

I'd like to make a suggestion to you.

27. 他 为 听 报告 买了 个 本子.

He bought a notebook for the purpose of listening to
reports.

But, before the verbal measure word — is generally not omitted. e. g.

28. 北京　圖書館　我　只　去过　一次.

I've been to the Peking Library only once.

42.3 了 and 过 了 and 过, as we know, are two verbal suffixes. 了 is used to indicate the completion of an action; a completed action always happens in the past. 过 is used to indicate experience, and experience also refers to past action. Since both bear relation to past actions, they are easily confused, though they are actually different from each other.

(1) When we wish to stress a completed action, we use the suffix 了 after the verb. e. g.

29. 在　联欢　会上，主席　请　他　唱了　一个　歌兒.

At the welcoming party the chairman asked him to sing a song.

30. 他　为　我們　准备了　不　少的　水菓　和　糖.

He prepared a lot of fruit and candy for us.

(2) When we wish to place special stress on a certain experience in the past, we use the suffix 过 after the verb. e. g.

31. 先生　到　我們　宿舍　来过　很　多　次.

The teacher's been to our dormitory many times.

32. 我　从前　没　有　参加过　这么　大　的　晚会，　这　是　第一次.

I have never participated in such a big party. This is the first time.

It is only because the point of emphasis is different, that in the above two groups of examples we cannot use the suffixes 了 and 过 interchangeably. However, when we wish to emphasize the completion of the action as well as the action as past experience, then 了 and 过 may be used together. e. g.

33. 那本 小説兒 雖然 看过了, 我 还 想 看.

Although I've already read that novel, I want to read it again.

34. 听过了 这个 报告 的 人 都 説 这个 报告 好.

Everyone who's heard this report says that it is good.

Occasionally in some sentences either 了 or 过 may be used, but we must understand that different suffixes imply different point of emphasis. e. g.

35. 他 到 那个 書店 去 了, (所以 不 在 宿舍里). *only a past action*

He's gone to that bookstore (so he's not in the dormitory).

36. 他 到 那个 書店 去过, (所以 他 認識 書店 在 什么 地方).

He's been to that bookstore (so he knows where the bookstore is). *emphasized experience*

課文 Kèwén Text

I

(a₁) 方东 同志, 先生 叫 我 通知 你 今天 下午 听 报告.

Comrade Fang Dong, the teacher asked me to notify you
to (go to) listen to a report this afternoon.

(b₁) 什么 报告?

What report?

(b₂) "国家 建設 方面的 几个 問題".
你 去 不 去?

"A few problems concerning (the aspect of) national
construction." Are you going?

(b₂) 一定 去. 这个 报告 应該 听听.
你 知道 誰 給 我們 講 嗎?

Definitely. One should listen to this report. Do you know
who's addressing us?

(a₃) 高子清 同志. 我 听过 一次 他
的 报告. 他 講得 好 極了.

Comrade Gao Zi-qing. I've heard his report once. He
delivered it exceedingly well!

(b₃) 在 哪兒 講? 是 不 是 在 礼堂?

Where is he reporting? Is it in the auditorium?

(a) 不 在 这兒. 在 人民 大学. 这
个 报告 是 为 三四个 大学 組
織 的.

Not here. At the People's University. This report has been
organized for three or four universities.

(b₄) 我 还 沒 有 去过 人民 大学 呢.

I haven't been to the People's University yet.

(a₅) 沒 关系, 我 去过, 我 認識. 我 可以 跟 你 一起 去.

It doesn't matter. I've been there. I know how to go there. I can go with you.

(b₅) 好 極了. 报告 几点 开始?

Splendid! When does the report start?

(a₆) 两点半. 现在 我 先 回去, 一 点半 再 来.

2:30. I'm going back now first. I'll come again at 1:30.

II

我 到 中国 来 的 时候兒, 有 八 九个 朋友 都 跟 我 说: "到了 中国, 你 要 常常 給 我們 写 信. 我們 希 望 知道 你的 情况, 也 希望 知道 中 国的 情况. 中国 是 我們的 好 朋友, 我們 应該 多多地 了解 中国的 人民 和 中国的 建设."

When I came to China, eight or nine of my friends said to me, "After reaching China you have to write us often. We hope to know about how you are doing. We also hope to know situations in China. China is our good friend. We should try to understand a lot about the Chinese people and China's construction."

到了中国以后，因为我学习很忙，只给他们写过两三次信。但是已经接到过他们十几封了。这个星期日上午我准备写信。我要告诉他们中国人民怎么样为社会主义建设努力工作。我也要告诉他们自己在学习中文方面有了一些进步。

Since reaching China, because I have been busy with my studies, I have written them only two or three times. Yet I've already received more than ten letters from them. This Sunday morning I plan to write letters. I want to tell them how the Chinese people work hard for the construction of socialism. I also want to tell them that I myself have made some progress in the (aspect of) studying of Chinese.

Lesson 43

生詞　Shēngcí　New Words

1.	时间	(名)	shíjiān	time
2.	工人	(名)	gōngrén	worker
3.	困难	(名)	kùnnán	difficulty
4.	骑	(动)	qí	to ride, to sit astride
5.	自行车	(名)	zìxíngchē〔辆〕	bicycle
6.	解放	(动、名)	jiěfàng	to liberate, liberation
7.	劳动	(名、动)	láodòng	labour, to labour
8.	饭	(名)	fàn	food, meal, cooked rice
9.	衣服	(名)	yīfú〔件〕	clothes, dress, clothing
10.	穿	(动)	chuān	to put on, to wear
11.	小组	(名)	xiǎozǔ	group
12.	锻鍊	(动、名)	duànliàn	to do (physical) exercise, training
13.	干	(动)	gàn	to do
14.	方便	(形)	fāngbiàn	convenient
15.	坏	(形)	huài	bad
16.	样子	(名)	yàngzi	sort, kind, style
17.	并且	(連)	bìngqiě	moreover, and
18.	家	(名)	jiā	home, family

語法　Yǔfǎ　Grammar

43.1　The Multi-verbal Form Indicating Purpose　In Chinese, besides the telescopic form (38.1), there are sentences containing complicated predicates. Sometimes two (or more) verbal constructions are used together in one sentence. We call such kind of sentence the sentence of the multi-verbal form. Here we shall deal with sentences of the multi-verbal form indicating purpose. e. g.

1. 我　要　进　城　买　东西.

   I want to go into town to shop.

2. 大家　去　礼堂　听　报告.

   Everyone goes to the auditorium to listen to reports.

Here 买东西 is the purpose of 进城 and 听报告 is the purpose of 去礼堂. In each sentence, the second action tells something about the first action.

There is a difference between the multi-verbal form and the telescopic form. The predicate in the telescopic form contains two verbs, belonging to different subjects. The subject of the first verb is the subject of the whole sentence, while the subject of the second verb is the object of the first verb. In the multi-verbal form, no matter how many verbal constructions there are in the predicate, all of them share one and the same subject — the subject of the whole sentence.

There is another point to be observed, that is, 来 or 去 is often used to connect the verbal construction of purpose with the verbal construction that stands before it. e. g.

3. 中国　同学　常常　到　我們　宿舍　来
   玩兒.

   Chinese schoolmates often come to our dormitory to have fun.

4. 他　要　到　合作社　去　买　鉛笔.

   He wants to go to the co-op to buy pencils.

In the above, 来 and 去 are used with reference to the direction of action. But 来 is sometimes rather vague in meaning, for it is only used to introduce the second action of purpose and bears no relation to the actual direction of action. e. g.

5. 学校 要 組織 一个 晚会 来 欢迎 那些 新 来 的 同学.

> The school wants to organize an evening party to welcome those new schoolmates (those schoolmates who have newly arrived).

43.2 The Multi-verbal Form Indicating Means   There is another kind of the multi-verbal form in common use, expressing the way or means by which an action takes effect. In general, a sentence of such a multi-verbal form contains two verbal constructions, and the first verbal construction indicating way or means assumes the function of an adverbial modifier in the whole sentence. e. g.

6. 先生 用 中文 講 語法.

> The teacher lectures on grammar in Chinese.

7. 他們 坐 汽車 去 首都 剧場 了.

> They have gone to the Capital Theatre in an automobile.

Here, 用中文 and 坐汽車 are used to describe the way of 講語法 and the means of 去首都剧場.

43.3 The Multi-verbal Form with 有... or 没有...

There is another kind of the multi-verbal form in which the first verbal construction is in the form of 有... or 没有... with a simple verb or a verb-object construction following it:

(1) A simple verb used after 有... e. g.

8. 我 有 錢 用.

> I have money to spend.

9. 他 沒 有 小說兒 看.

He doesn't have any novels to read.

In such sentences, the object of 有 or 沒有 is also the object of the second verb.

(2) A verb-object construction used after 有... e. g.

10. 下午 他 沒 有 時間 找 你.

He doesn't have time to look for you in the afternoon.

11. 我 有 問題 問 先生.

I have questions to ask the teacher.

In such sentences, the second verbal construction is used to tell something about the first verbal construction.

課文 Kèwén Text

I

1. 工人 同志 到 我們 学校 来 的 時候兒, 我們 都 到 門 外边兒 去 欢迎 他們.

When comrade-workers came to our school, we all went outside the gate to welcome them.

2. 我們 应該 想 个 方法 来 帮助 学習 困难 的 同志.

We should think of a method to help the comrades who have difficulties in learning.

3. 先生 每天 都 騎 自行車 来 上 課.

The teacher rides a bicycle to come to class every day.

4. 我們 用 鋼笔 或者 鉛笔 練習
   汉字, 都 可以.

We may use either a fountain pen or a pencil to practice writing characters.

5. 解放 以前, 劳动 人民 常常 没
   有 飯 吃, 没 有 衣服 穿.

Before the Liberation, working people often had neither food (to eat) nor clothes (to wear).

6. 我們 小組 每天 都 有 时間 鍛鍊
   身体.

Our group has time every day to do physical exercise.

II

(a₁) 下午 你 要 干 什么?

What do you want to do in the afternoon?

(b₁) 我 要 进 城 去.

I want to go into town.

(a₂) 进 城 去 干 什么?

What do you want to do in town?

(b₂) 去 买 东西

To do some shopping.

(a₃) 你 怎么 去——坐 汽車 去, 还是
    騎 自行車 去?

How are you going, by bus or by bicycle?

(b₃) 我 想 騎 自行車 去. 星期日 汽車 人 多, 騎 自行車 又 舒服 又 方便.

I'm thinking of going by bicycle. On Sundays there are a lot of people on the bus. Riding a bicycle is both comfortable and convenient.

(a₄) 你 要 去 買 什么?

What do you want to buy?

(b₄) 我的 鋼笔 坏 了. 上星期 我 一个 星期 沒 有 鋼笔 用, 非常 不 方便. 我 今天 要 去 買 一枝.

My fountain pen is broken. Last week I didn't have a fountain pen (to use) for the whole week. It was extremely inconvenient. I want to go buy one today.

(a₅) 学校的 合作社 也 有 鋼笔 卖, 你 不 知道 嗎?

The school co-op also carries fountain pens. Don't you know?

(b₅) 知道. 但是, 我 想 城里的 鋼笔 样子 多. 并且, 我 每天 都 上課, 沒 有 时間 看 朋友. 今天 星期日, 想 去 他們 家 看看.

Yes, I know. But I think there is more variety of fountain pens in town. Furthermore, I have classes every day and have no time to visit friends. Today's Sunday. I'd like to visit them at home.

(a₆) 你 先 买 鋼笔 还是 先 看 朋友？

Are you going to buy your pen first or visit friends first?

(b₆) 我 先 去 看 朋友，再 去 买 东西.

I am going to visit friends first and then shop.

課外練習　Kèwài liànxí　Home Work

1) Write proper interrogative sentences for the following declarative sentences (the words underlined show where the questions are):

(1) 那个 同学 到 圖書館 借書 去 了.

(2) 我們 用 汉俄 字典 看 中文 書.

(3) 我 沒 有 好 經驗 可以 在 会上 介紹.

2) Translate the following sentences into Chinese:
(4) He has gone home on bicycle.
(5) The elder brother is going to the city to buy two pieces of clothing.
(6) I have understood all. I have no question to ask the teacher.

3) Fill the following blanks with Chinese characters according to the given spellings; notice that different characters may have the same sound:

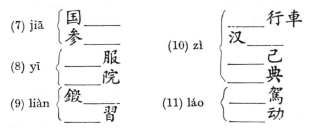

(7) jiā { 国 ＿＿＿
　　　 { 参 ＿＿＿

(8) yī { ＿＿＿服
　　　 { ＿＿＿院

(9) liàn { 鍛 ＿＿＿
　　　　 { ＿＿＿ 習

(10) zì { ＿＿＿行車
　　　 汉 ＿＿＿
　　　 { ＿＿＿己
　　　 { ＿＿＿典

(11) láo { ＿＿＿駕
　　　　 { ＿＿＿动

(12) fāng
{
___ 面
___ 便
___ 法
地 ___

(13) shí
{
___ 候兒
___ 个　小組
___ 間

汉字表　Hànzì biǎo　Chinese Characters

1	困	冂 困 困
2	騎	馬
		奇
3	行	彳
		于（二 于）
4	放	
5	动	云
		力
6	衣	丶 亠 广 忕 衣 衣
7	穿	宀
		牙（一 ㄈ 二 于 牙）
8	鍛	金
		段（丿 亻 个 作 皀 段）
9	鍊	金
		柬
10	便	亻
		更（一 百 更 更）

11	坏	土
		不
12	并	、 ⌣ 并
13	且	

Lesson 44

生詞 Shēngcí New Words

1.	正	（副）	zhèng	just (a word indicating the progressive aspect)
2.	才	（副）	cái	(a word expressing delay), just
3.	課文	（名）	kèwén	text
4.	计划	（名、动）	jìhuà	plan, to plan
5.	大声兒		dàshēngr	loud, loudly
6.	訂	（动）	dìng	to make (a plan)
7.	發音	（名）	fāyīn	pronunciation
8.	正确	（形）	zhèngquè	correct
9.	注意	（动、名）	zhùyì	to take care, to pay attention, attention
10.	机会	（名）	jīhuì	chance, opportunity
11.	改正	（动）	gǎizhèng	to correct
12.	錯誤	（名、形）	cuòwù	mistake, mistaken
13.	好处	（名）	hǎochù	advantage
14.	熟	（形）	shú	well versed, well acquainted
15.	鐘头	（名）	zhōngtóu	hour
16.	試	（动）	shì	to try

語法 Yǔfǎ Grammar

44.1 The Progressive Aspect   We know that in Chinese the aspect of an action, that is to say, the state of an action, is of great importance. When we want to express clearly that an action is in progress, we use the progressive aspect. There are several ways of expressing the progressive aspect. For example, if we want to stress the progressive aspect of the action in 我們上課, we may say:

1. 我們 上 課 呢!

We are having a class.

2. 我們 正 上 課 (呢)!

We are having a class.

3. 我們 在 上 課 (呢)!

We are having a class.

4. 我們 正 在 上 課 呢!

We are having a class.

Hence we know that ...呢, 正..., 在..., 正在... are all different ways of expressing the progressive aspect. Sometimes 正..., 在... or 正在 may be followed by 呢 at the end of a sentence.

The progressive aspect is not merely used for action of the present time. When we want to make clear that a past or future action was or will be going on at a certain time, or going on simultaneously with another action, we also use the progressive aspect. e. g.

5. 昨天 我 去 他 家 的 時候兒, 他 在 吃 飯.

Yesterday when I went to his house, he was having his meal.

6. 要是 你 明天 十二点 去 他 家, 他 一定 正在 吃 飯.

If you go to his house tomorrow at 12:00, he will definitely be having lunch.

The action in example 5 is in the past time and that in example 6 is in the future time. Generally speaking, we use the past progressive aspect quite often but rarely the future progressive aspect. Besides, in a sentence of future progressive aspect, some adverb must be used, (such as the word 一定 in example 6).

44.2   The Negative Form of the Progressive Aspect
We use the negative adverb 沒有 in a verb of negative progressive aspect. e. g.

7. 她 来 的 时候兒, 我們 沒 有 上 課.

When she came we were not in class.

8. 我 去 找 他 的 时候兒, 他 沒 有 学習.

When I went looking for him he was not studying.

In reply, if the answer is in the negative, we often use only 沒有 and do not repeat the question. e. g.

9、 你 在 看 小説兒 嗎?

Are you reading a novel?

10. 沒 有, 看 杂誌 呢!

No, I'm reading a magazine.

11. 他 来 的 时候兒, 你們 正 在 上 課 嗎?

When he came, were you just having a class (right in the middle of a class)?

12. 沒 有, 那 时候兒 我們 正 鍛鍊 呢!

No, we were exercising then.

13. 你 去 找 他 的 时候兒, 他 正
作 練習 嗎?

When you went to look for him, was he doing exercises?

14. 沒 有, 复習 語法 呢!

No, he was reviewing grammar.

44. 3 才 and 就 In Chinese, there are some adverbs which are often used to express the modal tone or the attitude of the speaker towards a matter or thing. Among them 才 and 就 are the most commonly used. When the speaker feels that an action is delayed or happens not promptly, he will use 才 before the predicate. e. g.

15. 今天的 晚会 七点 开始, 十点 才
开完 呢!

Tonight's party begins at 7; it won't be over until 10.

16. 我 敲 門 敲了 很 多 下兒, 他
才 听見.

I knocked on the door many times before he heard me.

When an action is not yet completed, the word 才 is always followed by the particle 呢, because these two words form an idiomatic word group (as in example 15); but after the word 才, we never use the particle 了, whether an action is completed or not (as in example 16).

就 is the exact opposite of 才 in meaning. When the speaker feels an action happens very soon or promptly, he will use 就 before the predicate. e. g.

17. 上星期六的 晚会 七点 开始,
十点 就 开完 了.

Last Saturday night's party started at 7; it was over by (as early as) 10.

18. 我 只 敲了 两下兒 門, 他 就 听見 了.

He heard me after I had knocked only twice.

就 must be followed by the particle 了, when an action is completed (or supposed to be completed).

It must be pointed out that "soon", "delayed", "promptly", "not promptly" are not absolute in sense, and are only the subjective feeling of the speaker Therefore, the speaker may use either 就….. (了) or 才….. (呢) for one and the same action, depending on his personal feeling. e. g.

19. 我 每天 都 十二点半 吃 飯, 今天 十二点 就 吃 了.

I have lunch every day at 12:30, but I ate at 12 today.

20. 我 每天 都 十一点半 吃 飯, 今天 十二点 才 吃.

I have lunch every day at 11:30; I did not eat until 12 today.

課文 Kèwén Text

(a₁) 你 在 干 什么? 正 在 作 練習 嗎?

What are you doing? Doing your exercises?

(b₁) 沒 有, 我 念 課文 呢.

No, I am reading the text.

(a₂) 你 为 什么 不 快 作 練習?

現在 已經 九点 了, 你 什么 时候兒
才 作 練習 呢?

Why don't you do your exercises right away? It's already 9.
When are you going to do your exercises?

(b₂) 我 一刻鐘 以后 就 作 練習. 我
有 一个 学習 計划: 每天 用
三刻鐘 大声兒地 念 課文. 現在
还 沒 有 念完 呢!

I'll do my exercises in fifteen minutes. I have a plan for
learning: every day I spend three quarters of an hour
reading the text aloud. I have not yet finished reading.

(a₃) 为 什么 訂 这样兒的 計划?

Why did you make such a plan?

(b₃) 發音 是 非常 重要的. 要是 希望
自己 說 的 話, 中国 人 能 听懂,
必須 發音 正确. 所以 我 从
开始 学習 起, 就 注意 發音 了.
有 机会, 我 就 請 先生 給 我
改正 錯誤.

Pronunciation is very important. If I wish the Chinese
people to understand what I say, I must pronounce
accurately. Therefore from the very beginning of my
studies I have paid a lot of attention to pronunciation.
Whenever I get a chance, I ask the teacher to correct my
mistakes.

(a₄) 所以 你的 發音 特别 正确. 但是

你 用 这么 多 时間 念 課文, 还
有 时間 記 生詞 复習 語法 嗎?

Therefore your pronunciation is unusually accurate. But if
you spend so much time reading the text, do you still have
time to memorize the vocabulary and to review the
grammar?

(b₄) 念 課文 好处 很 多. 要是 課文
念熟 了, 里边兒的 語法 也 懂 了,
生詞 也 記清楚 了.

There are many advantages in reading the text. If you
learn the text well, you'll understand the grammar in it,
and will also remember the vocabulary clearly.

(a₅) 你 每天 都 用 多少 時間 作
練習?

How much time do you spend every day doing the
exercises?

(b₅) 我 每天 用 半个多 鐘头 就
可以 作好 練習 了.

I need only a little more than half an hour every day to
finish my exercises.

(a₆) 你 給 我 介紹 的 这个 学習
方法 很 好, 我 明天 一定 試試.

This learning method that you've introduced to me is very
good. I'll definitely give it a try tomorrow.

課外練習 Kèwài liànxí Home Work

1) Make five sentences using different forms of the progressive
aspect of each of the following verbs or word groups:

(1) 鼓掌

(2) 穿 衣服

(3) 开 討論 会

(4) 建設

(5) 作 句子

2) Complete the following sentences using 才 or 就 and the modal particles:

(6) 这封 信 来得 很 快, 只用 五天.

(7) 你 可以 慢慢兒地 准备, 下星期 六＿＿＿＿＿.

汉字表 Hànzì biǎo Chinese Characters

1	正	一 丁 下 正 正
2	計	
3	划	
4	声	士 丰 韦 声 声
5	訂	言
		丁（一 丁）
6	音	
7	确	石（一 丆 石）
		角
8	注	氵
		主
9	机	才

		几	
10	改	フ コ 己 改	
11	誤	言	
		吳 (口 吕 吴 吴 吴)	
12	处	ノ 勺 久 处	
13	熟	孰	享 (丶 亠 言 享)
			丸
		灬	
14	試	言 ·	
		式 (一 工 式 式)	

Lesson 45

生詞 Shēngcí New Words

1.	着	(尾)	zhē	(a suffix)
2.	花兒	(名)	huār	flower
3.	屋子	(名)	wūzî 〔間〕	room
4.	間	(量)	jiān	(a measure word)
5.	簡單	(形)	jiǎndān	simple
6.	床	(名)	chuáng 〔張〕	bed
7.	放	(动)	fàng	to put
8.	白	(形)	bái	white
9.	顔色	(名)	yánsè	colour
10.	墙	(名)	qiáng	wall
11.	掛	(动)	guà	to hang
12.	画兒	(名)	huàr 〔張〕	picture
13.	空气	(名)	kōngqì	air
14.	躺	(动)	tǎng	to lie
15.	立刻	(副)	lìkè	at once, immediately
16.	笑	(动)	xiào	to smile
17.	关心	(动、名)	guānxīn	to concern oneself about, concern
18.	別的	(代)	biédè	other, others

語法　Yǔfǎ　Grammar

45.1　The Continuous Aspect　　If an action does not stop as soon as it happens, but remains in a continuous state, then this action belongs to the continuous aspect. In Chinese, the continuous aspect is indicated by adding the suffix 着 after the verb. e. g.

1. 我們　在　椅子上　坐着.

We were (are) sitting on chairs.

2. 先生　在　黑板　旁边兒　站着.

The teacher was (is) standing next to the blackboard.

坐 and 站 are verbs of action, but when followed by the suffix 着, the function of the two verbs is changed from expressing action to expressing state. Since the suffix 着 is an integral part of the verb, the object, if there is one, should be placed after the verb and the suffix. e. g.

3. 你　能　替　我　拿着　这本　字典　嗎?

Can you hold this dictionary for me?

4. 他　应該　記着　这件　事.

He should remember this (matter).

Notice that no extraneous element is allowed between the verb and the suffix 着, and no complement should ever be used after the verb with such a suffix.

Since a progressive action is very often at the same time a continuous one, therefore the suffix 着 may also be used together with the progressive aspect. e. g.

5. 大家　正　开着　会　呢!

We were having a meeting.

6. 他　跟　先生　談着　話　呢!

He is talking with the teacher.

Sometimes, when an action is already completed, and the result of the action continues, we also use the suffffix 着 after the verb. e. g.

7. 他 穿着 一件 新 衣服.

He is wearing a new garment.

8. 黑板上 写着 几个 汉字.

There are several characters written on the blackboard.

Here the actions of 穿 and 写 have already been completed, and the clothes are still on him and the Chinese characters still on the blackboard. So the suffix 着 is used to express the continuation of the result of an action.

45.2 The Negative Form of the Continuous Aspect Generally speaking, we also use the negative adverb 沒有 in a verb of negative continuous aspect. e. g.

9. 門 沒 有 开着, 窗户 开着 呢!

The door is not open; the window is (open).

45.3 The Multi-verbal Form Indicating Concomitant Action When there are two actions proceeding at the same time, and the first action describes the way or manner of the second action, then, we put the suffix 着 after the first verb. e. g.

10. 先生 站着 講 語法.

The teacher explains the grammar while standing.

11. 这些 問題 你們 可以 看着 課文 回答.

You may answer these questions while looking at the text.

In the above two examples, 站着 indicates the manner of explaining grammar and 看着課文 indicates how to answer the questions. Although in each of the above examples the two actions take place at the same time, the second action is pri-

mary in importance and the first action is only secondary.
The first verbal construction here assumes the function of an
adverbial modifier.

課文   Kèwén   Text

我 有 一个 朋友 病 了, 现在 正
在 医院 住着. 昨天 下午, 我 带着
花兒 和 水菓 去 看 他.

I have a friend who is ill, and is now staying at the
hospital. Yesterday afternoon I brought some flowers and
fruit (when I went) to visit him.

到了 医院, 我 找着了 我 朋友的 屋子,
就 敲 門 进去 了. 这 是 一间 又
干淨 又 舒服 的 屋子. 屋子里的 东西
很 简单. 有 一張 病床, 床 旁边兒 放着
一張 小 桌子 和 一把 椅子, 都 是 白
颜色 的. 墙上 掛着 一張 画兒. 两个
窗戸 都 开着, 屋子里 空气 非常 好.
我 进去 的 时候兒, 我的 朋友 正
躺着 看 画报 呢. 他 看見了 我 很
高兴, 立刻 笑着 讓 我 坐下.

After arriving at the hospital, and finding my friend's
room, I knocked on the door and went in. It was a clean
and comfortable room. The furniture (things) in the room
was very simple. There was a hospital bed. Next to the bed
were (placed) a small table and a chair. All of these were
white. On the wall there was a painting. Both windows
were open. The air in the room was very fresh (good).

When I entered, my friend was lying in bed reading a pictorial. When he saw me he was very glad. Smiling, he immediately asked me to sit down.

我 先 問了問 他 身体的 情况, 并且 告訴 他 同学們 都 很 关心 他的 病, 希望 他 早 (一)点兒 好. 他 告訴 我 他 在 这兒 休息得 很 好, 医院 很 关心 病人. 他 說 桌子上 放着 的 画报 和 花兒, 都 是 医院的 人 給 他 拿来 的. 以后, 我們 又 談了談 学校的 情况. 五点半, 别的 朋友 来 看 他, 我 就 回 学校 了.

First I asked him about the state of his health. I also told him that his fellow students were all concerned about his illness, and hoped that he would recover soon. He told me that he was resting very well there. The hospital was very concerned about the patients. (The hospital took good care of the patients.) He said that both the pictorials and the flowers on the table were brought to him by the staff in the hospital. Later on, we also talked about (the conditions of) our school. At half after five (some) other friends came to see him. Thereupon I came back to school.

課外練習 Kèwài liànxí Home Work

1) Complete the following sentences (care should be taken of the suffix of the continuous aspect).

(1) 明天 上午 我 要 带＿＿＿＿＿.

(2) 主席 台上 放＿＿＿＿＿.

(3) 台 中間兒＿＿＿＿＿一張 桌子.

(4) 主席 在 台上＿＿＿＿＿.

2) Translate the following sentences into Chinese:
   (5) When our Chinese friend was talking with us, some of us talked standing and some sitting.
   (6) The comrade who is making a report does it standing.
   (7) I am knocking at the door and asking, "Is Comrade Chang at home?"
   (8) Doctors all wear white gowns while (they are) working.

汉字表　Hànzì biǎo　Chinese Characters

1	花	⺾	
		化	亻
			匕
2	簡	⺮	
		間	
3	單	吅　吕　單	
4	床	广	
		木	
5	白		
6	顏	彥	文
			厂
			彡
		頁	
7	色	⼃　⼓　色	
8	墙	土	
		嗇（一　十　卡　去　去　嗇）	

9	掛	扌		
		卦	圭	
			卜	
10	空	穴		
		工		
11	气			
12	躺	身		
		尚（丨 丬 丬 丬 尚 尚）		
13	立			
14	笑	竹		
		夭（丿 夭）		
15	心			

Lesson 46

生詞 Shēngcí New Words

1.	革命史	（名） gémìngshǐ	history of revolution
2.	表演	（名、动） biǎoyǎn	performance, to perform
3.	小时	（名） xiǎoshí	hour
4.	当然	（副） dāngrán	of course
5.	自学	（动） zìxué	to study by oneself
6.	打(球)	（动） dǎ(qiú)	to play (ball)
7.	球	（名） qiú	ball
8.	够	（形） gòu	sufficient
9.	新闻	（名） xīnwén	news
10.	预习	（动） yùxí	to prepare (lessons)
11.	散步	（动） sànbù	to take a walk
12.	无线电	（名） wúxiàndiàn	radio
13.	什么的	（代） shénmǒdê	etc., and others
14.	睡	（动） shuì	to sleep
15.	上	（动） shàng	to go up, to go, to take (a lesson)
16.	睡觉	（动） shuìjiào	to sleep

語法 Yǔfǎ Grammar

46.1 Time-words Used as Complement   As adverbial modifiers, time-words are used to tell at what time or in what period of time an action or state happens or exists (25.3). But, when we want to express how long an action or a state has lasted, we use time-words as complements after verbs. e. g.

1. 他　昨天　工作了　十个　鐘头.

He worked for ten hours yesterday.

2. 先生　每年　休息　一个　月.

The teacher rests one month each year.

十个鐘头 and 一个月 are lengths of time spent in 工作 and 休息, they do not indicate "at what time" he works or the teacher rests.

When there is an object following the verb, there may be three arrangements:

(1) Reduplicate the verb after the verb-object construction, and place the time-words after the second form of the verb. e. g.

3. 他　每星期　上　中国　革命史　上　两个　鐘头.

Each week he has two hours of History of the Chinese Revolution.

4. 我們　学　中文, 学了　一个多　月了.

We have studied Chinese for more than a month.

Here, time-words are arranged in the same way as complements of degree: we know when there is an object, the complement of degree is also placed after the reduplicated verb. At the same time, the suffix and the adverbial modifier of the verb have to be placed together with the reduplicated verb. This rule holds true also for time-words when they are used as complements.

5. 他　每星期　上　中国　革命史　只
上　两个　鐘头.

Each week he has only two hours of History of the Chinese
Revolution.

6. 我們　学 中文, 已經　学了 一个多
月 了.

We have already studied Chinese for more than a month.

We cannot say 他每星期只上中国革命史, 上两个鐘史 or 我們
已經学了中文, 学一个多月了. At the same time notice that
the structural particle 得 should be used between the verb and
its complement of degree, it is never put before time-words
used as complement.

(2) When there is no reduplication of the verb, the time-
words are placed between the verb and its object. e. g.

7. 他　每星期　上　两个　鐘头(的)
中国　革命史.

Each week he has two hours of History of the Chinese
Revolution.

8. 我們 已經　学了 一个多 月(的) 中文
了.

We have already studied Chinese for more than a month.

Notice that the structural particle 的 may be used after
time-words.

(3) The object may be placed at the beginning of the sentence, especially when the object is stressed or when it is rather complicated. e. g.

9. 昨天的　表演 我 沒 看完, 只 看了
一个半　鐘头.

I didn't finish watching yesterday's performance. I watched it for only an hour and a half.

10. 怎么样 全面地 复習 詞彙 和 語法 的 問題, 我們 討論过 一个 下午.

We once discussed for one afternoon the problem of how to have an overall review of vocabulary and grammar.

46.2   The Negative Form of the Sentence with Time-words Used as Complement   A sentence with time-words used as complement can be either negated by 不 or 没有, according to different conditions:

(1) When an action or a state happens or exists frequently, or at the present time, or when it is a supposition, then we use 不. e. g.

11. 你 每天 都 鍛鍊 一个 鐘头 嗎?

Do you do an hour's physical exercise every day?

12. 不 鍛鍊 一个 鐘头, 只 鍛鍊 三刻鐘.

I don't do physical exercise for an hour. I only do it for three quarters of an hour.

13. 你 每天 念 課文 都 念 一小时 嗎?

Do you regularly read the text for an hour every day?

14. 每天 都 念 一小时, 要是 不 念 一小时, 就 不 熟.

Yes, I do. If I don't read it for an hour, I don't know it well.

Notice that 不 is an adverb, and it should be used before verbs and never before time-words. Therefore, we cannot say 不一个鐘头.

(2) When an action or a state did not last for a certain period of time in the past, we use 沒有. e. g.

15. 昨天 晚上 你 看 小説兒 看了 一(个) 晚上 嗎?

Last night did you read novels for the whole evening?

16. 沒 有 看 一(个) 晚上, 只 看了 两个 鐘头.

I didn't read for the whole evening. I read for only two hours.

17. 昨天 晚上 你 看了 一 晚上(的) 小説兒 嗎?

Last night did you read novels for the whole evening?

18. 沒 有, 只 看了 两个 鐘头.

No, I read for only two hours.

課文 Kèwén Text

(a₁) 你們 每天 上課 上 多少 时間?

How much time do you spend in classes each day?

(b₂) 上 四小时.

Four hours.

(a₂) 下 課 以后, 自己 还要 不要 学習?

After classes do you still have to study by yourself?

(b₂) 当然 要 学習. 我 差不多 每天 都 自学 四五(个) 小时.

Of course we have to. I almost invariably study by myself for four or five hours each day.

(a₃) 每天 下午 你 作 些 什么?

What do you do each afternoon?

(b₃) 我 每天 下午 要 复習 語法, 复習 半个多 鐘头. 練習 汉字 也 要 練習 半个多 鐘头. 大声兒 念 課文 可以 帮助 發音, 我 每天 都 念 一小时.

Every afternoon I have to review the grammar for more than half an hour. It also takes more than half an hour to practice writing the characters. (Since) reading out loud can help one's pronunciation, I read aloud every day for an hour.

(a₄) 你 不 鍛鍊 身体 嗎?

Don't you do any physical exercise?

(b₄) 我 鍛鍊 身体. 每天 都 打 一小时 (的) 球.

I do. Every day I play ball for an hour.

(a₅) 你 每天 用 多少 时間 看 报?

How much time do you spend every day reading the newspaper?

(b₅) 用 一小时. 我 觉得 要是 不 看 一小时, 就 不 够. 每天 报上 都 有 很 多 重要的 新闻, 我們 应該 关心 这些 大 事.

An hour. I feel if I don't read for an hour, it's not enough. Every day there is lots of important news in the newspaper. We have to be concerned about these important events.

(a₆) 晚上的 时間 你 干 什么?

What do you do during the evening (hours)?

(b₆) 作 練習. 先生 每天 都 讓 我們 作 練習.

I do the exercises. The teacher wants us to do exercises every day.

(a₇) 練習 你 要 作 一 晚上 嗎?

Do you have to spend the whole evening doing the exercises?

(b₇) 不, 現在 我們的 練習 还 很 簡單, 作 三刻鐘 就 夠 了. 每天 晚上 我 都 有 时間 預習 一下兒 第 二天的 語法. 有 时候兒 我 还 可以 散散 步、听听 无綫电 什么的. 听 无綫电 报告 新聞 也 可以 練習 听 中文.

No. Our exercises are still quite simple now. Three quarters of an hour is enough. Every evening I have time to preview a little grammar for the next day. Sometimes I even can take a little walk, listen to the radio (a bit), etc. Listening to the radio can also serve to practice comprehension of Chinese.

(a₈) 你 睡得 晚 不 晚?

Do you go to bed late?

(b₈) 不 晚. 我 十一点 以前 一定 上 床 睡觉, 每天 都 能 睡 八小时.

No. I always go to bed before eleven. I am able to sleep eight hours every day.

課外練習 Kèwài liànxí Home Work

1) Answer the following questions:

   (1) 我們 先生 從 一九五二年 起 教 書, 他 教过 几年 書 了?

   (2) 你們 每次 开 会 差不多 开 多少 时間?

   (3) 你 (是) 什么 时候兒 买 的 这枝 鋼笔? 用了 多少 时候兒 了?

   (4) 学習 專业 你 要 学習 几年?

2) Make sentences with the following groups of words (use the two words grouped together in the same sentence):

   (5) 当然　进步

   (6) 必須　夠

   (7) 預習　好处

汉字表　Hànzì biǎo　Chinese Characters

1	革	廿 苫 革
2	命	人 亼 合 命
3	史	口 史 史
4	当	⼁ ⼃ ⼩ ⼩ 当 当 当
5	打	扌
		丁
6	球	王
		求（一 十 寸 寸 求 求 求）
7	够	句
		多
8	闻	門
		耳
9	预	予
		頁
10	散	一 十 廿 世 昔 散
11	无	二 于 无
12	綫	糸
		戋
13	睡	目（⼁ 冂 月 月 目）
		垂（丿 二 乒 乒 垂 垂）

Lesson 47

生詞 Shēngcí New Words

1.	把	(介)	bǎ	(a preposition)
2.	丢	(动)	diū	to lose
3.	解决	(动、名)	jiějué	to solve, solution
4.	送	(动)	sòng	to send, to present, to see off
5.	参观	(动)	cānguān	to visit
6.	車間	(名)	chējiān	workshop
7.	亮	(形)	liàng	bright, light
8.	机器	(名)	jīqì〔架jià〕	machine, machinery
9.	愉快	(形)	yúkuài	cheerful, pleasant
10.	緊張	(形)	jǐnzhāng	busy, tense, energetic
11.	最后	(副)	zuìhòu	finally, last
12.	生产	(动)	shēngchǎn	to produce, production
13.	提前	(副)	tíqián	ahead of (schedule), in advance, to give precedence to
14.	完成	(动)	wánchéng	to complete, to fulfil
15.	祖国	(名)	zǔguó	fatherland
16.	偉大	(形)	wěidà	great, magnificent
17.	工业	(名)	gōngyè	industry

語法 Yǔfǎ Grammar

47.1 The Disposal Form   Generally speaking, in the sentence with a verbal predicate the verb always precedes its object. The sentence of the disposal form has also a verbal predicate, but its word order is not the same as that of the common sentence with a verbal predicate:

Subject — (把) — Object — Verb — Other Elements.

By using the preposition 把, the object is transposed to a position just before the verb, this is the structural characteristic of this kind of sentence. Thus it may also be termed the 把 sentence. In general, the object of 把 denotes some particular person or thing, and the action shown by the verb is active.

From the following two points we know why and when we use this kind of sentence:

(1) In the complicated predicate of a sentence, there is always a complement following the object (especially, a resultative complement which describes the change of the position or state of the person or thing denoted by the object); since the verb and its complement are a close unit we cannot separate them by inserting any object between them. Therefore we have to bring the object forward to a position just before the verb by using the preposition 把, so that the verb and its complement may be brought together. e. g.

1. 我 把 椅子 搬到 外边兒 去 了.

   I moved the chair outside.

2. 他 想 把 这本 小說兒 翻譯成 中文.

   He plans to translate this novel into Chinese.

3. 你 应該 把 桌子 放在 这兒.

   You should put the table here.

We cannot say 我搬椅子到外边兒去了，他想翻譯这本小說兒成中文 and 你应該放桌子在这兒.

(2) The disposal form is also used when the speaker wishes
for special emphasis. e. g.

4. 他 把 昨天的 报 丢 了.

He lost yesterday's newspaper.

5. 我 把 报告 准备好 了.

I have prepared the report.

Such expressions are more emphatic than 他丢了昨天的报了
and 我准备好了报告了.

47.2 Some Rules of the Disposal Form:

(1) After the verb there must be other elements (including the reduplicated form of the verb).

6. 晚上 睡觉 的 时候兒, 他 喜欢
把 窗戶 开着.

When he sleeps at night he likes to have the windows open.

7. 对不起, 我 把 这件 事 忘 了.

I am sorry. I forgot this thing.

8. 我們 必須 把 这个 問題 討論
討論.

We must discuss this problem a little.

9. 他 把 門 敲了 兩下兒 就 进来 了.

He knocked twice on the door and entered.

10. 你 应該 把 鐘 掛在 这兒.

You should hang the clock here.

11. 他 把 課文 念得 很 熟.

He studied the text thoroughly (until he knew it by heart).

But in the case where there is an optative verb, an adverb or an adverbial modifier before the predicate, some verbs may not be followed by other elements. e. g.

12. 今天的 小組 会 必須 把 这个 問題 解决.

Today's group meeting must solve this problem.

(2) We often use the 把 construction for verbal sentences with double objects, when the direct object is placed after the word 把 and the indirect object is placed after the verb as the "other element". e. g.

13. 我 把 花兒 送給 朋友 了.

I have given the flowers to a friend.

14. 他 要 把 那本 小説兒 借給 我.

He wants to lend that novel to me.

Notice the use of 給. It is often used to introduce the indirect object especially in the sentence of the disposal form. It always follows such verbs as 送, 借, 敎, 寄, 交, 介紹, 报告, etc.

(3) In a negative sentence, the negative adverbs 不 and 沒有 must be used before the preposition 把 and not before the verb. e. g.

15. 要是 你 不 把 身体 鍛鍊好, 就 不 能 很 好地 为 人民 服务.

If you don't train your body well, (then) you won't be able to serve the people very well.

16. 他 沒有 把 藥 吃完, 病 就 好 了.

His sickness was cured before he had finished taking the medicine.

(4) The optative verbs must also be placed before the preposition 把 and not before the verb. e. g.

17. 你 可以 把 學習 經驗 介紹給 別的 同学.

> You may introduce your learning experience to the other schoolmates.

18. 大家 都 应該 把 語法 复習复習.

> All of us should review the grammar.

課文　Kèwén　Text

星期日 上午 我們 去 参观了 一个 汽車 工厂. 到 中国 来 以后, 我 还 沒 有 去过 工厂, 这 是 第一次

> On Sunday morning we went to visit an automobile factory. Since coming to China, I had not yet gone to a factory. This was the first time.

到了 工厂, 那里的 一个 工作 同志 把 工厂的 情况 簡單地 給 我們 介紹了 一下兒. 他 講得 很 清楚, 很 多 同学 都 把 他 説 的 話 記在 本子里 了.

> After we arrived at the factory, a comrade worker there briefly introduced the conditions of the factory to us. He explained very clearly and many schoolmates wrote down in their notebooks what he said.

听完 介绍, 我們 就 开始 参观. 这个
工厂 很 大, 車間 很 多. 每个 車間
都 又 亮 又 干淨. 机器 都 是 新
的. 工人 正 在 車間里 愉快、緊張地
工作. 我們 最后 走到 的 那个 車間
很 大, 在 那里 我們 看到了 中国 工人
用 自己的 劳动 生产 的 新 汽車.
我們 都 高兴 極了, 站在 那里 看了
一刻多鐘 才 出来.

After listening to the introduction, we started the tour
(to visit). This factory was very big, and had many workshops. Every workshop was both bright and clean. All the
machinery was new. The workers were all working
happily and energetically in the workshops. The last workshop we came to was very large. There we saw some new
automobiles which were produced by the Chinese workers
with their own labor. We were all extremely happy and
stood there watching for more than a quarter of an hour
before coming out.

这个 工厂 每天 都 生产 很 多 輛
新 汽車, 每月 都 提前 完成 生产 計划.
中国 人民 都 这样地 积极 劳动, 一定
能很 快地 把 自己的 祖国 建設成 一个
偉大的 社会主义 工业 国.

This factory produces many new automobiles every day,
and every month it fulfills the quotas of the production

plan ahead of time. (Since) the Chinese people all work so enthusiastically, they can definitely develop (their) fatherland into a great socialistic, industrial country in a short time (very quickly).

課外練習 Kèwài liànxí Home Work

1) Change the following sentences into those of the disposal form:

(1) 他 試了 一下兒 这件 衣服.

(2) 大夫 治好了 我的 病.

(3) 先生 已經 告訴 我們 大声兒 念 的 好处 了.

(4) 他 沒 有 看完 这本 小説兒 就 借給 我 了.

2) Translate the following into Chinese sentences of the disposal form:

(5) My elder brother hung up the picture on the wall.

(6) He put the radio on the table.

(7) The teacher asks me to take this notice to my roommate.

汉字表 Hànzì biǎo Chinese Characters

1	丢	丢
2	决	冫
		夬
3	送	关
		辶
4	观	又

		見
5	亮	、 一 亠 亡 亮 亮
6	器	口
		口
		犬
		口
		口
7	愉	忄
		俞（人 𠆢 俞 俞）
8	緊	収（丨 刂 収）
		糸
9	最	曰
		取
10	祖	礻
		且
11	偉	亻
		韋（フ ⺈ 血 吾 吾 吾 韋 韋）

Lesson 48

語法复習　Yǔfǎ fùxí　Review

48.1　Time-words Used as Adverbial Modifiers and Complements　　We have learned up till now many words and word groups indicating time.　So far as their meaning is concerned, time-words can be divided into two kinds: one of these indicates a period of time. e. g.

1. 三个　鐘头

three hours

2. 半年

half a year

The other indicates a point of time. e. g.

3. 一九四九年　十月　一日

October 1, 1949

4. 两点　过　五分

five after two.

But this difference is not absolute.　There are some time-words which may indicate both period of time and point of time.　For example, the word 下午 in 今天下午 expresses a point of time, and that in 一个下午 expresses a period of time.

A time-word is always used as adverbial modifier giving the time when an action happens or a certain state exists.　In such a case, any time-word, whether indicating a period of time or a point of time, may be used as adverbial modifier. e. g.

5. 上星期六 我們 参观了 一个 自行车 工厂.

Last Saturday we visited a bicycle factory.

6. 每天 上午 七点 无綫电 报告 重要 新聞.

The radio reports important news every morning at seven.

上星期六 and 每天上午七点 are time-words indicating points of time. When we wish to express "at what time" something has or has not happened, we use time-words indicating points of time as adverbial modifiers. Other examples are:

7. 他 在 中国 学習, 两年 没 有 回 国 了.

He studies in China and hasn't gone back to his own country for two years.

8. 他 一个 星期 接到了 三封 信, 高兴 極了.

He received three letters in a week. He is exceedingly happy.

两年 and 一个星期 in the above examples indicate period of time. When we wish to express "during a certain period of time" something has or has not happened, we use time-words indicating periods of time as adverbial modifiers. Therefore an adverbial modifier of time may be a time-word indicating a period of time or a time-word indicating a point of time.

But if we wish to express how much time is taken in the course of a certain action or in the duration of a certain state, then we use a time-word as complement. Of course, such a complement can only be a time-word indicating a period of time. e. g.

9. 这课 語法 很 簡單, 我 昨天
   預習了 半个鐘头 就 看懂 了.

The grammar in this lesson is quite simple. I understood it
yesterday after having only prepared it for half an hour.

10. 星期日 他 請 我 到 他 家
    去 玩兒了 一天.

(Last) Sunday he invited me to spend the whole day at his
home.

When a time-word is used as complement, it is put immediately after the verb. If there is an object in the sentence,
we have to reduplicate the verb and put the complement after
the second form of the verb. e. g.

11. 我 每天 練習 發音 練習 半小时.

Every day I practice pronunciation for half an hour.

12. 他們 开 联欢 会 差不多 开了
    两个半 小时.

They had a reunion party for almost two and a half hours.
(Their reunion party lasted for almost two and a half
hours.)

There are other rules concerning the use of time-words:

(1) If there is an object, the time-word used as complement, such as we have just described, may also be put between
the verb and the object. Then the particle 的 may be placed
between the time-word and the object. e. g.

13. 我 每天 練習 半小时(的) 發音.

Every day I practice pronunciation for half an hour.

14. 他們 差不多 开了 两个半 小时
    (的) 联欢 会.

They had a reunion party for almost two and a half hours.

But the time-word cannot be used in this way, if the object is a complicated one, especially when it is modified by a demonstrative pronoun.

(2) If we wish to emphasize the object, or if .the object is not a simple one, then we move the object to the beginning of the sentence instead of reduplicating the verb, and we put the time-word as complement after the verb. e. g.

15. 中文 他 只 学过 一年, 俄文
他 学过 五六年, 当然 他 说
俄文 说得 好.

> He studied only one year of Chinese but (he studied) five or six years of Russian. Of course he speaks Russian better.

16. 那件 白 颜色的 新 衣服, 她
只 穿过 一天.

> She wore that new white dress for only one day.

48.2 着 This Chinese character is pronounced in two different ways. When it is used as suffix indicating aspect, it is pronounced "zhê"; when it is used as resultative complement, it is pronounced "zháo". As both uses are very common in speech, it is necessary for us to know more about this character:

When 着 is used as resultative complement, it often means "to achieve", "to get" or ' to attain". In the preceding lessons we have learned 借着, 买着 etc. 借着 means to have got something through the action of borrowing, and 买着 means to have got something through the action of buying. 着 is widely used in this way and it is very easy to give many such instances. e. g. the action of 睡(觉) may be expressed as: 我每天十一点睡(觉), in which 睡 (觉) is a simple action. But we may also say:

17. 我 躺下 就 睡着 了.

> As soon as I lay down I fell asleep.

18. 我 虽然 躺在 床上, 但是 没有
睡着.

Although I am lying in bed, I haven't fallen asleep.

睡着 in the above sentences means that one has really fallen asleep. Another example: the verb 打 in 我們打球 expresses a simple action. But we may also say:

19. 对不起, 我們 玩兒 球, <u>打着</u> 你 了 没 有?

     Sorry. We're playing ball. Did the ball hit you?

20. 没 关系, 没 有 <u>打着</u>, 打在 我的 自行車上 了.

     That's all right. It didn't hit me. (It) hit my bicycle.

Here 打着 means 打中 (to have hit). Another example: the verb 听 in 我們听报告 expresses a simple action. But we may also say:

21. 昨天的 报告 特别 好, 但是 我 有 别的 事, 没 <u>听着</u>.

     Yesterday's report was especially good, but I had other matters (to attend to), (therefore) I didn't get to hear it.

听着 means 听到. Therefore, when the word 着 is used as resultative complement, it means some action has reached some positive result.

    The suffix 着 is always used after the verb, but it differs from 着 used as resultative complement, for the suffix 着 indicates the aspect of action, that is to say, some action in a continuous state. e. g.

22. 作 报告 的 人 已經 来 了, 在 台上 <u>坐着</u> 呢.

     The person who is to give the report has already come. He is sitting on the rostrum.

23. 先生 念 課文 的 时候兒, 大家

都　注意地　听着.

When the teacher reads the text, everybody listens attentively.

All the above examples show that the actions are or were being continued. But, sometimes, even when an action is completed, the result of the action still remains, in that case we can use the continuous aspect. e. g.

24. 病人　都　穿着　医院的　白　衣服.

The patients are all wearing the hospital's white garments.

25. 黑板上　写着　开　会　的　通知.

The notice about the meeting is written on the blackboard.

The suffix 着 may also be used to express the concomitant action in sentences of the multi-verbal form (45.3). e. g.

26. 先生　站着　講　書.

The teacher lectures while standing (up).

27. 大夫　叫　他　不　要　躺着　看　書.

The doctor told him not to read lying down.

站着 and 躺着 are verbs used as adverbial modifiers to describe the main actions. Such verbs may also be followed by objects. e. g.

28. 騎着　自行車　去　書店　半个　鐘头
一定　可以　到.

If one goes to the bookstore on a bike, one can definitely arrive there in half an hour.

課文　Kèwén　Text

我　有　一个　中国　朋友　叫　張偉,

他 是 俄文 專業 三年級的 學生. 我
到 學校 的 第二天 班上的 工作
同志 就 把 他 介紹給 我 了. 那个
时候兒, 我 还 不 会 中文, 我們 就
用 俄文 談 話. 以后 我 上 課 了,
就 試着 用 學过 的 中文 跟 他
說 話. 現在 我們 能 用 中文 談 很
多 話.

I have a Chinese friend whose name is Zhang Wei. He is
a third-year student in (the special field of) Russian. The
working comrade in my class introduced him to me (as
early as) on my second day at school. I did not yet know
any Chinese then, so we conversed in Russian. Later on,
after I had (some) classes I tried to converse with him in
Chinese. Now we can talk about a lot of things in Chinese.

張偉 同志 非常 注意 我的 學習.
他 到 我 屋子 来 找 我 的
时候兒, 常常 先 問 我 學習 方面
有 沒 有 困难. 他 是 北京 人,
發音 很 正确. 我 常常 大声兒地 念
課文 給 他 听, 請 他 替 我 改正
錯誤. 有时候兒 我 把 不 清楚的 問題
記在 小 本子里, 看見 他 的 时候兒,
我 就 問 他. 他 帮助 我 解決了 不
少 問題. 在 別的 方面, 他 也 很 关

心我，給我很多幫助。他叫我每天一定要看报，要鍛鍊，也要休息。我們差不多每天下午要一起打一小时(的)球。有时候兒也一起騎着自行車到学校外边兒去玩兒。看电影兒或者看話劇的时候兒，他常常坐在我的旁边兒給我翻譯。有一次我病了，在医院里住了三天，他每天都来看我。虽然我們只認識了几个月，他已經成了我的好朋友了。

Comrade Zhang Wei pays a lot of attention to my studies. When he comes to my room to see me, he often asks me first whether I have any difficulty in learning. He is from Peking, so his pronunciation is quite accurate. I often read the text aloud to him and ask him to correct my mistakes. Sometimes I put down in my notebook the problems that puzzle me and ask him when I see him. He helped me solve a lot of problems. In other things (aspects) he is also concerned about me and give me a lot of help. He tells me every day I should read the newspaper, do physical exercises, and also rest. We play ball together for an hour almost every afternoon. Sometimes we also ride bicycles together to have some fun outside of the school. When we see movies or plays, he often sits by my side and translates for me. Once when I was sick and stayed in the hospital for three days, he came to see me every day. Although we have known each other for only a few months, he has already become my good friend.

Lesson 49

生詞 Shēngcí New Words

1.	天气	(名)	tiānqì	weather
2.	冷	(形)	lěng	cold
3.	将	(副)	jiāng	shall, will, about to
4.	还是	(副)	háishì	still
5.	詞	(名)	cí	word
6.	冬天	(名)	dōngtiān	winter
7.	毛衣	(名)	máoyī 〔件〕	woollen knitted garment
8.	街	(名)	jiē 〔条 tiáo〕	street
9.	百貨大楼	(名)	bǎihuòdàlóu	department store
10.	包	(量)	bāo	pack, parcel, (a measure word)
11.	紅	(形)	hóng	red
12.	黃	(形)	huáng	yellow
13.	藍	(形)	lán	blue
14.	綠	(形)	lù̈	green
15.	深	(形)	shēn	deep, dark (in colour)
16.	淺	(形)	qiǎn	light (in colour)

語法 Yǔfǎ Grammar

49.1 The Use of 要...了 When we wish to express an action or state that is about to take place, we use the construction 要...了 in the predicate. e. g.

1. 汽車 要 开 了.

   The automobile is about to start.

2. 天气 要 冷 了.

   The weather is going to get cold.

要 means "going to (do)" and 了 is a modal particle. This construction is used only when the speaker subjectively feels that an action or state will happen at once.

One of these adverbs 將, 就, and 快 is used as adverbial modifier before the word 要. 將 is often used in writing, while 就 and 快 are often used in speech. e. g.

3. 这个 工厂的 生产 计划 將 要 提前 完成 了.

   This factory's production plan is going to be accomplished ahead of time.

4. 现在 八点, 就 要 上 課 了.

   It's eight o'clock now, (we) are about to begin our class.

5. 我的 新 衣服 快 要 作好 了.

   My new clothing will soon be finished.

要 preceded by the adverbial modifier 就 or 快 deepens the feeling of the immediacy of an action, and the action expressed by 就要...了 happens even much sooner. 快要...了 does not, in general, take a time-word as modifier. We may say 三分鐘以后就要上課了, but we cannot say 三分鐘以后快要上課了.

49.2 Repetition of Measure Words Measure words may

also be used reduplicatively. The reduplication of a measure word implies the meaning of "each" or "every". e. g.

6. 間間 屋子 我 都 找过 了，还是 沒 有 找着 他.

I searched in every single room, yet I still did not find him.

7. 这个 学生的 發音 好 極了， 个个 字 他 都 念得 非常 正确.

This student's pronunciation is extremely good, he pronounces every single word very accurately.

間間屋子 means "every room" and 个个字 means "each word". Since such reduplication implies "every" or "each", the adverb 都 must be used in the predicate. Also, the reduplication of a word means emphasis, therefore the object modified by a reduplicated measure word must precede the clause or sentence.

We have learned that in Chinese there are some nouns which have in themselves the quality of measure words (14.1). Such nouns do not require other measure words when they are used with demonstrative pronouns or numerals. They can also be used reduplicatively as measure words with the implication of "every" or "each". e. g.

8. 人人 都 緊張、愉快地 工作着.

Everyone is working intensely and cheerfully.

9. 年年的 生产 計划 我們 都 提前 完成.

We accomplish in advance each year's production plans.

人人 means "everybody", and 年年 means "every year". Notice that when any of these nouns in reduplicated form is used as subject, 都 must be used in the predicate as adverbial modifier; when any of these nouns is used as object or adjective modifier of an object, the object must also be placed before the verb.

49.3 Repetition of Numerals and Measure Words   A numeral and a measure word, forming a word group, can also be used reduplicatively with the following two functions:

(1) When used as adverbial modifier describing the manner of an action. e. g.

10. 先生　叫　我們　两个两个地　到
黑板上　去　写　汉字.

> The teacher asked us to go two by two to write Chinese characters on the blackboard.

两个两个地 means that the action is done by two people at a time. In general, numerals are not very often used in this way except the numeral 一, and in that case, the second 一 may be omitted. e. g.

11. 他　把　买来　的　东西　一件(一)件地
都　放在　桌子上　了.

> He put on the table every single thing that he had bought.

12. 我　把　学过　的　語法一課(一)課地
都　复習　了.

> I have reviewed, one lesson at a time, all the grammar that we have learned.

Sometimes, after such numerals and measure words nouns may be used. e. g.

13. 先生　带着　我們　一个詞一个詞地
念.

> The teacher led us in reading, one word at a time.

(2) When used as adjective modifier describing the numerousness of things. e. g.

14. 書店的　窗戶里　放着　一本一本的
新　書, 我　都　想　买.

In the window of the bookstore there are copies and copies
of new books. I want to buy all of them.

15. 一輛一輛的　汽車　停在　学校　門
外边兒.

Lots and lots of cars are parked outside of the school gate.

When reduplication is used in this way, it implies there are
numerous things and also emphasizes the individual items of
a collective body.　In the above examples, though we may
change 一本一本的新書 into 很多本新書, and 一輛一輛的汽車 in-
to 很多輛汽車, it only means that "such things are numerous".
Therefore, if we wish to express only the "numerousness of
things", we cannot use the reduplicated form　For example,
we can never change such a sentence as 我买了很多本杂誌 into 我买了一本一本的杂誌.

課文　Kèwén　Text

冬天　就　要　到　了. 天气　快　要
冷　了. 天天　早上　或者　晚上　就
觉得　有　一点兒　冷. 我　必須　去　买
一件　毛衣.

Winter is coming soon. The weather is about to become
cold. Every morning or evening (I) feel a little bit cold. I
must go to buy a sweater.

今天　星期日, 上午　我　和　一个
朋友　进　城. 到了　城里, 看見　街上的
人　多　極了. 要　到　百貨　大楼　的
时候兒, 就　看見　很　多　人　从　里边兒
出来, 他們　都　拿着　一包一包的　东西.

Today is Sunday. In the morning, a friend of mine and I went to the city. When we arrived at the city, we saw there were lots of people in the streets. When we were about to reach the department store, we saw many people coming out from inside. They were all carrying packages and packages of things.

我們 进了 百貨 大楼, 到了 卖
毛衣 的 地方, 很 多 人 正 在 那兒
买 呢. 毛衣的 样子 很 不 少, 顏色
也 很 多————红的、黄的、藍的、綠的、
深的、淺的 都 有. 看着 那些件 毛衣,
件件 都 很 好看; 我 也 不 知道
应該 买 哪 一件. 我的 朋友 說 这件
深 藍的 好, 我 就 把 它 买来
了. 拿回 学校 以后, 别的 朋友 也
都 說 好. 今天 晚上 觉得 冷 的
时候兒 我 就 有 毛衣 穿 了.

We entered the department store building. After we arrived at the place where sweaters were sold, many people were buying. The sweaters came in lots of styles (the styles of the sweaters were not few) and they also came in many colors — red, yellow, blue, green, deep colors and light colors. Looking at those sweaters, I felt that every one of them was beautiful, and did not know which one to buy. My friend said that this deep blue one was good, so I bought it. After I brought it back to school, all my other friends also said that it was good. If I feel cold tonight I'll have a sweater to wear.

課外練習　Kèwài liànxí　Home Work

1) Re-write the following sentences using any of the constructions 要…了, 就要…了, 快要…了 and 將要…了:

(1) 今年的　工业　生产　计划　提前　完成.

(2) 中国　代表　回　国　来.

(3) 旧　杂誌　送到　圖書館　去.

(4) 欢迎　新　同学　的　晚会　七点　开始.

2) Re-write the following sentences by using the reduplication of measure words:

(5) 张友文　是　一个　很　好的　同志,
每个　人　都　很　喜欢　他.

(6) 这个　工人　每(个)　月　都　提前
完成　生产　计划.

3) Make sentences with reduplicated numerals and measure
words:

(7) 作状語 using them as adverbial modifier

(8) 作定語 using them as adjective modifier

汉字表　Hànzì　biǎo　Chinese Characters

1	冷	冫
		令(今 令)
2	将	丬 (丶 冫 丬)
		夕
		寸

3	冬		
4	街	彳	
		圭	
		亍	
5	百		
6	貨	化	
		貝	
7	楼	木	
		娄	米
			女
8	包	丿 勹 包	
9	紅	糸	
		工	
10	黃	一 十 廿 卄 苗 黃	
11	藍	艹	
		監	臥（一 丆 丆 丆 臣 臣 臣 臥 臥 臥）
			皿（丨 冂 冂 皿 皿）
12	綠	糸	
		彔（夕 彑 彐 彔 彔 彔 彔）	
13	深	氵	
		罙	宀
			八
			木

14	淺	シ
		淺

Lesson 50

生詞 Shēngcí New Words

1.	吧	（助） bā	(a particle)
2.	改	（动） gǎi	to correct, to change
3.	后天	（名） hòutiān	day after tomorrow
4.	所有（的）	（形） suǒyǒu(de)	all
5.	剛	（副） gāng	just, a moment ago
6.	真	（形） zhēn	real, really
7.	食堂	（名） shítáng	dining hall, refectory
8.	一会兒	yìhuǐr	a while, a few moments
9.	校园	（名） xiàoyuán	campus
10.	春天	（名） chūntiān	spring
11.	暖和	（形） nuǎnhė	warm
12.	义务	（名） yìwǔ	voluntary (labour for public interests), duty
13.	座	（量） zuò	(a measure word)
14.	楼	（名） lóu〔座〕	building
15.	决定	（动） juédìng	to decide
16.	需要	（动、名） xūyào	to need, to require, needs, necessity
17.	革命	（动、名） gémìng	to take revolution, revolution
18.	关	（动） guān	to close, to shut

語法 Yǔfǎ Grammar

50.1 The Modal Particle   We know that in Chinese the modal particle is used at the end of a sentence, it does not have any concrete meaning, but conveys a certain emotion and expresses some mood. One and the same particle may express different emotions and sentence mood under different conditions. We have learned that 嗎 indicates interrogation, 呢 continuous action and 了 completion, etc. In this lesson we shall introduce the particle 吧 and some other common uses of 呢 and 了.

50.2 The Modal Particle 吧   This particle is used chiefly to express uncertainty as to one's judgement. When we have formed an estimate of a thing, and yet we are not sure whether it is true, then we use the particle 吧 at the end of the sentence. e. g.

1. 那个 鐘 停 了 吧?

That clock must have stopped.

2. 我 作 的 这个 句子 不对 吧?
   要是 錯了, 你 替 我 改一改.

This sentence I made is wrong, isn't it? If it is wrong, please correct it for me.

吧 is always used at the end of a declarative sentence, thus changing the declarative sentence into an interrogative one. Since the particle 吧 implies uncertainty or a doubting mood, a sentence with 吧 is rather mild in mood.

When we express our consent or agreement to some contract, opinion, order or request, we may say 好, but 好吧 is more idiomatic. e. g.

3. 你們 把 球 拿到 宿舍 去 吧.

Please bring the ball back to the dorm.

4. 好 吧.

O.K.

50.3 The Modal Particle 呢　呢 is also used to express uncertainty or doubt, but it is different from 吧: 吧 is used at the end of a declarative sentence, expressing uncertainty, while 呢 is used at the end of an interrogative sentence. e. g.

5. 这个 汉字 念 什么 呢?

How is this character pronounced?

6. 这儿的 花儿 有 很 多 种, 买 哪种 送 他 呢?

There are many kinds of flowers here. Which kind shall I buy for him?

If there is no particle 呢 after such sentences, they are still interrogative; but when the particle 呢 is added, of course such sentences are much softened in mood. We have studied five kinds of interrogative sentences, all of them can be followed by 呢, with the exception of the interrogative sentence with 嗎. e. g.

7. 天气 不 好, 去 不 去 参观 呢?

The weather is bad. Should we go on the tour?

8. 后天 开 讨論 会, 是 你 去 通知 他 还是 我 去 通知 他 呢?

There is a discussion meeting day after tomorrow. Are you going to notify him or shall I notify him?

9. 那个 字 怎么 写 呢?

How does one write that character?

10. 是 不 是 还 有 别 的 方法 呢? 大家 可以 想一想.

Is there any other method? Let's all think a little.

呢 is also always used after a word or word group (which is in fact an essential element of the sentence), thus forming an elliptical interrogative sentence. e. g.

11. 我　现在　去　开　会，你　呢？

I am going to a meeting now. How about you?

12. 这　是　他的　本子，你　自己的　呢？

This is his notebook. How about your own?

In this way, 呢 is used in a sentence asking "how" or "where", but its exact meaning is determined by context.

50.4 The Modal Particle 了　　We have learned that 了 can be used as a verbal suffix indicating the perfective aspect, and can also be used as a modal particle (27.1). As a modal particle, besides indicating the completion of an action, it can also mean that some new situation or state has come about. 了 may be used in the sentence with a substantive predicate. e. g.

13. 从前　他　在　一个　工厂　工作，
现在　他　是　北京　大学的　学生　了.

Formerly he used to work in a factory. Now he is a student at Peking University.

14. 今天的　新　中国　是　人民的　了.

The new China of today belongs to the people.

The sentence with an adjectival predicate may also denote a new situation or state by using 了. e. g.

15. 已经　把　窗户　开开　了，屋子里
不　热　了.

The window(s) is (are) already open. It is not hot in the room any more.

16. 訂了 學習 計划 以后, 他的 进步
就 很 快 了.

After his study plans have been made, his progress will be fast.

了 may also be used in the sentence with a clause predicate to indicate a change in situation or state. e. g.

17. 到 别的 地方 休息了 一个 月,
他 身体 好 了.

After he had gone elsewhere to rest for a month, his health improved.

In the sentence with a verbal predicate, the particle 了 is always used, of course, to indicate completion, but it may also indicate a new situation or state. e. g.

18. 解放 以后, 所有的 工人 都 有
學習 的 机会 了.

Since the Liberation, all workers have an opportunity to study.

19. 因为 有 一件 重要的 工作, 他
不 来 参加 我們的 联欢 晚会 了.

He can no longer come to participate in our reunion party in the evening because an important job has come up (he has an important job to do).

課文 Kèwén Text

(a₁) 你 吃完 飯 了 吧?

You have finished your meal, haven't you?

(b₁) 吃完 了. 你 呢?

Yes, how about you?

(a₂) 我 也 剛 吃完. 今天 天气 真 好,
我們 一起 去 散散 步, 好 嗎?

I have also just finished my meal. The weather is so good today, let's go for a walk together, O.K.?

(b₂) 好 吧! 我 每天 从 食堂 出来
都 散 一会兒 步.

Fine. I always take a little walk every day after coming out of the dining hall.

(a₃) 我 很 喜欢 我們的 校园. 春天的
时候兒, 天气 暖和 了, 花兒 都
开 了, 那 时候兒 一定 好 看
極了.

I like our campus very much. In the spring, when the weather has warmed up and the flowers have started to bloom, it must be very pretty.

(b₃) 对了. 你 看, 一个多月 以前 我
們 在 这兒 参加 义务 劳动, 現
在 这兒 已經 是 一座座的 大
楼 了.

That's right. Look, a month ago we were participating in voluntary labor here. Now many buildings (one next to the other) have come up.

(a₄) 建設得 真 快, 我們 走到 哪兒
来 了? 前边兒 就 是 新 圖書館
了. 你 在 这兒 借过 書 嗎?

The construction is going on really fast. Where have we

come to? The new library is already in front of us. Have you ever borrowed books here?

(b₄)　借过. 这兒的 书 很 多. 我
已經 决定 学 中国 革命史 了.
以后 我 需要 的 书 这兒 都
有.

Yes. There are lots of books here. I have decided to study the History of the Chinese Revolution. This library has all the books I am going to need in the future.

(a₅)　你 决定 学 中国 革命史 了, 那
真 好! 中国 有 很 多 非常 好
的 革命 經驗, 应該 学習.

(So) you have decided to study the History of the Chinese Revolution. That's wonderful! China has a lot of wonderful revolution experiences. One must study them.

(b₅)　今天 星期日, 圖書館 开 門 不
开 門 呢? 我 想 查 一本 書.

Today's Sunday. Is the library open? I would like to look up something in a book.

(a₆)　我 星期日 来过, 不 关 門. 我
跟 你 去 查 吧!

I have been here on Sundays before. It's open. I will go to look it up with you.

课外練習　Kèwài liànxí　Home Work

1) Copy the following sentences and fill the blanks with the particle 吧 or 呢:

(1) 那件 紅 衣服 是 誰的_____?

(2) 他的 意見 不 太 正确＿＿＿＿?

(3) 你 喜欢 穿 淺 顏色的 衣服＿＿＿＿?

(4) 明天 講 第五十一課, 你 什么 时候兒 預習＿＿＿?

2) Make three sentences with the particle 了 to express new conditions or states:

(5) A sentence with a substantive predicate
(6) A sentence with an adjectival predicate
(7) A sentence with a verbal predicate

汉字表 Hànzì biǎo Chinese Characters

1	吧	口
		巴
2	真	一 ナ 自 直 真 真
3	食	人
		良 (` 良)
4	园	门 园 园
5	春	三 丰 夫 春
6	暖	日
		爰 (´ ⺈ ⺈ ⺈ 乆 爭 爰)
7	需	雨
		而 (一 ㄧ 丆 丙 而 而)

Lesson 51

1. 更　（副）　gèng　more, further
2. 合适　（形）　héshì　suitable, proper
3. 故事　（名）　gùshi　story
4. 最　（付）　zuì　most
5. 一样　（形）　yíyàng　the same
6. 文化　（名）　wénhuà　culture
7. 像　（动）　xiàng　to resemble
8. 天　（名）　tiān　day
9. 妹妹　（名）　mèimei　younger sister
10. 容易　（形）　róngyì　easy
11. 比較　（动、副）　bǐjiǎo　to compare, comparatively
12. 复杂　（形）　fùzá　complicated, complex
13. 深　（形）　shēn　profound, deep (in meaning)
14. 流利　（形）　liúlì　fluent
15. 語言　（名）　yǔyán　language, speech
16. 特点　（名）　tèdiǎn　characteristic, feature
17. 掌握　（动）　zhǎngwò　to master
18. 習慣　（名、动）　xíguàn　habit, get used to

語法 Yŭfǎ Grammar

51.1 更 We know that in Chinese the adjectival predicate of a sentence often implies comparison (14.3). But when two persons or things are compared for some special quality, we often use the adverb 更 as adverbial modifier before the predicative adjective to express greater or less degree. e. g.

1. 二年級的 學生 多, 三年級的 學生 更 多.

There are many second-year students but there are more third-year students.

2. 这件 衣服 不 合适, 那件 衣服 更 不 合适.

This piece of clothing does not fit (and) that piece fits even less (well).

The adverb 更 is not only used as adverbial modifier before an adjective, but also before a verb or an optative verb. e. g.

3. 你 喜欢 看 話剧, 我 更 喜欢 看 話剧.

You like to watch plays; I like to watch them even more.

4. 你 会 說 故事, 他 更 会 說 故事.

You know how to tell stories well; he knows how to tell stories even better.

And so, when two different conditions or states of one and the same thing are compared, the adverb 更 is also used as adverbial modifier. e. g.

5. 我 希望 你 以后 学習得 更 好.

I hope you will study even better in the future.

This sentence does not imply that you are not doing well at present, but that you have been doing rather well.

51.2   最   The adverb 最 is used to indicate the superlative degree.   As we know, the adverb 更 is used to compare two or two groups of persons or things, however, when there are more than two or two groups of persons or things to be compared, we must use the adverb 最. e. g.

6. 二年級的 學生 多, 三年級的 學生 更 多, 一年級的 學生 最 多.

> The second year has many students. The third year has even more (students). The first year has the most.

7. 你 喜欢 看 話劇, 我 更 喜欢 看 話劇, 他 最 喜欢 看 話劇.

> You like to watch plays, (but) I like to watch plays even more (and) he likes to watch plays the most.

8. 你 会 說 故事, 她 更 会 說 故事, 她 同屋 最 会 說 故事.

> You know how to tell stories, (but) she knows even better how to tell stories (and) her roommate knows best how to tell stories.

51.3   跟.. 一樣   一樣 is an adjective, and may be used as predicate. e. g.

9. 這 兩件 衣服的 顏色 一樣.

> The colors of these two pieces of clothing are the same.

10. 他們 用 的 練習 本子 都 一樣.

> The exercise books they use are all the same.

Sometimes, it is used together with the preposition 跟 which serves to bring together the two things compared. e. g.

11. 一年級的　教室　<u>跟</u>　二年級的　教室
一樣.

The first-year classroom and the second-year classroom are the same.

12. 他　用　的　練習　本子　<u>跟</u>　你的
一樣.

The exercise book he uses is the same as yours.

跟…一樣 (the same as…), these two words are always used together to form an idiomatic word group. The object of 跟 may be a rather complicated construction. e. g.

13. 他　寫　的　汉字　很　好看,　<u>跟</u>　<u>先生</u>
<u>寫的</u>　一樣.

The Chinese characters he writes are beautiful, as beautiful as those written by the teacher.

14. 我們　在　中国　很　愉快,　跟　<u>在</u>
<u>自己的　国家里</u>　一樣.

We are happy in China, just as in our own country.

跟…一樣 may also be used as adjective or adverbial modifier to express comparison. e. g.

15. 我　要　买　一枝　<u>跟　你　这枝　一樣</u>
<u>的</u>　鋼笔.

I want (or am going) to buy a pen like this one of yours.

16. 参加　劳动　<u>跟　学　文化　一樣</u>(地)
重要.

Participating in labor is as important as studying culture (getting an education).

The construction 跟...一样 may be negated by the word 不, but there are two possible positions in the sentence for the word 不, that is to say, it may be placed either before the word 跟 or before the word 一样. e. g.

17. 这个 词的 意思 不 跟 那个 词 一样.

The meaning of this word (term) is not the same as that one.

18. 这件 毛衣 跟 那件 毛衣 不 一样 长.

This sweater and that one are not of the same length.

51.4 像...一样 像 is a verb, and may be used as the predicate of a sentence. e. g.

19. 他 穿着 白 衣服, 像 一个 大夫.

He has some white clothes on, and looks like a doctor.

20. 他的 身体 这么 好, 不 像 七十 岁的 人.

His health is so good; he does not look like a man seventy years old.

But 像 and ...一样 are always used together as a word group, which may also express comparison when it is used as predicate, adjective modifier or adverbial modifier. e. g.

21. 那天的 天气 很 冷, 像 冬天 一样.

The weather that day was cold like winter.

22. 我 喜欢 像 天 一样 的 藍 顏色.

I like the same shade of blue as the sky.

23. 住在 城外 像 住在 城里 一样 方便.

Living outside the city is as convenient as living inside the city.

課文 Kèwén Text

I

(a₁) 你 是 張 同志的 妹妹 嗎?

Are you comrade Zhang's sister?

(b₁) 对了, 你 怎么 知道?

Yes. How did you know?

(a₂) 因为 你 很 像 他. 你 是 几年级的 学生?

Because you look like him. Which year are you in?

(b₂) 我 是 一年級的. 你 呢?

I am a freshman. How about you?

(a₃) 我 是 二年级的, 你們 学了 几課 語法 了?

I am a sophomore. How many lessons of grammar have you already studied?

(b₃) 学了 三課 了.

We have studied three lessons.

(a₄) 你 覺得 怎么样?

How do you feel about them?

(b₄) 我 覺得 現在的 課文 不 太 容易 了. 我們 班的 同学 都 說: 第一課 比較 容易, 第二課 有点兒 难, 第三課 更 难.

I feel that the present text is getting difficult. The students in our class all say, "The first lesson is comparatively easy, the second lesson is a little bit difficult, and the third one is even more difficult."

(a₅) 为 什么 你們 覺得 第三課 更 难 呢?

Why do you feel that the third lesson is even more difficult?

(b₅) 因为 这一課 生詞 比較 多, 語法 也 有 点兒 复杂. 我 覺得 現在 預習 更 重要 了. 要是 不 預習, 有 些 地方 就 不 容易 听懂.

Because there are comparatively more new words in this lesson and the grammar is somewhat complicated. I feel it is even more important to prepare now. If I don't prepare, some places will be hard to understand.

(a₆) 你 說得 很 对. 以后的 課文 会

更 深, 所以 更 需要 好好兒地
預習.

What you have said is true. The future texts will be even
more difficult. Therefore it is even more necessary to
prepare carefully.

(b₆) 我 很 希望 你 能 幫助 我. 我
覺得 你 說 中文 說得 非常
流利. 我 什么 時候兒 才 能
說得 跟 你 一樣 好 呢?

I hope very much that you can help me. I think that your
Chinese is extremely fluent. When will I be able to speak
as well as you do?

(a₇) 不, 我 不 是 說得 最 好的. 但是
我 一定 幫助 你. 我 想: 要是
你 努力 學習, 一定 會 有 更
大的 進步.

No, I am not the one who speaks the best. However, I will
certainly help you. I think if you study diligently, you
certainly will make even greater progress.

II

張友文 是 我們 班 最 好的 學生. 他
作 的 練習 錯誤 很 少; 汉字 寫得
也 很 好; 中国 話 說得 更 好, 又

流利、又 正确, 像 中国 人 一样. 他
非常 注意 中文 跟 他 自己 祖国
語言 不 一样 的 地方. 常常 比較 两国
語法的 特点. 所以 他 掌握 語法 掌握得
特別 好, 用 詞 也 用得 很 合适,
有时候兒 用得 跟 中国 人的 習慣
一样.

Zhang You-wen is the best student in our class. The exercises which he does have very few mistakes; his characters are well written too, and he speaks Chinese even better, not only fluently but also accurately, just like a Chinese. He pays a lot of attention to the differences between Chinese and the language of his own country. He often compares the special grammar points of the languages of the two countries. Therefore, he handles the grammar especially well and uses the words very appropriately too, sometimes as idiomatically as the Chinese.

課外練習　Kèwài liànxí　Home Work

1) Write down ten adjectives from your memory.

2) Make sentences with 跟...一样 and each of the following groups of words. e. g.

"新床、旧床、長":

新 床 跟 旧 床 一样 長.

(1) 我 学 的 專業、他 学 的 專業、重要

(2) 深 黄的 花兒、淺 黄的 花兒、好看

(3) 哥哥、妹妹、喜欢 唱 歌兒

3) Make sentences with 更, 最, 像, and 像…一样 respectively.

汉字表   Hànzì biǎo   Chinese Characters

1	更		
2	适	舌	
		辶	
3	故	古	
		攵	
4	化		
5	像	亻	
		象（ノ ク ク ケ 乃 乃 鱼 多 免 象 象 象）	
6	妹	女	
		未（一 未）	
7	容	宀	
		谷	八
			人
			口
8	易	日	
		勿（ノ ク 勺 勿）	
9	比	匕 匕 比	
10	較	車	

		交
11	流	氵
		㐬（丶 亠 厶 㐬 㐬 㐬）
12	利	禾
		刂
13	言	
14	握	扌
		屋
15	慣	忄
		貫 乚 口 毌 毌 貫

Lesson 52

1.	过	（动） guò	to pass
2.	跑	（动） pǎo	to run
3.	又	（副） yòu	again, too
4.	再	（副） zài	again, once more, any more
5.	遍	（量） biàn	(a measure word)
6.	树	（名） shù〔棵'kē〕	tree
7.	叶子	（名） yèzi	leaves (leaf)
8.	母亲	（名） mǔqīn	mother
9.	便宜	（形） piányi	cheap
10.	完全	（副） wánquán	completely
11.	放假		fàngjià	to take (have) a holiday
12.	一块兒	（副） yíkuàir	together
13.	旅行	（动） lǚxíng	to travel
14	批評	（动、名） pīpíng	to criticize, criticism
15.	犯	（动）	fàn	to commit (a mistake)
16.	重	（形）	zhòng	heavy

語法　Yúfǎ　Grammar

52.1 The Compound Directional Complement　　We have already learned that 来 and 去 may be used after verbs as simple directional complement (34.1). e. g.

1. 她 从 宿舍里 出来 了.

She came out of the dormitory (toward the speaker).

2. 先生 从 礼堂 前边兒 过去 了.

The teacher went by the auditorium (away from the speaker).

Such a verb-complement construction as 出来 or 过去 may also be used after a verb as complement. Then such a construction is the compound directional complement to that verb. e. g.

3. 她 从 宿舍里 跑出来 了.

She came running out of the dormitory.

4. 她 从 宿舍里 跑出去 了.

She went running out of the dormitory.

5. 先生 从 礼堂 前边兒 走过来 了.

The teacher has walked by the auditorium (toward us).

6. 先生 从 礼堂 前边兒 走过去 了.

The teacher has walked by the auditorium (away from us).

The words 来 and 去 in the compound directional complement are used in the same way as in the simple directional complement. The word 来 is used when the action proceeds towards the speaker; and if the action proceeds away from the speaker, we use the word 去.

Besides 出来, 出去, 过来 and 过去 given above, we also use the following verb-complement constructions as compound directional complements; 上来, 上去, 下来, 下去, 进来, 进去, 回来, 回去, and 起来.

52.2 The Compound Directional Complement and the Object   The object after the compound directional complement may occupy different positions in a sentence, when it is different in function:

(1) If the person or thing denoted by the object does not change its position under the influence of an action, the object has to be inserted into the compound directional complement, that is to say, it must be placed before the word 来 or 去. e.g.

7. 那个 工人 走进 車間 来 了.

The worker has walked into the machine shop.

8. 那輛 汽車 开出 工厂 去 了.

That car has been driven out of the factory.

(2) If the person or thing denoted by the object changes its position under the influence of an action, the object is, in general, also placed within the compound directional complement, that is to say, it is placed before 来 or 去. e. g.

9. 他 从 桌子上 拿起 一本 書 来.

He lifted (picked up) a book from the table.

10. 張 同志 买回 水菓 来 了.

Comrade Zhang has bought (and brought back) some fruit.

But the object may also be placed after the compound complement. e. g.

11. 他 从 桌子上 拿起来 一本 書.

He lifted a book from the table.

12. 張 同志 买回来 水菓 了.

Comrade Zhang has bought some fruit.

Generally speaking, we put the object after the entire verb-complement construction, only when the action is a completed one. Yet, it is much more idiomatic to use the disposal form. e. g.

13. 他 从 桌子上 把 那本 書 拿起来 了.

He lifted that book from the table.

14. 張　同志　把　水菓　買回來　了.

Comrade Zhang bought (and bought back) the fruit (we wanted).

52.3　又 and 再　　Both these two adverbs indicate repetition of action, but they are different in use:

(1) 又 shows that the repetition of an action or a state has taken place. e. g.

15. 昨天　他　來　了，今天　他　又　來　了.

He came yesterday. Today he came again.

16. 上次　晚會　她　沒　有　參加，這次　她　又　沒　有　參加.

She did not participate in the evening party last time; this time again she did not participate.

Sometimes, an action is not yet repeated (especially a periodic action), but the speaker is very sure that the action is bound to be repeated, then 又 is also used. e. g.

17. 明天　又　是　星期六　了.

Tomorrow is Saturday again.

18. 回　國　的　時候兒，又　可以　看見　從前的　朋友　了.

When you (we) are back in your (own) own country, you (we) will be able to see your (our) old friends again.

(2) 再 also expresses repetition, meaning "once more". In general, it means an action is going to be repeated (or not to be repeated). e. g.

19. 那本　小說兒　好　極了，我　想　再　看　一遍.

That novel is very good. I'd like to read it once more.

20. 那个 歌兒 我 已經 学会 了，不 需要 再 学 了.

I have learned that song. I don't have to learn it any more.

If we wish to say that the repetition of an action did not happen in the past, we use 再 instead of 又, and in such a case 再 is placed after the word 沒有 and before the verb. e. g.

21. 他 上次 来过 以后，沒 有 再 来.

Since he came here last time, he has not come again.

22. 我 复習了 一遍 以后，沒 有 再 复習.

After having reviewed it once, I did not review it again.

52.4 再 and 还   再 expresses a repetition which is not yet realized, 还 may also express such a repetition. Their different uses are as follows:

(1) In the interrogative sentence, we use 还, not 再. e. g.

23. 今天 进了 城，明天 还 进 城 嗎?

After going into town today, are you going again tomorrow?

(2) In the declarative sentence, when there is an optative verb, 还 is used before the optative verb, and 再 after it in the same clause. e. g.

24. 这个 話剧 好 極了，我 看了 两次 还 想 (再) 看.

This play is very good. I have seen it twice but want to see it again.

課文　Kèwén　Text

I

1. 我 要 把 这张 画兒 掛上去.

I want to hang up this picture.

2. 天气 冷 了, 树上的 叶子 都 掉下来 了.

The weather has turned cold. The leaves on the trees have all fallen down.

3. 他 听見 他的 同学 在 楼下 叫 他, 就 跑下去 了.

He went running down upon hearing his schoolmates calling him from downstairs.

4. 汽車 要 开过来 了. 我們 准备 上 車 吧.

The car is about to be driven over (here). Let's get ready to get in.

5. 我 买回来 一輛 新 自行車, 又 好 又 便宜.

I bought (and brought back) a new bicycle. It's both good and inexpensive.

II

6. (a) 那些 問題 都 解决 了 嗎?

Are all those problems solved?

(b) 前天　討論了　一次,　昨天　又
討論了　一次,　已經　完全　解決
了;　明天　不　再　开　会　了.

We discussed them once the day before yesterday, and once again yesterday. They have all been solved now. We are not going to have any meetings tomorrow.

7. (a) 快　放　假　了!　我們　又　可以
一塊兒　去　旅行　了.　上次
旅行　你　去过　了.　这次　还
去　嗎?

We are about to begin our vacation. We can go traveling together again. You went traveling last time. Are you going again this time?

(b) 我　不　想　再　去　了.

I am not going again.

8. (a) 同志們　批評了　他　以后,　他
怎么样?

How has he been since the comrades criticized him?

(b) 很　好,　他　沒　有　再　犯过　那种
錯誤.

Quite good. He has not made that same mistake again.

9. (a) 昨天　他　沒　有　来　上　課,　今天
又　沒　有　来　上　課.　他　病　了　吧?

He did not come to class yesterday. He did not come again today. Is he sick?

(b) 对了. 大夫 說 他的 病 很 重,
已經 搬进 医院 去 了.

Yes. The doctor said he is seriously ill. He has been taken into the hospital.

10. (a) 这課 語法 比較 复杂, 你 掌握
了 嗎?

The grammar in this lesson is relatively complicated. Have you mastered it (gained good control of it)?

(b) 我 还 沒 有 掌握好. 昨天
我 复習了 一遍. 今天 上午
我 又 复習了 一遍, 晚上 我
还 想 再 复習 一遍.

I haven't mastered it (to satisfaction). I reviewed it once yesterday. This morning I reviewed it once more. I am planning to review it once again tonight.

課外練習　Kèwài liànxí　Home Work

1) Make sentences with each of the following verb-complement constructions:

(1) 借回来

(2) 騎出去

(3) 走过来

(4) 站起来

2) Copy the following sentences and fill the blanks with 再, 又, or 还:

(5) 那个 地方 很 有意思, 今年 放
假 的 时候兒 我 想＿＿＿＿去
一次.

(6) 上次 他 因为 病 了, 沒 有 去 旅行, 这次 因为 工作 忙, ________ 沒 有 去.

(7) 課文里 有 一个 句子 很 复杂, 先生 給 我們 講了 一遍________ 講了 一遍.

(8) 要是 你 想 把 这些 汉字 都 記住, 你________要________写 几遍.

汉字表 Hànzì biǎo Chinese Characters

1	跑	足
		包
2	遍	扁(户 户 启 启 扁 扁)
		辶
3	树	木
		对
4	叶	口
		十
5	母	ㄥ 马 母 母 母
6	亲	立
		木
7	宜	宀
		且
8	假	亻

		叚（¬ ¬ ⼫ ⼫ ⼫ ⼫ ⼫ 叚 ）
9	旅	方（⽅ ⽅ ⽅ ⽅ ⽅ 旅 ）
10	批	扌
		比
11	評	言
		平（¬ ¬ ¬ 平 ）
12	犯	犭（／ 犭 犭 ）
		㔾（¬ 㔾 ）

Lesson 53

生詞 Shēngcí New Words

1. 代表 (名、动) dàibiǎo — to represent, representative, delegate
2. 农民 (名) nóngmín — peasant, farmer
3. 夏天 (名) xiàtiān — summer
4. 收 (动) shōu — to harvest, to gather
5. 包 (动) bāo — to pack, to wrap
6. 研究 (动、名) yánjiū — to study, to research; study, research
7. 外国 (名) wàiguó — foreign country
8. 节目 (名) jiémù — performance, item
9. 最近 (形) zuìjìn — recent
10. 播送 (动) bōsòng — to broadcast
11. 爱 (动) ài — to love
12. 織 (动) zhī — to knit, to weave
13. 漂亮 (形) piàoliǎng — beautiful, good-looking
14. 洗 (动) xǐ — to wash
15. 秋天 (名) qiūtiān — autumn

語法 Yǔfǎ Grammar

53.1 **The Extended Use of the Compound Directional Complement**   We have learned that the compound directional complement indicates the direction of an action. e. g.

1. 先生　走进　教室　的　时候兒，同学
都　站起来　了.

When the teacher came into the classroom, the fellow students all stood up.

2. 球　掉下去　了.

The ball has fallen down.

Here 起来 and 下去 both have their practical meaning. But compound directional complements often possess extended meanings. Here we will deal with the extended meanings of some compound complements in daily use.

53.2　The Extended Use of 起来　The directional complement 起来 is often used in its extended meaning. It is generally used in the following three ways:-

(1) After a verb showing that an action has begun. e. g.

3. 朋友　听了　我的　話，就　笑起来
了.

Having heard what I said, (my) friend started to laugh.

4. 工作　时間　还　沒　到，他們　已經
干起来　了.

It's not working time yet (working time has not yet arrived), but they have already begun to work.

When there is an object, we have to put it between 起 and 来.

5. 他　剛　表演完，大家　就　鼓起掌
来　了.

As soon as he finished performing, everybody started to clap.

6. 人民 代表 进了 工厂, 就 跟 工人
談起 話 来 了.

As soon as the people's representative entered the factory,
he started talking with the workers.

起来 is also often used after an adjective, showing that
some person or thing will possess the quality expressed by the
adjective. In such a case, the adjective assumes the function
of a verb. This is a characteristic of the adjective in the
Chinese language. e. g.

7. 到 中国 以后, 我 認識 的 中国
朋友 慢慢兒地 多起来 了.

Since I arrived in China, I have known more and more
Chinese friends.

8. 我們 学 的 語法 已經 复杂起来
了.

The grammar we are studying has already become more
and more complicated.

(2) After a verb to stress the actual progress of an action,
or after an adjective stress the actual existence of some quality. e. g.

9. 这件 事, 說起来 容易, 作起来
难.

This (affair) is more easily said than done.

10. 天气 热起来 的 时候兒, 我們 每天
七点 一刻 就上課.

When the weather gets hotter we start our class (as early
as) at 7:15 every day.

(3) After certain verbs to show the state of being organized or put together. e. g.

11. 农民　都　組織起来　了.

The peasants have all been organized.

12. 冬天　来了,　夏天的　衣服　可以
收起来　了.

Winter has come; summer clothing can be stored away now.

13. 合作社的　工作　同志　把　糖　給
我　包起来　了.

The working comrade of the co-op has wrapped up the candies (OR: sugar) for me.

53.3 The Extended Use of 下去　As a complement, 下去 is often used after a verb to indicate the continuation of an action. e. g.

14. 先生　叫　我　念下去.

The teacher asked me to read on.

15. 你　在　中国　住下去,　一定　可以
把　中文　說得　非常　流利.

If you stay on in China, you will certainly be able to speak Chinese very fluently.

When there is an object in such a sentence, it is better, in general, to transpose the object to the beginning of the sentence, or to turn the sentence into the disposal form. e. g.

16. 那个　工作　他們　决定　作下去.

They decided to continue (doing) that work.

17. 他們 決定 把 那个 工作 作下去.

They decided to continue (doing) that work.

53.4 The Extended Use of 出来   The direction of an action expressed by the directional complement 出来 after a verb is often not entirely definite. e. g.

18. 我的 自学 計划 还 沒 有 訂出来 呢!

My self-study plan has not been mapped out yet.

19. 第二个 問題 很 难, 我 还 沒 有 研究出来.

The second question is very difficult; I have not yet figured it out (by researching it).

Sometimes it is very vague in meaning, and expresses a meaning that can only be inferred from the action expressed by the verb. e. g.

20. 他 說 中国 話, 說得 跟 中国 人 一样; 我 沒 有 听出来 他 是 外国 学生.

He spoke the Chinese language like a Chinese. I couldn't tell (by listening) that he was a foreign student.

21. 他 有 几个 汉字 写得 不 对, 先生 立刻 就 看出来 了.

He wrote several characters improperly; the teacher spotted them right away.

課文 Kèwén Text

I

(a₁) 新聞 报告完 了，要 不 要 把 无綫电 关上？

The news report is over. Do you want to turn off the radio?

(b₁) 我 还 想 听下去，但是 不 知道 下边兒 是 什么 节目？

I still want to continue listening, but I don't know what the next program is.

(a₂) 下边兒的 节目 是 唱 歌兒. 你 听，已經 唱起来 了.

The next program is singing. Listen! They have already begun to sing.

(b₂) 唱的 是 什么 歌兒？你 听出来 了 嗎？

What is this song they are singing? Can you tell (by listening)?

(a₃) 这个 歌兒 最近 无綫电 差不多 天天 播送，叫 "社会主义好".

Recently the radio (station) has been broadcasting this song almost every day. It is called "Socialism is Good."

(b₃) 对，是 "社会主义好"，我 常 听

中國 同學 唱 這個 歌兒. 我 也
很 愛 唱 這個 歌兒.

Right! It *is* "Socialism is Good." I have often heard my
Chinese schoolmates sing this song. I love to sing this song
too.

II

(a₄) 你 這件 毛衣 很 好看, 是 新
買 的 吧?

This sweater of yours is very pretty. It must be newly
bought.

(b₄) 不 是, 這 是 一件 旧 毛衣, 我
母親 給 我 織 的, 已經 穿了
兩三年 了.

No, this is an old sweater. My mother knitted it for me,
and I have worn it for two or three years already.

(a₅) 真的 嗎? 看起来 跟 新的 一样
—— 颜色 还 很 漂亮, 我 真
沒 有 看出 它 是 旧的 来.

Really? It looks like a new one—the color is still very
beautiful. I really could not tell (by looking) that it is old.

(b₅) 我 每年 春天 穿完了 以后, 一定
先 把 它 洗干淨了 再 收起来.

秋天 要 穿 的 时候兒, 拿出来
就 可以 穿.

Every spring, after I finish wearing it, I always wash it
clean before I store it away. When I want to wear (it) in
the autumn, I can wear it as soon as I take it out.

(a₆) 你 洗得 干淨, 收得 好, 所以 跟
新的 一样.

You wash it clean and you store it well, therefore it is like
new.

課外練習　Kèwài liànxí　Home Work

Copy the following sentences and put the words 起来, 下去
and 出来 into their proper places:

(1) 放完了 假, 我們 就要 忙＿＿＿＿
了.

(2) 时間 不 早 了, 我們 不 能 再
談 ＿＿＿＿＿ 了.

(3) 要是 想 后天 去 旅行, 現在
应該 組織 ＿＿＿＿＿ 了.

(4) 剛才 表演 的 是 張 同志, 但是
我 沒有 看 ＿＿＿＿＿.

(5) 因为 昨天的 討論 会 沒 有 把
所有的 問題 都 解决, 今天 会
还 要 开 ＿＿＿＿＿.

(6) 这种 鋼笔 虽然 看 ＿＿＿＿＿ 不
特別 漂亮, 但是 用 ＿＿＿＿＿ 真
好.

(7) 我 在 外边兒 就 听 ———— 是
你 在 説 話 了.

汉字表 Hànzì biǎo Chinese Characters

1	代	イ イ 代 代
2	农	丶 冖 少 农 农 农
3	夏	一 百 頁 夏
4	收	丩
		攵
5	研	石 石 石 研 研
6	究	穴
		九
7	目	
8	近	斤
		辶
9	播	扌
		番
10	爱	丿 ⺈ ⺈ ⺊ 爫 爱
11	漂	氵
		票
12	洗	氵
		先
13	秋	禾
		火

Lesson 54

語法复習 Yǔfǎ fùxí Review

54.1 The Simple Directional Complement and the Compound Directional Complement. We know that the simple directional complement (34.1) and the compound directional complement (52.1) are very commonly used in Chinese. In this lesson we are going to sum them up as follows:

(1) The directional complements 来 and 去 are used after verbs, showing the direction of action. If an action proceeds towards the speaker, we put the complement 来 after the verb; on the contrary, if an action proceeds away from the speaker, we use the complement 去. e. g.

1. 那封 信 是 从 哪国 寄来 的?

From which country was that letter sent?

2. 从 这个 门 出去, 就 是 大 街 了.

If you go out of this door, the main street is right there.

When the word 来 or 去 is part of a compound directional complement, it has the same function as when it is used as a simple directional complement, that is to say, it expresses the relation between the direction of an action and the speaker. But the other part of the compound directional complement (such as 上, 下, 进, 出, 起, 过, or 回) is used only to show the direction of the action itself. e.g.

3. 妹妹的 球 从 楼上 掉下来 了.

Little sister's ball has fallen down from upstairs.

In the above sentence, 来 is used because the speaker is downstairs, and 下 is used because the ball has fallen down from the upstairs. If the speaker is upstairs, we must use 去 instead of 来. e.g.

4. 誰 在 楼 下? 妹妹的 球 掉下去 了,
能 不 能 給 她 拿上来?

Who is downstairs? Little sister's ball has fallen down. Can you bring it up to her?

Note: Here the word 下 remains unchanged, because the falling action of the ball still proceeds from upstairs to downstairs.

(2) When there is an object, we must pay attention to its position in the sentence, whether the directional complement is simple or compound:

(a) If the person or thing denoted by the object does not change position under the influence of an action, the object should be placed before the word 来 or 去 e.g.

5. 張 先生 到 外国 去 了.

Mr. Zhang has gone abroad.

6. 那个 大夫 走进 医院 来 了.

That doctor has walked into the hospital (toward the speaker).

(b) If the person or thing denoted by the object changes position under the influence of an action, it is also often placed before the word 来 or 去. e.g.

7. 我 朋友 給 我 带了 一封 信 来.

My friend brought me a letter.

8. 母亲 买回 很 多 花兒 来.

Mother (bought and) brought back lots of flowers.

Note: Such objects may also be placed after the entire verb-complement constructions. But, in general, such actions are often completed ones. e.g.

9. 他　带来了　一封　信.

He brought a letter.

10. 母亲　买回来　很　多　花兒.

Mother brought back lots of flowers.

We have to remember that compound directional complements always have extended meanings. e.g.

11. 中国　人民　都　組織起来　了.

The Chinese people have organized themselves.

12. 这个　話剧　只　演了　一半兒, 休息
以后　还　要　演下去.

Only half of the play has been performed. It will go on after the intermission.

13. 要是　注意　發音　方面的　錯誤, 你
自己　也　能　听出来.

If you pay attention to the mistakes in pronunciation, you can even detect them yourself.

In the above examples, 起来, 下去 and 出来 have already lost their original meaning of direction.

54.2　The Modal Particle 了 and the Suffix 了　We have learned the modal particle 了 (50.4) and the suffix 了 of completed aspect (27.1.). Since these two words are the same in pronunciation and in form, it is necessary for us here to distinguish their different uses:

(1) The suffix 了 is used to show the completion of an action, so it always comes after a verb or a verbal construction; while the particle 了 is placed only at the end of a sentence. Therefore, when 了 is found in the middle of a sentence, it must be a suffix. e.g.

14. 今年 春天 他們 放了 三天 假.

Last spring (of this year) they had three days of vacation.

15. 我們 前天 鍛鍊了 一小时.

Day before yesterday we did physical exercises for an hour.

In a conditional sentence, 了 is used in the conditional clause, meaning that the completion of the first action is the condition for accomplishing the second action; in such a case, 了 is a suffix with or without an object after the verb. e.g.

16. 复習好了, 才 能 作 練習.

One can do exercises only after one has finished reviewing.

17. 放了 假 就 可以 去 旅行 了.

After the vacation starts, we may go traveling.

There are certain verbs that are so closely bound to their resultative complements or directional complements, that the suffix 了 can only be used after the entire verbal construction. e.g.

18. 他 从 合作社 买来了 一大包 水菓.

He bought (and brought) a big package of fruit from the co-op.

19. 无綫电 播送完了 这个 节目, 就 报告 新聞.

The radio will report the news after it finishes broadcasting this program.

(2) All modal particles are used at the end of a sentence, the particle 了 is no exception. As 了 is put at the end of a sentence, there may be a noun or pronoun before it. e.g.

20. 已經 是 秋天 了, 大家 都 穿上了 暖和的 衣服.

It is already fall. (Fall is already here.) Everybody has put on some warm clothing.

21. 下次的 主席 是 你 了, 你 应該 早
作 准备.

It's your turn to be the chairman next time. You should make some early preparations.

Sometimes there may be an adjective before the particle 了. e. g.

22. 現在 汽車 多 了, 进 城 更 方便
了.

There are lots of cars (OR: buses) now. It is even more convenient to go into town now.

23. 学完 語法 以后, 再 看 这本 書
就 不 困难 了.

If you read this book after you have finished studying the grammar, there won't be any difficulties.

Sometimes there may be a numeral and a **measure** word before the particle. e.g.

24. 时間 过得 真 快, 十二月 了.

Time goes by really fast. It is December now.

25. 六点多 了, 天 亮 了.

It's after six now. It's dawning.

26. 他 十八岁 了, 可以 参加 工作 了.

He is eighteen now. He may join the work force (take part in working) now.

When there is a verb before 了 and the verb is preceded by an optative verb, 了 is still considered a particle. e.g.

27. 那个 病人 能 坐起来 了.

That patient can sit up now.

28. 他 已經 能 用 中文 談 話 了.

He is now able to talk in Chinese.

When there is some other element before a verb showing an incomplete action, 了 after the verb is also a particle. e. g.

29. 他 因為 有 事, 不 來 了.

He is not coming any more because he is busy.

30. 代表們 要 到 了.

The representatives are about to arrive.

All the particles in the above sentences are used to express new states or situations.

(3) When 了 not only comes after a verb or a verbal construction, but also at the end of a sentence, then it assumes both the function of a particle and that of a suffix, and may be called a particle indicating completed action. e.g.

31. 我的 朋友 旅行去 了.

My friend has gone traveling.

32. 母亲 从 楼上 下来 了.

Mother came down from upstairs.

33. 他 把 那个 无綫电 关上 了.

He has turned off the radio.

When there is an object in a verbal construction, the word 了 after the object is also a particle. e.g.

34. 北京 大学 放(了) 假 了.

Peking University is on vacation now.

35. 我 下午 接到(了) 通知 了.

I received the notice in the afternoon.

If the object or the complement contains a numeral and a

measure word, and if at the same time we wish to express that an action is still to be continued, then we must use the particle 了 in addition to the suffix. e.g.

36. 我們 解決了 第一个 問題 了, 現在 可以 討論 第二个 了.

We have solved the first problem. Now we may discuss the second one.

37. 他 研究 这个 問題 已經 研究了 半年 了, 还 要 研究下去.

He has done research on this topic (problem) for half a year. He is going to continue the research.

課文 kèwén Text

I

(a₁) 你 在 北京 住了 多少 时候兒 了?

How long have you lived in Peking?

(b₁) 快 要 三年 了. 你 是 新 来 的 吧?

Almost three years. Did you come recently?

(a₂) 对了. 我 只 来了 两个 月. 北京的 天气 怎么样? 你 已經 習慣 了 吧?

Right. I have been here for only two months. How is the climate in Peking? You must have got used to it by now.

(b₂) 我 很 喜欢 这兒的 天气, 冬天 不 太 冷, 夏天 不 太 热.

I like the climate here. It's not too cold in the winter and not too hot in the summer.

(a₃) 北京的 春天 怎么样？

How is the spring in Peking?

(b₃) 很 好，但是 比較 短．年年 都
是 剛 暖和 起来，夏天 就 来 了．
秋天 比較 長，天气 也 更 好．
所以 我 喜欢 北京的 春天，更
喜欢 北京的 秋天．

Very good, but relatively short. Every year when it has
barely warmed up, summer is on us already. Fall is longer,
and the weather is even better. Therefore though I like
Peking's spring, I like Peking's fall even better.

II

我 学習 中文，已經 学了 两个 多
月 了．现在 想起 从前的 情况 来，
真 有意思：第一次 看見 汉字 的 时候兒，
我 想："一个一个的 汉字 都 跟 画兒
一样，我 怎么 能 記住 呢！"但是 要
学 中文，就 必须 会 写 汉字，所以
我 决定 用 最 大的 努力 掌握 它．我
天天 練習．有的 汉字 簡單，有的 汉字
复杂．我 都 一个一个地 一遍一遍地
看了 又 看，写了 又 写．这样，我
慢慢兒地 学会了 很 多 汉字，也 觉得

汉字　容易　了．我　要　繼續　努力，掌握
更　多的　汉字，学好　中文．

I have studied Chinese for more than two months. Now that I come to think of what happened before, it is very interesting. When I saw the Chinese characters the first time, I thought: "Every single character is like a picture. How can I remember them all?" But if I wanted to study Chinese I had to be able to write characters, so I decided to master them with the greatest effort. I practiced every day. Some characters were simple, some complicated. I wrote each one of them again and again, and looked at each one of them over and over. In this way, I gradually learned quite a few characters and now feel Chinese characters are easy to learn. I want to continue my effort so that I can master even more characters and learn Chinese well.

Lesson 55

生詞 Shēngcí New Words

1. 下（雪） （动）xià (xuě) to fall, to snow
2. 雪 （名）xuě snow
3. 刮 （动）guā to blow (the wind blows)
4. 風 （名）fēng wind
5. 安静 （形）ānjìng quiet, silent
6. 別 （副）bié don't
7. 勿 （副）wù don't
8. 吸 （动）xī to smoke, to inhale
9. 烟 （名）yān〔枝,包〕cigarette, smoke
10. 雨 （名）yǔ rain
11. 团結 （动、名）tuánjié to unite, union
12. 推 （动）tuī to push
13. 克服 （动）kèfú to overcome
14. 棵 （量）kē (a measure word)
15. 倒 （动）dǎo to fall down
16. 倒 （动）dào to pour
17. 茶 （名）chá tea
18. 客气 （形）kèqì formal, polite
19. 互相 （副）hùxiāng each other, one another, mutually

語法   Yŭfǎ   Grammar

55.1   The Sentence with an Indeterminate Subject   In Chinese, the majority of sentences consist of two parts: the subject and the predicate. There are also sentences consisting of only one part; a sentence that is composed of a predicate is called the sentence with an indeterminate subject.

The sentence with an indeterminate subject is different from the sentence in which the subject is omitted; in the latter what has been omitted is very obvious and can be easily put in according to context, while the former expresses a complete and definite thought by itself, where a subject is either impossible or unnecessary. Here we will deal with two common kinds of sentences with indeterminate subjects:

(1) Sentences describing natural phenomena, e. g.

1. 下着 雪 呢!

It is snowing.

2. 刮 風 了.

The wind has begun to blow.

(2) Sentences in which the subject is understood. e. g.

3. 开 会 了.

The meeting has begun.

4. 現在 上 課.

Now we begin our class.

55.2   The Telescopic Form with an Indeterminate Subject   In Chinese, there are sentences with indeterminate subjects beginning with the verb 有; in such sentences there are usually cther elements following the verb 有 and its object. e. g.

5. 有 人 敲 門.

There is someone knocking at the door.

6. 从前 有 一个 农民 叫 張和,......

Once upon a time, there was a peasant named Zhang He, ...

Both sentences have only one part — the predicate. 人 and 农民 are the objects of 有; they are also the subjects of 敲門 and 叫張和. Therefore, 人 and 农民 are double-function words, and such sentences are in the telescopic form with indeterminate subjects. In example 6 there is an adverbial modifier 从前 at the beginning of the sentence.

55.3 The Imperative Sentence   Here we are going to deal with the imperative sentence, the affirmative and the negative respectively, in the following:

(1) The affirmative:

7. 請 坐!

Please sit down.

8. 請 安靜!

Please be quiet!

9. 坐下!

Sit down.

10. 安靜!

Be quiet!

The word 請 expresses politeness and it can only be used before the predicate and not after the predicate.

(2) The negative:

11. 請 不 要 說 話!

Please don't talk!

12. 別 进来!

Don't come in!

13. 請 勿 吸 烟.

Please don't smoke!

In general, we use 不要 or 別 to express prohibition in speech. 勿 also expresses prohibition, but it is only used in writing.

Aside from these affirmative and negative forms of the imperative sentence, there are three more rules to be observed:

(1) At the end of an imperative sentence, there is often a particle 吧 to soften the tone of the sentence, especially in a negative sentence. e. g.

14. 准备好 了, 现在 开始 吧!

We are ready. Let's start now!

15. 别 回 家 了 吧! 雨 下得 很 大, 住 这儿 吧!

Don't go home. It is raining hard. You had better stay here.

(2) When the word 請 is used, we may not omit the subject in the second person. e. g.

16. 我 不 太 懂, 请 您 再 讲 一遍.

I don't quite understand, please explain it once more.

17. 节目 要 开始 了, 请 大家 坐好!

The program is going to start. Every one please be seated.

(3) The subject may be in the first person, in that case the word 讓 is generally used before the subject. e. g.

18. 讓 我 代表 我們 小组 谈谈 我們的 意見.

Let me represent our group to talk about our opinions.

19. 讓 我們 團結起来 吧!

Let's unite.

As we know, the word 讓 is causative in meaning, and often used in sentences of the telescopic form, but here it is not so definite in meaning.

課文 Kèwén Text

I

1. 下 雨 了, 快 把 自行車 推到 里边兒 来!

It has begun to rain. Hurry up and push the bicycle inside!

2. 要 开 車 了, 快 上去 吧!

The train (OR: bus) is going to start. Get on quickly!

3. 时間 到 了, 現在 开 会. 請 大家 安静!

The time has come. The meeting is beginning now. Will everyone please be quiet?

4. 刮起 風 来 了, 快 把 窗戶 关上 吧!

The wind has begun to blow. Hurry up and close the windows.

5. 想 去 旅行 的, 請 把 名字 写下来!

Those who want to go on the trip, please write down your names.

6. 現在 是 自學 時間, 別 大声兒
唱 歌兒!

Now is the time for self-study; don't sing out loud.

7. 讓 我們 一起 来 克服 这些
困难 吧!

Let's overcome these difficulties together.

8. 前天 刮 大 風, 有 两棵 树
刮倒 了.

The wind blew very hard day before yesterday; two trees
were blown down.

9. 有 一包 东西, 是 你 母亲 給
你 寄来 的.

There is a parcel of things that your mother sent to you.

10. 前天的 晚会 有 一个 节目
特别 好.

There was one especially good program at the evening
party day before yesterday.

11. 有 很 多 工厂 提前 完成了
今年的 生产 计划.

(There are) many factories (which) have completed this
year's production plan ahead of schedule.

II

有一天下午，我正坐在屋子里
自学的时候儿，听见外边儿有人
敲门．我说："請进!"門开开
了，进来的是我的中国朋友．
看见他我非常高兴，立刻請他
坐下，給他倒茶．我的朋友說："别
客气，你繼續学習吧!"我說："不
忙，我差不多已經复習完了，我們
談談吧!"

One afternoon, just as I was sitting in (my) room
studying by myself, I heard someone outside knocking at
the door. I said, "Come in, please!" The door opened and
in came my Chinese friend (and the one who came in was
my Chinese friend). Seeing him, I was extremely happy.
(I) immediately asked him to sit down and poured tea for
him. My friend said, "Don't be so polite, go on with your
studying." I said, "There is no hurry. I have almost
finished reviewing. Let's have a chat."

因为我現在还不能看中文
报，我的朋友就把这两天报上的
新聞給我講了講，我也把
我們国家的情况給他介紹了一下儿．
以后我們又談到学習．我的朋友
問我这两天学習方面有什么

問題. 我 告訴 他 这 兩天 我 学 的 語
法 都 掌握 了, 沒 有 問題. 我 看見 他
拿着 一本 俄文 小説兒, 就 問 他 "这本
書 你 能 完全 看懂 嗎?" 我的 朋友 説:
"有 几个 地方 我 沒 看懂, 請 你 給
我 講講, 可以 嗎?" 我 説: "当然 可以.
讓 我們 一塊兒 看看 吧 !"

Because I still cannot read Chinese newspapers now, my friend told me a little about the news in the newspapers of the past two (few) days and I introduced a little about our country's situation to him. Afterwards, we also talked about our studies. My friend asked me what problems I had regarding my studies during the last few days. I told him that I grasped all the grammar I had learned the last few days, (so) there was no problem. I saw him holding a Russian novel, so I asked, "Can you (read and) understand this book completely?" My friend said, "There are several places that I do not understand. Please explain them to me, O.K.?" I said, "Of course, let's take a look together!"

我 帮助 他 把 他的 問題 解決 了
最后 他 説: "謝謝 你的 帮助." 我 説:
"不 謝, 不 謝. 你 帮助 我的 更 多.
讓 我們 互相 帮助、互相 学習 吧!"

I helped him solve his problems. Finally he said, "Thank you for your help!" I said, "Not at all. You helped me even more. Let's help each other and learn from each other!"

課外練習   Kèwài liànxí   Home Work

1. Make a sentence with an indeterminate subject.

2.   Make a telescopic sentence with an indeterminate subject.
3.   Make an imperative sentence with the word 請.
4.   Make an imperative sentence with the word 別.
5.   Make an imperative sentence with the word 讓.
6.   Make an imperative sentence with the particle 吧.

汉字表   Hànzì biǎo   Chinese Characters

1	雪	雨 雪 雪 雪		
2	刮	舌		
		刂		
3	風	丿 几 凡 風		
4	安	宀		
		女		
5	静	青		
		争		
6	勿			
7	吸	口		
		及		
8	烟	火		
		因		
9	雨			
10	团	门 闭 团		
11	結	糹		
		吉	士	

			口		
12	推	扌			
		隹			
13	克	古			
		儿			
14	楪	木			
		果			
15	倒	亻			
		到			
16	茶	艹			
		人			
		朩			
17	客	宀			
		各	夂		
			口		
18	互	一	工	丏	互
19	相				

Lesson 56

生詞　Shēngcí　New Words

1. 百	(数)	bǎi	hundred
2. 千	(数)	qiān	thousand
3. 万	(数)	wàn	ten thousand
4. 亿	(数)	yì	hundred million
5. 零	(数)	líng	zero, naught
6. ...分之...		...fēnzhī...	(the formula of fractions
7. 倍	(量)	bèi	times
8. 去年	(名)	qùnián	last year
9. 数目	(名)	shùmù	number
10. 女	(形)	nǚ	female
11. 增加	(动)	zēngjiā	to increase
12. 男	(形)	nán	male
13. 全	(形)	quán	all
14. 遊行	(名、动)	yóuxíng	demonstration, to demonstrate or parade
15. 队伍	(名)	duìwǔ	paraders, troops
16. 举	(动)	jǔ	to hold up, to raise, to lift
17. 喊	(动)	hǎn	to shout, to cry
18. 口号兒	(名)	kǒuhàor	watchword, slogan
19. 兴奋	(形)	xīngfèn	excited

20. 万岁　　　　　　　wànsuì　　long live...

21. 中华人民共和国

Zhōnghuá rénmín gònghéguó
The People's Republic of China

語法　Yǔfǎ　Grammar

56.1 Enumeration from 100 Upward　　We have already learned that enumeration below 100 is by means of multiplication and addition (22.1). Enumeration from 100 upward is the same; the only difference is that there are more units in such numbers. In reading big numbers we must follow this unit order:

亿 (yì) ....hundred million
千万 (qiānwàn) ....ten million
百万 (bǎiwàn) ....million
十万 (shíwàn) ....hundred thousand
万 (wàn) ....ten thousand
千 (qiān) ....thousand
百 (bǎi) ....hundred
十 (shí) ....ten
个 (gè) ....digit.

Count from right to left according to the unit order. After reaching the biggest unit, we read the number from left to right. For example: 234 has three units, 个, 十 and 百, so it reads:

1. 二百　三十四(个)

5,762 has four units, 个, 十, 百, and 千, so it reads:

2. 五千　七百　六十二(个)

84.193 has five units, 个, 十, 百, 千 and 万, so it reads:

3. 八万　四千　一百　九十三(个)

7,456,823 has seven units, 个, 十, 百, 千, 万, 十万 and 百万, so it reads:

4. 七百　　四十五万　　六千　　八百
二十三(个)

617,458,293 has nine units, 个, 十, 百, 千, 万, 十万, 百万, 千万 and 亿, so it reads:

5. 六亿　一千　七百　四十五万　八千
二百　九十三(个)

There are three points to be noticed about enumeration of big numbers:

(1) As shown above, there are nine units in big numbers in Chinese, but 个, 万 and 亿 are basic units compared with others. e. g. 18 is:

6. 十八

180,000 is:

7. 十八万

1,800,000,000 is:

8. 十八亿

18,000 is:

9. 一万　八千

We cannot say 十八千.

1,800 is:

10. 一千　八百

We cannot say 十八百.

(2) When a number of three units or more is used to indicate the year or the number of a room or some other thing, we simply read the numerals, without using the units. e. g.

11. 你們　在　哪个　教室　上　課？

In which classroom do you have classes?

12. 在　二一三号.

In room 213.

13. 那輛　自行車　多少号?

What is the number of that bicycle?

14. 五一三二八四 (号).

513284 (five one three two eight four)

(3) In interrogation, we often use 几 before 百, 千, 万 etc. e. g.

15. 这个　礼堂　能　坐　几千　人?

How many thousands of people can this auditorium seat?

16. 那本　小説兒　有　几十万　字?

How many hundred thousand characters does that novel have?

56.2　The Use of 零　Sometimes there are zeros in a big number. In order to read the number accurately, we use the word 零. Attention should be paid to the following rules in using the word 零:

(1) In a big number, if the second unit is "0", this zero must be read. If "0" happens to be in any other unit, it may or may not be read. e. g. 208 is:

17. 二百　零　八

70,504 is:

18. 七万　(零)　五百　零　四

(2) In a big number, when there are two or more zeros in succession, we read only one "0". e. g. 80,024 is:

19. 八万　零　二十四

800,024　is:

20. 八十万　零　二十四

(3) Whether there is one zero or more at the end of a big number, "0" is not read. e. g. 120 is:

21. 一百　二(十)

12,000 is:

22. 一万　二(千)

In the spoken language, we need not read the last units, such as 十 and 千 in the above examples, because we can tell what the last unit is from the preceding unit without difficulty. But the last unit must be read on a formal occasion.

(4) "0" must be used when we read the numerals of a number. e. g.

23. 他　坐　的　汽車　是　200306

(二零零三零六)号.

The number of his car (OR: The car in which he came) is 200306.

56.3 Fraction and Percentage In Chinese we use …分之… to indicate fractions. The denominator is placed before the numerator. e. g. 1/3 reads:

24. 三分之　一　　2/5 reads: 25. 五分之　二

1/3 means that one whole is divided into three equal parts and one part is taken out of three; 2/5 means two parts out of five parts of a whole. So …分之… means so many parts out of the so many parts of a whole.

Percentage is also a kind of fraction, and is expressed in the same way as fraction. As the denominator is always "100", we put 百分之… before the numerator. e. g. 25% reads:

26. 百分之　二十五

150% reads:

27. 百分之　一百　五(十)

56.4 Multiple Numbers Multiple numbers are formed by adding the word 倍 after numerals. e. g.

28. "二"的 四倍 是 多少?

How much is four times two?

29. 是 "八".

(It's) eight.

30. "七十五" 是 "二十五"的 几倍?

Seventy-five is how many times twenty-five?

31. 三倍.

Three times.

課文 Kèwén Text

I

(a₁) 你們 学校 有 五六千(个) 学生 吧?

There must be five or six thousand students in your school.

(b₁) 去年 有 六千 五百多(个) 学生, 今年 学生的 数目 是 七千 四百 零 八个.

Last year there were a little over sixty-five hundred students. This year the number of students is seven thousand four hundred and eight.

(a₂) 解放 以前, 这兒 有 几千 学生, 呢?

Before the Liberation, how many thousands of students were there?

(b₂) 那 时候兒 只 有 七百多 人,
現在 差不多 是 从前的 十倍.

There were only a little over seven hundred then. There
are now almost ten times as many as before.

(a₃) 發展得 真 快. 这些 学生里 有
百分之 多少 是 女生?

The growth is really fast. What percentage of the present
student body is (made up of) female students?

(b₃) 百分之 三十几. 女生的 数目
增加得 更 快. 一九五〇年 男生
是 女生的 五六倍; 現在 全校的
学生里 有 三分之 一 是 女生
了.

Over 30%. The number of female students has increased
even faster. In 1950, the number of male students was five
or six times that of the female students. Now one third of
the entire student body is female.

II

(a₄) 你 看了 今年 十月 一日的 遊行
了 嗎?

Did you see the October first parade this year?

(b₄) 看 了, 遊行的 队伍 真 長, 参加
遊行 的 人 真 多.

I did. The parade was really long. Quite a lot of people
participated in the parade.

(a₅) 是的. 那天 參加 遊行的, 有 五
十多万 人. 遊行 的 队伍 好看
不 好看?

Right. More than five hundred thousand people took part
in the parade that day. Was the parade pretty?

(b₅) 好看 極了. 工人 队伍 和 农民
队伍 在 最 前边兒. 学生的 队伍
在 后边兒.

Extremely pretty. The worker and farmer paraders were
at the very front; the student paraders were at the end.

(a₆) 北京 大学的 队伍 你 看見 沒 有?

Did you see the parade of Peking University?

(b₆) 看見 了. 你 也 參加 遊行 了 嗎?

I did. Did you also participate in the parade?

(a₇) 那天 我 也 在 北京 大学的
队伍 里边兒. 我們 都 把 最 好的
衣服 穿出来 了, 女 同学 穿得
特別 漂亮.

That day I was also among the Peking University paraders.
We all wore our best clothes. The women students were
especially prettily dressed.

(b₇) 我 看見 北京 大学的 队伍 过来
了, 就 注意 找 我的 朋友; 因为
人 太 多, 沒 有 找着. 只 看見

你們 举着 花兒, 大声兒地 喊着
口号兒.

When I saw the Peking University paraders marching by, I immediately looked for my friends; but because there were too many people, I did not find any of them. I only saw all of you holding flowers and loudly shouting slogans.

(a₈) 我們 走到 主席 台 前边兒, 看見
毛 主席 在 主席 台上, 大家 都
兴奋地 喊: "毛 主席 方岁!" "中华
人民 共和国 方岁!"

We walked up in front of the chairman's platform and saw Chairman Mao up there. Everybody shouted excitedly: "Long Live Chairman Mao! Long live the People's Republic of China!"

(b₉) 我 听着 你們 喊 口号兒 也 兴奋
极了, 也 跟 你們 一起 喊起来 了.

Hearing you all shouting slogans, I also became very excited and started to shout with you.

课外練習   Kèwài   liànxí   Home Work

1) Write out the following numbers in Chinese:
   (1) 218   (2) 580   (3) 202
   (4) 20,200   (5) 7,009   (6) 185,673
   (7) 600,532,147   (8) 23,500,000
   (9) 85%   (10) 5/8

2) Write out questions for the following answers: (try to ask questions using the words underlined in the following sentences)

(11) 那个　書店　在　王府井　(Wángfǔjǐng)
大街　147　号.

(12) 我們的　先生　有　五分之　三　是
女的.

(13) 这个　工厂的　生产　增加了　两倍.

(14) 遊行　队伍里　有　两三万个　农民.

汉字表　Hànzì biǎo　Chinese Characters

1	千	ノ 千		
2	万	一 丆 万		
3	亿	亻		
		乙		
4	零	雨		
		令		
5	之	丶 ㇇ 之		
6	倍	亻		
		音	立	
			口	
7	数	娄		
		攵		
8	女			

9	增	土
		曾（丶 丷 丷 丷 丷 丷 丷 曲 曾)
10	男	田
		力
11	遊	斿（方 方 方 斿)
		辶
12	队	阝
		人
13	伍	亻
		五
14	举	丶 丷 丷 丷 丷 兴 丼 举
15	喊	口
		咸（一 厂 厂 后 咸 咸 咸)
16	口	
17	华	化
		十

Lesson 57

生詞　Shēngcí　New Words

1.	干部	(名) gànbù	cadre
2.	修理	(动) xiūlǐ	to repair
3.	髒	(形) zāng	dirty
4.	篇	(量) piān	(a measure word)
5.	文章	(名) wénzhāng 〔篇〕	article, essay
6.	远	(形) yuǎn	distant, far
7.	排	(名) pái	row, rank
8.	近	(形) jìn	near, close
9.	观众	(名) guānzhòng	audience
10.	水平	(名) shuǐpíng	level, standard
11.	低	(形) dī	low
12.	着急	(动) zhāojí	to be anxious, to be impatient,
13.	音乐	(名) yīnyuè	music
14.	怕	(动) pà	to be afraid, to fear
15.	淺	(形) qiǎn	shallow, easy
16.	票	(名) piào 〔張〕	ticket

57.1 The Potential Complement　Besides optative verbs, the potential complement may also be used to express possi-

bility. It is idiomatic in Chinese to use the potential complement, especially when a verb carries a resultative complement
or a directional complement. The potential complement is
formed by putting the structural particle 得 between the verb
and its resultative or directional complement. e. g.

1. 你 記得住 这些 詞的 意思 嗎?

Can you remember the meaning of these new words?

2. 那張 桌子 不 大, 他 搬得上去.

That table is not large; he can move it up.

記得住 means 能記住，and 搬得上去 means 能搬上去.

If a directional complement has an extended meaning, it
can still be turned into a potential complement by adding 得.
e. g.

3. 那个 同志 是 哪国 人, 你 看得出
来 嗎?

What nationality is that comrade, can you tell (by looking
at him)?

4. 这个 詞 是 什么 意思, 你 好好兒地
想想, 一定 想得 起来.

As to what this word means, if you think about it carefully
you certainly can (think of it) recall.

Note: In most cases a potential complement is used instead of an optative verb, but 能 cannot be replaced by a
potential complement, when it expresses request or permission
and not ability. For example, when we say: 我能进来嗎, in
asking one's permission, we must use the optative verb. Here
we cannot say 我进得来嗎.

57.2 The Negative Form of the Potential Complement
As mentioned above, the affirmative potential complement

is formed by putting the word 得 before the resultative or directional complement. Its negative is formed by using 不 instead of 得. e. g.

5. 我 記不住 那些 同志的 名字.

I can't remember the names of those comrades.

6. 那張 画兒 掛得 很 好, 掉不下来.

That painting is well hung, it can't fall down.

記不住 is the negative form of 記得住, and 掉不下来 is the negative form of 掉得下来.

57.3 Some Rules of the Potential Complement:

(1) If a verb is followed by a potential complement and an object, the object should stand after the complement. e. g.

7. 两个 干部 作得完 这些 工作 嗎?

Can two cadres complete this work?

8. 我 剛 鍛鍊完, 吃不下 飯.

I finished exercising, so I cannot eat anything.

But, if the object is rather long and complex, it should be transposed to the beginning of the sentence. e. g.

9. 我 推来 的 那輛 自行車, 明天 修理得好 嗎?

Can the bicycle which I pushed here be repaired by tomorrow?

10. 讓 大家 后天 来 开 会 的 通知, 明天 寄得到 嗎?

Can the notice which tells everybody to come to the meeting the day after tomorrow reach everybody by mail by tomorrow?

(2) The potential complement can be used in all interrogative sentences. In the alternative interrogative sentence, the affirmative and the negative forms of the potential complement appear together. e. g.

11. 黑板上的 字 你 看得清楚 看不清楚?

Can you see the words on the blackboard clearly?

12. 无線电 播送 的 新聞, 你 听得懂 听不懂?

Can you understand the radio news broadcast?

(3) The negative form of the potential complement makes use of the word 不 and not the particle 得; while the negative form of the complement of degree makes use of both the words 得 and 不 at the same time. e. g.

13. 這件 衣服 太 髒, 她 一定 洗不干淨. (可能补語)

This garment is too dirty; she certainly can't wash it clean. (potential complement)

14. 她 洗 衣服 洗得 不 干淨. (程度补語)

She does not wash clothes clean. (complement of degree)

But the affirmative form of the potential complement is the same as that of the complement of degree, and can only be distinguished from the context. e. g.

15. 這件 衣服 這么 髒, 她 洗得干淨 洗不干淨?

(Since) this garment is so dirty, will she be able to wash it clean? (potential complement)

16. 虽然　髒，但是　洗得干凈. （可能补語）

Although it is dirty, she can still wash it clean. (potential complement)

17. 她　洗　衣服　洗得　干凈　不　干凈？

Does she wash clothes clean? (complement of degree)

18. 洗得　干凈. （程度补語）

She does (She washes them clean). (complement of degree)

Moreover, the potential complement may be followed by an object; so example 15 may be changed into 她洗得干凈这件衣服嗎. But the complement of degree is never followed by any object, so we must say 她洗衣服洗得干凈.

(4) But in sentences of the disposal form, optative verbs are always used instead of potential complements. We can say 我能把这个窗戶推开, but we cannot say 我把这个窗戶推得开.

(5) Sometimes an optative verb can be used together with a potential complement. e. g.

19. 后天　就　要　开　联欢　会　了，这些　节目　两天　可以　准备得出来　嗎？

We are going to have the reunion day after tomorrow. Can these programs be prepared within two days?

20. 你　一定　能　写得好　这篇　文章.

You certainly can write this article well.

課文　Kèwén　Text

I

(a₁)　上星期六　你　看的　話剧　怎么样？

How was the play you saw last Saturday?

(b₁) 不错. 但是 我的 座位 比較 远,
在 楼下 十五排, 看得 不 太
清楚. 要是 近 一点兒, 就 看得
清楚 了.

Pretty good, but my seat was relatively far. It was in the fifteenth row downstairs, and I did not see very clearly. If it had been a little bit closer I would have been able to see clearly.

(a₂) 你 听得 怎么样?

How did you comprehend (by listening)?

(b₂) 观众 都 很 安静, 所以 听得
很 清楚. 但是 自己的 中文 水平
太 低, 很 多 地方 听不懂.

The audience was all very quiet, so I heard clearly. But my Chinese level is too low, so there were many places that I could not understand.

(a₃) 别 着急! 慢慢兒地 就 能 完全
听得懂 了. 这个 星期六 有 音乐
会, 你 想 去 吗?

Don't worry. Gradually (you'll) be able to understand completely. There is a concert this Saturday. Do you feel like going?

(b₃) 当然 想 去, 我 是 最 爱 听
音乐 的.

Of course I feel like going. I love to listen to music the most.

(a₄) 我 也 想 去. 我們 一起 去, 好
不 好?

I also feel like going. Let's go together, O.K.?

(b₄) 好.

O.K.

II

(a₅) 現在 你 能 不 能 看 中文 报?

Can you read Chinese newspapers now?

(b₅) 我 試着 看过 一兩次, 还 看不懂.
报上的 文章 太 深 了. 我 只
看得懂 又 短 又 淺的 文章 和
簡單的 小 故事. 有时候兒 先生 給
我們 講 的 故事, 我 都 听 得懂.

I have tried to read them once or twice, but still can't
understand them (by reading). Newspaper articles are too
advanced. I can only understand short and easy articles
and simple little stories. Sometimes when the teacher tells
us stories, I can understand all of them.

(a₆) 先生 給 你們 講 故事 的 时候兒,
他 說 几遍?

When the teacher tells you stories, how many times does he
tell them?

(b₆) 說 兩遍, 第一遍 慢, 第二遍 比較
快. 要是 不 这样兒, 我們 有时候兒
就 听不懂.

Twice, the first time slowly, the second time relatively
quickly. If it is not done this way (If he does not do it this
way), sometimes we cannot understand.

(a₇) 要是 讓 你 自己 說 这个 故事,
說得出来 說不出来 呢?

If you were to tell the story yourself (If he makes you tell the story yourself), could you tell it or not?

(b₇) 說得出来. 但是 說不流利, 并且 会
有 語法 錯誤.

I could but I couldn't tell it fluently and furthermore (I) might make grammatical mistakes.

(a₈) 沒 关系. 多 練習練習, 就 說得好
了.

That doesn't matter. (If you) practice more you'll be able to tell it well.

課外練習　Kèwài liànxí　Home Work

1) Re-write the following sentences using the potential complement:

(1) 要是 你 把 音乐 会的 票 丢 了,
就 不能进去 了.

(2) 因为 我 不去 看 电影, 我 想 我
今天 能看完 这本 小说兒.

(3) 别 着急, 你 要是 努力, 一定
能 学好 中文.

(4) 这个 句子 很 容易, 我 能 翻譯
出来.

2) Write three sentences using potential complements with each of the following verb-complement constructions:

(5) 学会

(6) 拿起来

(7) 关上

汉字表　Hànzì biǎo　Chinese Characters

1	部	咅
		阝
2	修	亻（亻 亻）
		攵
		彡
3	理	王
		里
4	髒	骨（丶 冂 冂 冎 咼 骨）
		葬（丷 丷 艹 莚 莚 葬 葬）
5	篇	竹
		扁
6	章	立
		早
7	远	元
		辶
8	排	扌
		非
9	众	人

		人
		人
10	平	
11	低	亻
		氏（氏 氏）
12	急	刍（丿 ⺈ 刍 刍 刍）
		心
13	乐	ノ 匚 乐
14	怕	
15	票	

Lesson 58

生詞　Shēngcí　New Words

1. 了　　　(动) liǎo　　　to complete, to finish, to settle
2. 孩子　　(名) háizî　　　child
3. 照(像)　(动) zhào(xiàng)　to photograph, to take a photograph
4. 动　　　(动) dòng　　　to move, to touch
5. 像片兒　(名) xiàngpiānr 〔張〕　photograph, snapshot
6. 累　　　(形) lèi　　　tired, weary, fatigued
7. 戏　　　(名) xì〔出〕　play, opera
8. 白毛女　(名) Báimáonǚ　a white-haired girl (the name of a story)
9. 女兒　　(名) nǚêr　　daughter
10. 喜兒　　(名) Xǐêr　　(a proper name)
11. 受　　　(动) shòu　　to suffer
12. 地主　　(名) dìzhǔ　　landlord
13. 压迫　　(动) yāpò　　to oppress, oppression
14. 追　　　(动) zhuī　　to run after, to catch up, to overtake
15. 山　　　(名) shān〔座〕　hill, mountain
16. 头髪　　(名) tóufả　　hair
17. 八路軍　(名) Bálùjūn　Eighth Route Army

18.	爱人	（名）	àirén	lover, sweetheart,(also denoting husband and wife)
19.	大春	（名）	Dàchūn	(a proper name)
20.	分	（动）	fēn	to get a portion of, to divide, to separate
21.	地	（名）	dì	land
22.	結婚	（动）	jiéhūn	to get married
23.	幸福	（形）	xìngfú	happy
24.	生活	（动、名）	shēnghuó	to live, life

語法 Yǔfǎ Grammar

58.1 了 Used as Potential Complement   The verb 了 is rather peculiar, because it is rarely used as predicate or resultative complement (especially as affirmative resultative complement), but it is always used as potential complement. As potential complement, it means that there is (or there is not) the possibility of carrying on some action. e.g.

1. 明天 早上 七点 你 来得了 嗎?

Can you come (as early as) (at) 7:00 in the morning?

2. 这种 翻譯 工作 他 作得了 作不了?

Can he do this kind of translation work?

来得了 means 能来，作得了 and 作不了 mean 能作 and 不能作.

了 sometimes means "to finish", when it is used as potential complement after certain verbs. e.g.

3. 你 用得了 这么 多 紙 嗎?

Can you use this much paper? (Do you need this much paper?)

4. 我 吃不了 这些 水菓.

I can't eat this much fruit.

用得了 means 用得完, and 吃不了 means 吃不完.

了 is also often used as potential complement after an adjective. e.g.

5. 我 給 这个 孩子 照 像 的 时候兒,
   他 动 了. 这張 像片兒 好不了,

When I took a picture of this child, he moved. This picture can't be good.

6. 合作社 就 在 宿舍 后边兒 从
   这兒 过去 錯不了!

The co-op is right behind the dormitory. If you go over from here, you won't miss it (you couldn't go wrong).

58.2 动 Used as Potential Complement   The verb 动 is also often used as potential complement, meaning that the person or thing denoted by the subject has (or hasn't) the strength to carry on some action and to move away from the original position through this action. e.g.

7. 这么 远, 你 走得动 嗎?

It's so far away. Can you make it there (by walking)?

8. 我 真 累 極了, 跑不动 了.

I am really exhausted. I can't run any more.

There is no object in the above examples, and 动 indicates the movement of the person or thing denoted by the subject. If there is an object, 动 will mean that there is (or there is no) possibility of moving the person or thing denoted by the object away from the original position through some action. e.g.

9. 你們 搬得动 这个 机器 嗎?

Can you move this machine?

10. 他 拿不动 这包 書.

He can't move (carry) this package of books.

58.3   下 Used as Potential Complement   The verb 下
implies direction, but when it is used as potential complement,
it is not so definite in meaning. e.g.

11. 他 因为 工作 放不下, 决定 不 去
旅行 了.

Because he could not leave his work, he decided not to go
traveling.

But 下 is more often used to indicate whether there is
space enough to make certain accommodation. e. g.

12. 这种 最 新的 大 汽車 坐得下
八十 人.

This kind of most (very) modern bus can seat eighty
people.

13. 礼堂 前边兒 地方 大, 停得下
六七十辆 汽車.

The space in front of the auditorium is quite big. Sixty or
seventy cars can be parked there.

14. 那間 宿舍 放不下 四張 床, 当然
住不下 四个 人.

That dormitory room does not have room for four beds. Of
course it cannot accommodate four people.

坐得下 and 停得下 mean that there is space enough for
people to sit in or for the cars to park in, while 放不下 and 住
不下 mean that there is not enough space to put in four beds
and allow four people to live in.

58.4　上来 used as Potential Complement　The verbal construction 上来 indicates the final direction of an action. As a potential complement, it expresses whether there is a possibility for a person or thing to ''get up'' as the result of an action. e. g.

15. 那張 桌子 很 重, 你 搬得上来 嗎?

That desk is heavy. Can you move it up (here)?

But this verbal construction is often used in its extended meaning. As a potential complement, it may indicate whether one has ability (in knowledge, skill etc.) to carry on some action. e. g.

16. 所有的 問題, 他 都 回答得上来.

He could answer all the questions.

17. 先生 講 的 故事 我 听得懂, 但是 自己 说不上来.

I could understand the story the teacher told us, but I could not tell it myself.

課文　Kèwén　Text

(a₁) 昨天 晚上 你 到 哪兒 看 戏 去 了?

Where did you go to see a play last night?

(b₁) 首都 剧場.

The Capital Theatre.

(a₂) 我 还 沒 有 去过 那兒 呢! 那个 剧場 怎么样?

I have not been there yet. How is that theatre?

(b₂) 那个 剧場 又 好 又 大, 可以 坐得下 一千多 人, 座位 也 很 舒服.

That theatre is both good and big. It can seat more than a thousand people. The seats are also very comfortable.

(a₃) 你 看 的 是 什么 戏?

What play did you see?

(b₃) "白毛女".

"The White-Haired Girl."

(a₄) 这个 戏 很 有名, 我 还 沒 有 看过, 演得 怎么样?

This play is very famous. I have not seen it yet. How was it (performed)?

(b₄) 非常 好. 我們 看到 那个 农民的 女兒 喜兒 受不了 地主的 压迫, 从 地主 家里 跑出来 的 时候兒, 都 很 緊張. 特別 是 她 跑不 动 了, 地主 快 要 追上 她 的 时候兒, 我們 都 替 她 着急.

Exceedingly good (well). When we saw Xi'er, the daughter of a farmer, escape from the landlord's house because she could not stand the oppression any more, we were all quite excited. We were all worried for her, especially when she could not run any more and the landlord was about to overtake her.

(a₅) 以后 怎么样 呢?

What happened next?

(b₅) 以后 喜兒 跑到 山里 去 了,
在 山里 过了 几年, 头髮 都 白
了. 这 时候兒, 八路軍 来 了,
把 这个 地方 解放 了. 她的
爱人 大春 也 在 八路軍的 队
伍里. 大春 在 山里 找到了 喜兒,
这 时候兒 地主 也 跑不了 了.
农民 組織起来 打倒了 那个 地主,
分到了 地; 喜兒 和 大春 結了
婚, 开始了 幸福的 生活.

Later on, Xi'er ran into the mountains. She spent a few
years in the mountains and her hair all turned white. At
this time the Eighth Route Army came and liberated the
area. Her lover, Dachun, was also in the Eighth Route
Army. Dachun found Xi'er in the mountains, and by this
time the landlords could not run any more. The peasants
organized themselves, struck down that landlord, and
received their shares of land. Xi'er and Dachun were
married and began a happy life.

(a₆) 演 喜兒 的 那个 演員 是 誰?

Who played Xi'er?

(b₆) 是 一个 很 有名的 演員, 她
还 到 苏联 表演过, 但是 我
叫不上来 她的 名字 了 这个 戏

非常 好, 演員 演得 很 好. 你
真 应該 去 看看.

She is a famous actress. She has even performed in Russia
but I can no longer recall her name. This play is very good.
The actors and actresses all performed very well. You
should go see it.

(a₇) 要是 買得着 票, 我 明天 就
去 看.

If I can get a ticket, I will go see it tomorrow.

課外練習 Kèwài liànxí Home Work

1) Re-write the following sentences using potential complements:

(1) 下 雨 的 时候兒, 能 照 像 嗎?

(2) 那个 礼堂 很 大, 能 坐 一兩千 人.

(3) 要是 不 常常 鍛鍊, 跑 一会兒 就 不 能 跑 了.

(4) 我 还 記得 这个 詞的 意思, 但是 不 会 念 了.

2) Copy the following sentences and fill the blanks with proper potential complements:

(5) 这張 紙 太 小, 写不____五百 汉字.

(6) 先生 告訴 我 的 話, 我 都 好好兒地 記着, 忘不____.

汉字表 Hànzì biǎo Chinese Characters

1	孩	子
		亥
2	照	

3	片		
4	累	田	
		糸	
5	戏	又	
		戈	
6	受	⼀ ⼃ ⼃⼃ ⺥ ⼝ 受	
7	压	厂 圧 压	
8	迫	白	
		辶	
9	追	𠂤 (⼃ ⼁ 𠂤 𠂤 𠂤 𠂤)	
		辶	
10	山		
11	路	足	
		各	
12	髮	髟 (⼀ 厂 F F 王 镸 髟)	
		发 (友 发)	
13	軍	⼌	
		車	
14	婚	女	
		昏	氏
			日
15	幸		
16	福	礻	

		畐 (一 � 畐)
17	活	氵
		舌

Lesson 59

生詞 Shēngcí New Words

1. 不但 ... 而且 ...　búdàn...érqiě

   not only...but also

2. 一 ... 就 ...　yī...jiù...　as soon as..., no sooner... than

3. 臉　(名)　liǎn　face

4. 越 ... 越 ...　yuè...yuè...　the more...the more

5. 只要 ... 就 ...　zhǐyào...jiù...

   if only...(then)

6. 大禹　(名)　Dàyǔ　(a proper name)

7. 水　(名)　shuǐ　water, river

8. 历史　(名)　lìshǐ　history

9. 發生　(动)　fāshēng　to happen, to take place

10. 水災　(名)　shuǐzāi　calamity caused by flood

11. 庄稼　(名)　zhuāngjià　crops

12. 淹　(动)　yān　to drown, to inundate

13. 餓　(动、形)　è　to hunger, hungry

14. 死　(动)　sǐ　to die

15. 領导　(动)　lǐngdǎo　to lead

16. 办法　(名)　bànfǎ　method, way

17. 經过　(动、名)　jīngguò　to pass by, history

18.	門口兒	（名）	ménkǒur	door, gate, entrance
19.	滿意	（形、动）	mǎnyì	satisfactory, satisfied, to satisfy
20.	劝	（动）	quàn	to advise, to persuade
21.	任務	（名）	rènwù	mission, task

語法 Yǔfǎ Grammar

59.1 不但…而且　　When we introduced the conjunction for the first time, we said that some conjunctions in Chinese (such as 和) are used mainly to connect nouns and pronouns (17.4). But there are other conjunctions used to connect verbs, adjectives, verb phrases and adjective phrases, such as the word 而且. When we say 这个医院很大，而且很有名, it means that this hospital is both big and famous. When we say this, we emphasize both elements 大 and 有名 at the same time. But when we not only lay emphasis on the two elements, but also show that the second action or state is more important or outstanding, then we use the construction 不但…而且. e. g.

1. 这个　医院　不但　很　大．而且　很　有名．

This hospital is not only large but also famous.

2. 第四十四課的　課文，他，不但　念了，而且　念得　很　熟．

He has not only studied the text of the forty-fourth lesson but has also mastered it.

3. 我們　到　中国　来，不但　要　学好　專业，而且　要　了解　中国的　情况．

We have come to China not only to learn a special field well but also to understand the situation in China.

In each of the above examples emphasis is laid on the two parallel elements of the predicate. If we want to emphasize two parallel clauses, we may use the same construction. e. g.

4. 不但　二年級的　同學　聽懂了　這個
　　報告. 而且　一年級的　也　聽懂了.

> Not only did the second-year students understand (by listening) this report, but the first-year students also understood it.

In such a case, we often use the adverb 也 in the predicate of the second clause.

59.2　一... 就...　Both 一 and 就 are adverbs. In Chinese two adverbs may be used together as one relative connective, and the construction 一... 就... is a typical example. This construction is chiefly used in two ways:

(1) Meaning that two actions are closely connected in time, e. g.

5. 主席　一　報告完,　音樂　會　就
　　開始了.

> As soon as the chairman finished the report, the concert began.

6. 他　一　上　汽車　就　買好了　票.

> As soon as he got on the bus he bought his ticket.

(2) Expressing condition, e. g.

7. 他　一　著急,　就　臉　紅.

> Whenever he is anxious, his face turns red.

8. 他　一　興奮,　就　睡不着　覺.

> Whenever he is excited, he cannot sleep.

The construction 要是... 就..., which we have learned, also expresses condition, therefore it may be used instead of 一...

就… in a conditional sentence. But there is a difference: —…
就… expresses a general condition, that is to say, something
always happens under such a condition; while 要是… 就… expresses not only a general condition but also a particular condition, for example, in such a sentence, 今天要是下雨, 就别去打
球, we can only say 要是… 就…, but never —… 就….

59.3 越…越   越 is an adverb, it can never be used
alone but always reduplicatively. When we wish to show that
two actions or states are correlative to each other, we prefer
this construction. e. g.

9. 我 觉得 工作 越 紧張, 越 愉快.

I feel that the more exciting the work is, the more pleasant
it is.

10. 他 越 学習, 越 觉得 自己 知道
的 少.

The more he studies, the more he feels that he knows very
little.

In general, the word 越 is placed before the predicate, but
when there is a complement of degree in the sentence, it may
also be placed before the complement. Therefore, example 10
may be rewritten as follows:

11. 他 学習得 越 多, 越 觉得 自己
知道 的 少.

The more he studies, the more he feels that he knows very
little.

59.4 只要… (就)…   This construction is the emphatic
form of 要是… 就…. e. g.

12. 只要 您 說得 慢, 我 就
听得懂.

As long as you speak slowly, I can understand.

13. 你 只要 努力， 就 可以 克服 困难.

As long as you strive to, (you) can overcome difficulties.

In the above two examples we can also use the construction 要是… 就…, but the construction 只要… 就… is more emphatic. The word 就 may be omitted, but another adverb must be used instead. e. g.

14. 只要 您 說得 慢， 我 一定 听得懂.

As long as you speak slowly, I can definitely understand.

15. 你 只要 努力， 当然 可以 克服 困难.

As long as you strive to, of course you can overcome difficulties.

課文 Kèwén Text

大禹 治 水 是 中国 一个 很 有名的 历史 故事.

Da Yu's (The Great Yu's) controlling of the flood is a very famous historical Chinese story.

四千多年 以前 中国 發生了 一次 很 大的 水災. 把 庄稼 都 淹 了, 不 少 人 都 餓死 了.

More than four thousand years ago a great flood occurred in China. It inundated all the crops and a lot of (not a few) people starved to death.

大禹 領导着 很 多 人 治水；他們
不但 不 怕 困难， 还 想出了 很 多
办法. 他們 每天 都 很 緊張地 工作，
大禹 常常 几天 不 睡 覺.

Da Yu led many people to control the flood. They not
only were unafraid of the difficulties but they also thought
of many methods. They worked very energetically every
day, Da Yu frequently not sleeping for several days.

有 一次 大禹 帶着 很 多 人 經过
自己的 家 門口兒，他 想 进去 看看；
但是 一 想 到 工作 很 緊張， 就
走过去 了.

Once Da Yu, bringing along many people, passed by the
door of his own home. He wanted to go in to have a look.
But as soon as he thought of the urgency of the work, he
passed by.

几年 以后， 他 又 从 自己 家
門口兒 經过， 这 一次 还是 沒 进去.
他 想：只要 把 水 治好，我 就 满意 了；
我 回 家 不 回 家 沒 关系.

Several years later, he again passed by the door of his
own home. This time, he still did not go in. He thought:
"If only we could bring the water under control, then I
would be satisfied. Whether I return home or not does not
matter."

水 快 治好 了. 大禹 第三次 走过
家 門口兒， 大家 都 劝 他："这次 你

可以 回 家 看看 了". 大禹 說:
"越 是 任務 快 完成 的 時候兒,
就 越 緊張. 要是 我 回去, 大家
也 都 可以 回去, 這樣兒 我們的 工作
就 完成不了 了." 他 还是 沒 有
回去.

When the water was about to be brought under control, Da Yu passed by the door of his home for the third time. Everyone encouraged him: "This time you can return home and take a look!" Da Yu said, "The closer a mission comes to its completion, the more tense (demanding) it is. If I go back, everyone can also go back. This way, our work won't be completed." He still did not go back.

大禹 和 大家 在 一起 忙着 治水,
經过 十三年的 努力, 他們 最后 把
水 治好 了.

Da Yu, together with all the others, worked busily at controlling the water, and after thirteen years of great effort, they finally brought the water under control.

課外練習　Kèwài liànxí　Home Work

1) Re-write the following sentences using 不但… 而且…

(1) 那个 翻譯 同志 中文 很 好,
　　并且 有 很 多 工作 經驗.

(2) 十月 一日 我 又 参加了 遊行,
　　又 参加了 晚会.

2) Re-write the following sentences using 一... 就...:

(3) 我 每次 遇見 困难 都 找 先生 談.

(4) 汽車 停了 以后, 我們 都 立刻 下来 了.

3) Re-write the following sentence using 越... 越...:

(5) 他 因为 每天 鍛鍊, 身体 就 更 好 了.

4) Re-write the following sentences using 只要... 就...:

(6) 要是 你 決定 研究 中国 历史, 就 有 人 帮助 你.

(7) 要是 你 把 东西 都 好好兒地 放在 桌子上, 找起来 就 方便 了.

汉字表　Hànzì biǎo　Chinese Characters

1	而	
2	臉	月
		僉
3	越	走
		戉（一 厂 戊 戉 戉）
4	禹	ノ 白 户 户 禹 禹 禹
5	历	厂

		力	
6	災	く 巛 巛 災	
7	庄	广	
		土	
8	稼	禾	
		家	
9	淹	氵	
		奄	大
			电
10	餓	食	
		我	
11	死	一 歹 死	
12	領	令	
		頁	
13	导	巳	
		寸	
14	办	力 办	
15	满	氵	
		萳(艹 芇 芇 莤 萳)	
16	劝	又	
		力	
17	任	亻	
		壬(丿 二 千 壬)	

Lesson 60

語法复習 Yǔfǎ fùxí Review

60.1 The Potential Complement and the Complement of Degree   We have already discussed potential complements (57.1), which, we know, are extensively used in Chinese, and some of which have even idiomatic meaning. e. g.

1. 他 跑得快 嗎?

Can he run fast?

2. 只要 是 学过 的 汉字, 他 就 写得上来.

So long as they are characters he has learned before, he can write them.

We know that verbs may be followed by potential complements formed by adjectives or verbs (or verbal constructions), and that the structural particle 得 should be used before potential complements.

We have also studied complements of degree (21.2), which are also used after verbs and require the same structural particle. e. g.

3. 雨 下得 大 了, 快 把 窗户 关上 吧!

It's raining harder now. Quickly close the window.

4. 观众　看　表演　都　看得　满意
極了.

The audience was all pleased with (watching) the performance.

Now we will deal with the differences between the potential complement and the complement of degree:

(1) They are different in meaning. The potential complement indicates possibility, while the complement of degree indicates degree. Besides, we can make out from the context whether a complement is potential or one of degree. e. g.

5. 这个　故事　这么　复杂，他　講得
清楚　嗎？　(可能補語)

This story is so complicated, can he tell it clearly? (potential complement)

6. 他　講完了　以后，先生　說　他
講得　清楚.　(程度補語)

After he finished explaining, the teacher said he had spoken very clearly. (complement of degree)

Since the complement of degree indicates degree, an adjective used as such a complement is often modified by an adverb. e. g.

7. 这个　故事　他　講得　特別　清楚.

He told this story especially clearly.

8. 这个　故事　他　講得　清楚　極了.

He told this story exceedingly clearly.

In general, the potential complement can never take any adjunct.

(2) The affirmative form of the potential complement is like that of the complement of degree, but their negative forms are different. In the potential complement the word 不 is used instead of the particle 得; while in the complement of degree the word 不 is used after the particle. e. g.

9. 这个 故事 复杂, 我 怕 他 讲 不清楚. (可能补語)

This story is complicated. I am afraid he can't tell it clearly. (potential complement)

10. 因为 这个 故事 复杂, 他 讲得 不 清楚. (程度补語)

Because this story was complicated, he did not tell it clearly. (complement of degree)

Therefore, we come to a conclusion that the potential complement and the complement of degree are like each other in the affirmative form, but they are entirely different in the negative form; accordingly they are also different in the interrogative form. The different forms of these two kinds of complements are shown in the following table:

	肯 定 The affirmative	否 定 The negative	疑 問 The interrogative		
可 能 补 語 The potential complement	講得清楚	講不清楚	講得清楚 嗎?	講不清楚 嗎?	講得清楚 講不清楚?
程 度 补 語 The comple- ment of degree	講得清楚	講得不清 楚	講得清楚 嗎?	講得不清 楚嗎?	講得清楚 不清楚?

(3) The potential complement is definite in form, consisting only of a single adjective or verb (or verbal construction, such as 起来, 下去 etc.). A verb carrying a potential comple-

ment can take an object. But the complement of degree cannot be followed by an object, moreover, it has many forms——it may be a single word or it may be a whole sentence. e. g.

11. 他 説得 <u>大家 都 笑起来 了</u>.

He spoke in such a way that everybody started laughing.

The above example means "what he had said was so interesting that everybody laughed"; 大家都笑起来了 has every reason to be considered a complete sentence.

60.2 On the Uses of 的, 得 and 地   It is one of the characteristics of the Chinese language to use particles, and they are difficult to master. In addition, these three structural particles 的, 得 and 地 have the same pronunciation, and are likely to be confused. It is advisable here to sum up their various uses we have learned as follows:

(1) 的   This word is used chiefly as a connective between an adjective modifier and its central word, but we must notice that not every adjective modifier requires it under all conditions.

a) When 的 has to be used   When an adjective modifier is composed of a verb (or a verbal construction), a subject-predicate construction, an adjective with an adverbial modifier or a reduplicated adjective, the word 的 must be used. e. g.

12. <u>要 去 参观 的</u> 同学 都 来得 很 早.

The schoolmates who wanted to go on the visit all came very early.

13. 我 有 一个 <u>很 爱 照 像 的</u> 朋友.

I have a friend who likes to take pictures very much.

14. 这本 书 太 深, 水平 低 的
    同志 翻譯不了.

This book is too difficult. Comrades with a low level (of training or knowledge) can't translate it.

15. 我們 解决了 一个 非常 复杂的
    問題.

We solved a very complicated problem.

16. 这 孩子 紅紅的 小 臉 真 好看.

This child with rosy cheeks is really pretty.

b) When 的 is not used   When a measure word is used as an adjective modifier, or when an adjective modifier and its central word have already formed a stable unit, the word 的 is not used. e. g.

17. 这枝 鉛笔 是 紅 的.

This pencil is red.

18. 树 叶子 都 掉下来 了.

The leaves have all fallen down.

If the sentence is rather long and has a number of adjective modifiers, 的 is also often omitted. e. g.

19. 我們 可以 看到 最 新的、
    外国(的) 进步(的) 电影.

We may see the most recent, foreign, progressive movies.

Besides, 的 is always used in the construction 是...的. We have learned two kinds of such constructions: the first kind is used in the sentence with a substantive predicate (2). e. g.

20. 这个　語法　特点　<u>是　我們　应該　注意　的</u>.

This grammatical peculiarity is what we must be careful about.

21. 上次　旅行　<u>是　很　有意思　的</u>.

The parade last time was a very interesting one.

的 and the words before it have the function of a substantive construction. Therefore the particle 的 cannot be omitted.

The other kind of the construction 是...的 is used in the sentence with a verbal predicate. e. g.

22. 他　（是）　最近　把　这本　历史　<u>写好　的</u>.

It was recently that he finished writing this history book.

23. 我　（是）　在　城里　买　<u>的</u>　表.

It was in the city that I bought the watch.

In the above examples 的 must be used. but the word 是 may be omitted.

(2) 得　This is the structural particle used before the complement of degree and the potential complement. See section 60.1

(3) 地　This structural particle is used after the adverbial modifier, but we must pay attention to the following:

a) When an adverb, a monosyllabic adjective or a prepositional construction is used as adverbial modifier, the particle 地 is not used. e. g.

24. 我們的　生产　任务　已經　早　完成　了.

Our production mission was completed long ago.

25. 車 要 开 了, 快 把 东西 拿上去!

The bus (car) is about to start. Take the things on immediately.

26. 新 中国的 干部 都 在 努力地 为 人民 服务.

New China's cadres are all diligently serving the people.

b) When an adjective used as adverbial modifier is modified by another adverbial modifier, the particle 地 has to be used. e. g.

27. 我們 非常 愉快地 劳动了 四小时.

We labored extremely happily for four hours.

28. 他 很 快地 改正了 自己的 错误.

He very quickly corrected his own mistakes.

These three particles are pronounced in the same way in colloquial speech. There are some people who use only one 的 for all three in writing. But 得 and 地 are quite different in function, so they should not be used interchangeably.

課文 Kèwén Text

颐和园 (Yíhéyuán) 是 北京 城外 一个 很 有名的 地方. 外国 朋友們 到了 北京 都 要 到 那兒 去 看看. 我 一 到 北京 就 有 朋友 带 我 去过 了. 以后, 我 也 常常 到 那兒 去 玩兒.

Yiheyuan [the Summer Palace] is a very famous place outside of the city of Peking. Foreign friends, after arriving in Peking, all want to go there to have a look. As soon as I arrived in Peking some friends (already) took me there. Ever since then, I have been there often to enjoy myself.

有 一天, 下 雪 了, 我的 朋友 跟 我 說: "今天 頤和园 一定 更 好看 了, 我們 去 照照 像 吧!" 我 也 早 就 想 在 頤和园 照 两張 像片兒 寄 回 国 去. 这样, 我們 就 一塊兒 高高兴兴地 出發 了.

One day, it snowed. My friend said to me, "Yiheyuan must be even prettier today. Let's go to take some pictures." Since I also had wanted for a long time (wanted to, a long time ago) to take a couple of pictures of Yiheyuan to send back to my own country, we started out happily together.

到了 頤和园, 雪 不但 沒有 停, 而且 下得 更 大 了. 树上、 楼上、 山上 都 是 白的, 頤和园 像 穿 上了 白 衣服 一样. 这 一天 去 玩兒 的 人 很 少 —— 跟 我們 每次 去 的 时候兒 不 一样. 我們 都 說: "今天 这兒 真 安静 極 了."

When we reached Yiheyuan, the snow not only had not stopped but was coming down faster. The trees, the buildings, the hills, were all white. It seemed as if

Yiheyuan had put on a white garment. On that day there were very few visitors — quite different from the other times when we were there. We both said, "It's really extremely quiet here today."

我們 慢慢兒地 走, 只要 遇見 好看的
地方 就 停下来 照 像. 我 朋友 照
像 照得 很 好, 但是 我 照 像 的
經驗 不 多. 所以 我 就 問 他:
"今天 下着 雪, 我們的 像片兒 照得好
照不好?" 朋友 説: "我 从前 在 下 雪
的 时候兒 也 照过, 可以 照得好."

We walked slowly on. Whenever we came to a scenic spot, we stopped to take pictures. My friend takes very good pictures, but my experience at picture-taking is rather limited, so I asked him, "It's snowing today. Can we take good pictures?" My friend said, "I have taken pictures while it was snowing before. You can take good pictures."

雪 越 下 越 大, 也 越 深 了.
我們 在 雪里 走得 很 慢, 差不多 要
走不动 了. 我們 走出 颐和园 的
时候兒, 天 已經 晚 了.

It snowed harder and harder and the snow was getting deep. We walked very slowly in the snow, and almost could not walk any more. When we walked out of Yiheyuan, it was already dark.

Lesson 61

生詞 Shēngcí New Words

1. 旗(子) (名) qí(zi) 〔面〕 flag, banner
2. 南 (名) nán south
3. 除了…以外… chúle…yǐwài… in addition to, except, besides
4. 古 (形) gǔ ancient
5. 傳説 (名) chuánshuō legend
6. 路 (名) lù 〔条 tiáo〕 road, way, path
7. 湖 (名) hú lake
8. 条 (量) tiáo (a measure word)
9. 态度 (名) tàidù attitude
10. 能力 (名) nénglì ability
11. 高 (形) gāo high, tall
12. 馬 (名) mǎ 〔疋 pǐ〕 horse
13. 車 (名) chē 〔輛〕 vehicle
14. 赶(車) (动) gǎn(chē) to drive (a cart, or carriage)
15. 往 (介) wǎng towards, to
16. 北 (名) běi north
17. 楚国 (名) Chǔguó Ch'u State(kingdom)
18. 箱子 (名) xiāngzi box, trunk
19. 条件 (名) tiáojiàn condition

20. 方向　　（名）　fāngxiàng　　direction
21. 結果　　（名）　jiéguǒ　　result, effect, consequence

語法　Yǔfǎ　Grammar

61.1 The Verbal Sentence Showing Existence, Emergence or Disappearance　We have already learned that the verbal sentence is used chiefly to describe some action, behavior or change (16.1); in this lesson we shall deal with a special kind of verbal sentence, which is used not chiefly for narrating something, but for telling the appearance, existence, or disappearance of some person or thing at a certain place or time. This kind of sentence is rather peculiar in its word order:

Noun of place or Time—Verb—Noun of Person or Thing

Here we will explain this kind of sentence in the following:

(1) Indicating existence:

1. 楼上　放着　很多　床.

There are many beds placed upstairs.

2. 車間里　掛着　一面　紅旗.

There is a red flag hanging in the workshop.

楼上 and 車間里 are words of place, and the verbs 放 and 掛 with their continuous suffixes express states, not actions, that is to say, they tell in what state are the beds and the red banner. When the speaker has no wish to stress the continuation of an action (or the result of an action), and has in mind only the completion of an action, he may say:

3. 楼上　放了　很多　床.

Many beds had been placed upstairs.

4. 車間里　掛了　一面　紅旗.

A red flag had been hung up in the workshop.

(2) Indicating emergence or disappearance: The order of words is the same as shown above. e. g.

5. 南边兒　走过来　两个　干部.

Two cadres came walking from the south.

6. 十点　一刻　开来了　一辆　汽车.

At 10:15, an automobile drove up (toward the speaker).

These two sentences tell respectively at what time and at what place the cadres and the motor-car appeared. More examples are:

7. 宿舍里　搬走了　两个　同学.

Two schoolmates moved out of the dormitory.

This example relates how the school-mates disappeared.

In short, this kind of sentence is not only different in structure from the general verbal sentence, but each element of the sentence has also its own peculiar form:

a) At the beginning of the sentence, we must use a time-word or a noun of locality; if it is a noun denoting place (such as "宿舍"), it is often used together with a noun of locality (e. g. 宿舍里).

b) If there is no 了 or 着 after the verb, the verb must generally be followed by a resultative or directional comple-ment. It may also be followed by a 了 and a complement at the same time (examples 5, 6, 7).

c) At the end of the sentence we must use a noun denot-ing person or thing, but in most cases what it denotes is inde-finite, such as example 7 meaning "two students moved away from the dormitory".

61.2 The Construction 除了…以外   This construction is very commonly used. It has two different uses:

(1) Meaning "in addition to":

8. 校园里　除了　小　山　以外, 还有　一个　湖.

On the campus, besides a small hill, there is also a lake.

9. 除了 他 以外, 这班 还 有 五 个 男生.

In addition to him, this class has five other male students.

The above two examples mean that "there are not only a hill but also a lake in our school campus", and "there are six boy students in this class".

Not only are nouns and pronouns used in this construction, but verbs or adjectives may also be used. e. g.

10. 星期日 除了 玩兒 以外, 我 还 学习了 一 晚上.

On Sunday, in addition to playing, I also studied all evening.

11. 住在 这条 街上, 除了 方便 以外, 也 很 安静.

Living on this street, in addition to being convenient, is also very quiet.

Sometimes, a subject-predicate construction or a verb-object construction may also be inserted into this construction. e. g.

12. 他 除了 工作 态度 好 以外, 工作 能力 也 很 高.

In addition to his good working attitude, (his) working ability is also high.

13. 我 除了 爱 骑 自行车 以外, 还 爱 骑 马.

Besides enjoying riding bicycles, I also like to ride horses.

It should be noted that in such sentences we always use the adverbs 还, 又 and 也, indicating addition.

(2) Meaning "with the exception of": It is always used together with the adverb 都. e. g.

14. 除了 第四十五課 以外, 我 都 復習 了.

Except for Lesson 45, I have reviewed everything.

15. 除了 她 以外, 別的 都 是 男 同學.

Except for her, all the others are male schoolmates.

The above examples mean that "he has already reviewed all the lessons with the exception of lesson forty five", and that "all the students but she are boys."

Not only are nouns and pronouns used in this construction, but a verb-object construction or a subject-predicate construction may also be used. e. g.

16. 他 除了 晚上 在 家 以外, 別的 時候兒 都 在 學校.

Except for being at home in the evening, the rest of the time he is always at school.

17. 除了 他 學 歷史 以外, 我們 都 學 語言.

With the exception of his studying history, we all study languages.

課文 Kèwén Text

古 時候兒, 中国 有 这样 一个 傳說.

In ancient times, there was such a legend in China.

大路上　过来了　一辆　车，车上
坐着　一个　人，还有　一个　赶车的.
车　很　快地　往　北　走，看起来　他们
是　要　到　很　远的　地方　去　的. 路
旁边儿　走过来　一个　人，看见了　坐
车　的　就　说："先生，您　到　哪儿
去?" 坐车　的　回答："我们　到　楚国
去." 走路的　一　听　就　说："您
走错　了! 楚国　在　南边儿，您　为　什么
往　北　走　呢?"

A chariot was coming along the highway. In the chariot
sat a man, and there was also a driver. The chariot
traveled quickly toward the north. It seemed that they
wanted to go to a very distant place. There came a man
walking along the side of the road. When he saw the man
seated in the chariot, he said, "Sir, where you are going?"
The man in the chariot answered, "We are going to the
state of Chu." As soon as he heard this, the passer-by said,
"You have taken the wrong road! Chu is in the south. Why
do you travel toward the north?"

坐车　的　说："没　关系，你　看，
我的　马　又　高　又　大，走起来　快得
很."

The man in the chariot said, "It does not matter. Look!
My horses are both tall and big. When they run they run
very quickly."

走　路　的　说："马　虽然　好，但是
这条　路　不　对. 您　快　回去　吧!"

The passer-by said, "Although the horses are good, this road is still not correct. Go back quickly!"

坐 車 的 說: "怕 什么! 除了 馬
好 以外, 我 箱子里 还 放着 很 多
很 多 錢."

The man in the chariot said, "What is there to be afraid of? In addition to good horses, there is lots and lots of money in my trunk."

走 路 的 又 說: "您 虽然 有
錢, 但是 这 不 是 去 楚国 的
路!"

The passer-by again said, "Although you have much money, this is not the road to the state of Chu."

坐 車 的 又 回答 說: "别 着急!
你 看, 我 这个 赶 車 的 能力
特别 高."

The man in the chariot again answered, "Don't worry. Look! The ability of this driver of mine is especially great."

虽然 坐 車 的 有 很 多 好 条件,
但是 他的 方向 錯了, 結果 就 要
越 走 越 远.

Although the man in the chariot had many good qualifications, his direction was wrong. As a result, the more he traveled the further he got (from his destination).

課外練習　Kèwài liànxí　Home Work

1) Complete the following sentences showing existence, emergence or disappearance:

(1) 山上 _____ .

(2) 湖　旁边兒 _____ .

(3) 街　北边兒 _____ .

2) Re-write the following sentences using 除了…以外:

(4) 北京　圖書館　有　这本　書，別的
地方　都　沒　有.

(5) 大家　都　參加了　討論　会，只　有
有　病　的　人　沒　有　參加.

3) Change the following sentences into verbal sentences showing emergence, existence or disappearance:

(6) 有　两个　新　同学　在　教室里
坐着.

(7) 昨天　有　很　多　參观　的　来　了.

汉字表　Hànzì biǎo　Chinese Characters

1	旗	方 方 方 旗
2	南	一 十 占 古 南 南
3	除	阝
		余（人 仐 余）
4	傳	亻
		專
5	湖	氵

		胡	古
			月
6	条	夂	
		朩	
7	态	太	
		心	
8	度	庑	
		又	
9	馬		
10	趕	走	
		干	
11	往	彳	
		主	
12	箱	竹	
		相	
13	佝	ノ 亻 勹 佝	
14	果		

Lesson 62

生詞 Shēngcí New Words

1. 比 (介) bǐ than, to compare
2. 頁 (名) yè (a measure word)
3. 提高 (名) tígāo to raise, to heighten
4. 考試 (动、名) kǎoshì to examine, examination
5. 快乐 (形) kuàilè happy
6. 家庭 (名) jiātíng family
7. 父亲 (名) fùqin father
8. 一直 (副) yìzhé up to the present, all the time, straight ahead
9. 姐姐 (名) jiějiě elder sister
10. 饱 (形) bǎo (having eaten to the) full, enough
11. 小学 (名) xiǎoxué primary school
12. 加入 (动) jiārù to join
13. 少年先鋒队 shàonián xiānfēngduì the young pioneers
14. 得 (动) dé to get
15. 分兒 (名) fēnr marks

語法　Yǔfǎ　Grammar

62.1　比 as a Word of Comparison　　When we compare two persons or things with each other, we use the following formula:

A — 比 — B — the Result of Comparison　e. g.

1. 这个　办法　<u>比</u>　那个　（办法）　好.

This method is better than that one.

2. 那个　教室　<u>比</u>　这个　（教室）　大.

That classroom is bigger than this one.

The adverbs 更 and 还 may be used as adverbial modifiers before the predicative adjective. e. g.

3. 这个　办法　比　那个　（办法）　<u>更</u>
好.

This method is even better than that one.

4. 那个　教室　比　这个　（教室）　<u>还</u>　大.

That classroom is even bigger than this one.

The use of 更 or 还 also implies that 那个办法 is already pretty good, and 这个教室 is already rather big. Therefore, the use of this adverbial modifier affects the meaning of the sentence.

62.2　Some Rules Concerning 比:

(1) In addition to the sentence with an adjectival predicate, there are certain sentences with verbal predicates in which 比 may also be used in a comparison. e. g.

5. 他　比　我　<u>了解</u>　那个　学校的
情况.

He understands the situation of that school better than I do.

6. 我 同屋 比 我 还 <u>关心</u> 报上的 新闻.

My roommate is even more concerned than I am about the news in the paper.

(2) When there is a complement of degree, the word 比 may either be placed before the reduplicated form of the verb or before the complement. e. g.

7. 他 說 中文 <u>比</u> 我 說得 流利.

He speaks Chinese more fluently than I do.

8. 他 說 中文 說得 <u>比</u> 我 流利.

He speaks Chinese more fluently than I do.

(3) In a negative sentence, 不 is placed in general before the word 比 and not before the predicate. e. g.

9. 这篇 文章 不 比 那篇 容易.

This article is not any easier than that one.

(4) When we wish to show that there is some difference between two things, we may use 一点兒 or 一些 after the predicate, meaning that the difference is not great. e. g.

10. 那課 課文 比 这課 深 <u>一点兒</u>.

The text of that lesson is a bit harder than this one.

11. 这个 箱子 比 那个 重 <u>一些</u>.

This suitcase (OR: trunk) is somewhat heavier than that one.

When the difference is great, it is expressed by the word 多 as complement with the structural particle 得. e. g.

12. 新 宿舍 比 这座 楼 <u>漂亮得多</u>.

The new dormitory is much better-looking than this building.

13. 昨天的　観众　比　前天　晚上的
多得　多.

Last night's audience was much bigger than the audience the night before.

(5) When we wish to express the difference between two things in actual number or ratio, we use a numeral and a measure word as complement after the predicate. e. g.

14. 二年級的　学生　比　一年級　少
二十个.

The second year has twenty students less than the first year.

15. 这包　烟　比　那包　烟　便宜　一毛
五.

This package of cigarettes is fifteen cents cheaper than that one.

16. 那本　杂誌　比　这本　多　十頁.

That magazine has ten more pages than this one.

17. 男　先生的　数目　比　女　先生
多　两倍.

The number of men teachers is twice as much as that of the women teachers.

18. 这个　車間　从　用了　新　方法　以后,
他們的　生产　比　上月　提高了　百
分之　八十.

Ever since this machine shop adopted a new method, its production has increased 80% over last month's.

(6) When we wish to show the actual difference between the time or result of one action and that of another action, we use one of the following words 早, 晚, 多 and 少 as adverbial modifier and words expressing the actual difference come after the predicate. e. g.

19. 每天 早上 八点 零 五分 上
課, 我們 比 先生 早 来
五分鐘.

Every morning we start our class at 8:05. We come five minutes earlier than the teacher.

20. 我們 比 这些 同学 晚 来 一年.

We came one year later than these schoolmates.

21. 他 比 你 多 穿了 一件 衣服.

He wore one more piece of clothing than you did.

22. 这次 考試 我 比 他 少 回答
一个 問題; 他 都 回答 了. 我
沒 有 回答 最后的 一个.

In this examination, I answered one less problem than he did. He answered everything, (but) I did not answer the last one.

62.3 比 as a Word Indicating the Change of a Thing with the Passage of Time   If a thing undergoes change in the passage of time, we may also use 比 to show such a change. e. g.

23. 他 翻譯得 比 以前 好 了.

Now he translates better than before.

We may use a complement to show how great the change is. e. g.

24. 他　現在　翻譯得　比　從前　好得
多　了.

Now he translates much better than before.

62.4 一天比一天 as Adverbial Modifier　Sometimes we use 一天比一天 or 一年比一年 before the predicate as adverbial modifier to indicate the gradual change of something with the passage of time. e. g.

25. 天气　一天　比　一天　冷　起来　了.

The weather is getting colder day by day.

26. 学生的　数目　一年　比　一年　增加
了.

The number of students increases year by year.

課文　Kèwén　Text

我　有　一个　非常　快乐的　家庭. 我
家里　有　父亲、母亲, 还　有　一个　哥哥、
一个　姐姐　和　一个　妹妹.

I have a very happy family. In my family there are my father, my mother, (also) an elder brother, an elder sister and a younger sister.

我的　父亲　一直　在　工厂里　工作.
解放　以前, 我們　家的　生活　非常　困难,

常常 吃不飽、穿不暖. 解放 以后 工厂
是 国家的 了; 父亲 工作得 很 愉快,
我們的 生活 也 一天 比 一天 好了.

My father has always been working in the factory.
Before the Liberation, life in our family was very difficult;
we often did not have enough food or clothing. [Notice the
potentials: *chībubǎo, chuānbunuǎn.*] After the
Liberation, the factory became the property of our
country. My father is very happy at work and our life
improves day by day.

我的 母亲 从前 一个 字 也 不
認識, 现在 每天 晚上 也 到 工厂
的 学校里 去 学 文化 了. 她 学習
很 努力, 学习得 很 好, 现在 可以
看 报, 写 信 了.

My mother used to be illiterate (didn't know one single
character); now she goes to the factory school every night
to be educated. She studies very hard and learns very well.
Now she can read the newspaper and write letters.

我的 哥哥 比 我 大得 多, 从前
找 不 到 工作, 解放后 很 快地 就
参加了 工作.

My elder brother is much older than I am. He was
formerly unable to find jobs. After the Liberation he
quickly found a job (took part in working).

我的 姐姐 比 我 大 一点兒, 我們
都 在 这个 学校里 学習. 她 在 三年級,
比 我 早 来 两年.

My elder sister is a little older than I am. We both study in this school. She is in the third year, having come to school two years before I did.

妹妹 比 我 小得 多, 今年 才 九岁.
她 是 小学 三年级的 学生, 快要 加入
少年先锋队 了. 她 学习 很 努力, 最近
一年 学得 特别 好, 比 从前 进步得
更 快 了. 上次 考试 她 得了 五个
五分儿, 父亲 和 母亲 都 很 高兴,
我们 也 都 希望 她 继续 努力.

My younger sister is much younger than I am. She is only nine years old this year. She is a third-grader and is about to join the Young Pioneers. She studies very diligently. She has been doing especially well during the past year and has progressed even faster than before. At her last examination, she received five five-points. My father and mother were very happy and we all hope that she keeps on working hard.

我们的 家庭 生活 是 非常 幸福的,
我 很 爱 我的 家庭.

My family life is very fortunate. I love my family very much.

課外練習　Kèwài liànxí　Home Work

1) Complete the following sentences:

(1) 哥哥　每小时　看　二十頁　中文
小說兒,　姐姐　每小时　看　十八頁,
哥哥　比　姐姐　看————.

(2) 第一課 有 十五个 生詞, 第二課
有 十三个 生詞, 第二課的 生詞
比 第一課 ————.

2) Make comparative sentences with the following words or word groups:

(3) ...... 得多

(4) ......一点兒

(5) 一天 比 一天

3) According to the example given below, make comparative sentences by combining each pair of sentences in the following, using 早 or 晚, 多 or 少 as adverbial modifier:

{ 姐姐 織了 兩件 毛衣.
妹妹 織了 三件 毛衣. } ⟶

姐姐 比 妹妹 少 織了 一件 毛衣.

妹妹 比 姐姐 多 織了 一件 毛衣.

(6) { 我 進 城 用了 十五塊 錢.
同屋 進 城 用了 十块 錢.

(7) { 我 (是) 2:40 来 的.
主席 (是) 2:50 来 的.

汉字表 Hànzì biǎo Chinese Characters

1	頁			
2	考	土 耂 耂 考		
3	庭	广		
		廷	壬	
			又	

4	父	ハ ゲ 父
5	姐	女
		且
6	飽	食
		包
7	入	
8	鋒	金
		夆 (夂 夆 夆)

Lesson 63

生詞 Shēngcí New Words

1. 船 (名) chuán 〔只〕 boat, ship
2. 飞机 (名) fēijī 〔架〕 aeroplane
3. 架 (量) jià (a measure word)
4. 啊 (助、嘆) ā (a particle and an interjection)
5. 从来 (副) cónglái hitherto
6. 那么 (副) nènmò then, in that case, that
7. 等 (动) děng to wait
8. 杯 (量) bēi (a measure word), cup
9. 凉 (形) liáng cool, cold
10. 开(水) (动) kāi(shuǐ) boiling, boiled (water)
11. 喝 (动) hē to drink
12. 胜利 (名、动) shènglì victory, to triumph (over)
13. 公社 (名) gōngshè commune
14. 农村 (名) nóngcūn village, countryside
15. 热情 (形、名) rèqíng enthusiastic, enthusiasm
16. 不断 (副) búduàn incessantly
17. 改善 (动、名) gǎishàn to improve, improvement
18. 共产党 (名) gòngchǎndǎng the Communist Party
19. 公社化 (动) gōngshèhuà to switch over to people's communes

語法 Yǔfǎ Grammar

63.1 The Object Placed before the Verb　We know that an object may be placed at the beginning of a sentence, when the predicate is rather complicated or when we wish to lay stress on the object (29.1). But when we wish the object to be more conspicuous, we may also put it after the subject and before the verb. Such word order is always adopted when the object is simple or when there are two parallel constructions in a sentence. e. g.

1. 我 生詞 完全 記住 了, 練習 还 沒 作完 呢.

> I have completely memorized the words, but I have not yet finished doing the exercise.

2. 我 船 也 坐过, 飞机 也 坐过.

> I have traveled both by boat and by airplane.

The first example sets forth a contrast, and the second describes two things in succession. If the parallel constructions of two things in succession are expressed in the form of a compound object, we may use the following word order: Subject — Object — Verb; at the same time we must use the adverb 都 as adverbial modifier before the verb. e. g.

3. 我 船 和 飞机 都 坐过.

> I have traveled both by boat and by airplane.

4. 这个 星期 她 电影、話剧 都 不 看, 她 要 写 文章.

> This week she will see neither a movie nor a play. She wants to write an essay.

63.2 Rhetorical Question　An interrogative sentence is used chiefly to ask a question. But there are some interrogative sentences which are not used to ask a question but to express emphasis in a rhetorical way. In a rhetorical question, the use of a negative adverb serves to stress the affirmation; if there is no negative adverb, the negative meaning is stressed. There are many kinds of rhetorical questions, the following two kinds are most commonly used. e. g.

(1) 不是…嗎 is used to emphasize affirmation. e. g.

5. 那本 書 你 不 是 已經 從 圖書館 借着 了 嗎? 为 什么 还 要 买 呢?

Haven't you already borrowed that book from the library? Why do you still want to buy it?

6. 那架 机器 不 是 已經 修理好 了 嗎?

Hasn't that machine already been repaired?

(2) 哪兒 is used to express emphasis. In most cases, we use 哪兒 to stress negation. e. g.

7. 你 沒 告訴 我, 我 哪兒 知道 你 在 这兒 啊!

You did not tell me. How could I know that you were here?

8. 北京的 冬天 哪兒 冷 啊—— 比 我們 那兒 暖和得 多.

How can you say that Peking's winter is cold? — it is much warmer than where we are.

The above examples are more impressive than the general negative sentences, such as 我不知道你在这兒 and 北京的冬天 不冷.

哪兒 is sometimes used in a negative sentence to stress affirmation. e. g.

9. 他 非常 关心 同志, <u>哪兒</u> 能 不
帮助 你 啊!

He is very concerned about comrades. How could he not
help you?

The above sentence means "he will certainly help you".

When a rhetorical question is composed of 哪兒, whether
it is in the affirmative or in the negative, the modal particle
啊 is always used at the end of the sentence. This final particle
attracts attention and is persuasive in effect, and heightens the
mood of affirmation.

63.3 The Double Negative. Two negatives amount to
an affirmative in sense, but the sentence mood is much more
impressive. The double negative is used chiefly in the following
two ways:

(1) The negatives are used separately in the two clauses
of a composite sentence, and the clauses are connected by the
word 就. e.g.

10. <u>不</u> 發展 生产 就 <u>不</u> 能 提高
生活 水平.

If we don't develop our production, we won't be able to
raise our standard of living.

11. <u>沒 有</u> 批評 就 <u>沒 有</u> 进步.

If there is no criticism, there will be no progress.

Here the word 就 is the same 就 of the construction 要是…就.
In fact, 要是… may also be used in such sentences.

(2) In a simple sentence the element to be emphasized
is put between the two negative adverbs. e. g.

12. <u>沒 有</u> 人 <u>不</u> 知道 这个 新聞.

There is no one who does not know about this news.

13. 义务 劳动 他 <u>没</u> <u>有</u> 一次 <u>不</u> 参加.

He never once missed participating in voluntary labor.
(LIT: He never once did not participate . . . .)

The two examples above mean "everybody knows this news," "he joins the voluntary labour every time." Another example is:

14. 学习上 <u>没</u> <u>有</u> 克服<u>不了</u> 的 困难.

In studying there are no unconquerable difficulties.

克服不了 is composed of a verb and a negative potential complement; the whole sentence also contains a double negative, meaning "all the difficulties in the world can be overcome."

課文 Kèwén Text

I

(a₁) 請 坐, 吸 枝 烟 吧!

Please sit down, (and) have (smoke) a cigarette!

(b₁) 謝謝, 我 不 会.

Thank you, (but) I don't (know how to) smoke.

(a₂) 别 客气 啊!

Don't be polite!

(b₂) 我 哪兒 客气 啊! 我 从来 不 吸 烟.

(No) I am not being polite at all. I never smoke.

(a₃) 那么, 你 等 我 給 你 倒 杯 茶 来 吧.

Then let me pour (and bring) a cup of tea for you.

(b₃) 你 不 是 有 凉 开水 嗎? 就 喝 凉 开水 吧!

Don't you have cooled boiled water? Let's just drink cooled boiled water.

(a₄) 到 中国 来 以后, 我 也 喜欢 喝 茶 了. 我們 喝 茶 吧!

Since coming to China, I have also begun to like tea. Let us drink tea.

II

(a₅) 我們 后天 去 参观 胜利 人民 公社, 你 去过 那兒 嗎?

Day after tomorrow we are going to have a tour of the People's Commune "Victory." Have you been there before?

(b₅) 我 沒 有 去过.

No, I haven't.

(a₆) 你 不 是 参观过 很 多 地方 了 嗎?

Haven't you toured many places already?

(b₆) 我 工厂 参观过 不 少, 但是 农村 还 沒 有 去过.

I have toured quite a few factories, but (I) have never been to a farming village.

(a₇) 我們　一起　去　吧!

Let's go together.

(b₇) 好,　我　一定　去.　听　朋友　說
农村　組織了　人民公社　以后,
农民的　生产　热情　高　极了.　生产
不断　提高,　人民的　生活　不断
改善.

All right, I will certainly go. I heard from (my) friend that since the (farming) villages organized people's communes, the peasants' enthusiasm for production has been been very high and the level of production has continuously improved.

(a₈) 是　的,　大家　都　说,　沒　有　共产党,
就　沒　有　新　中国;　公社化　以后
人民的　生活　更　幸福　了.

Right. Everybody says that had there been no Communist Party, there would be no new China. Since communization, the people's lives have become even more fortunate.

課外練習　Kèwài liànxí　Home Work

1) Change the following sentences into those with objects standing before verbs:

(1) 他們　改善了　工作　条件,　也　改善
了　生活　条件.

(2) 他 掌握了 語法, 但是 他 不 很
掌握 詞彙.

2) Re-write the following sentence using 哪兒 or 不是... 嗎:

(3) 你 預習 了, 請 你 給 我 講講
这課.

3) Write two sentences in the double negative form:

4) Fill the following blanks with proper measure words:

一 _____ 凉 开水   两 _____ 船

三 _____ 飞机   那 _____ 机器

这 _____ 路   哪 _____ 車

几 _____ 像片兒   那 几 _____ 楼

这一 _____ 树

汉字表   Hànzì biǎo   Chinese Characters

1	船	舟		
		𠘧	几	
			口	
2	飞	㇟	㇟	㇟
3	架	加		
		木		
4	啊	口		
		阿	阝	
			可	
5	等	𥫗		
		寺		

6	杯	才	
		不	
7	凉	冫	
		京	
8	喝	口	
		曷	日
			匄（ノ 勹 勺 匄）
9	胜	月	
		生	
10	村	才	
		寸	
11	断	乴	
		斤	
12	善	丶 丷 半 兰 羊 姜 善	
13	党	当	
		儿	

Lesson 64

生詞 Shēngcí New Words

1. 連...也（都）... lián...yě(dōu)... even...(too)

2. 老　　（形）　lǎo　　old

3. 默（寫）（动）　mò(xiě)　to write from dictation, to write from memory

4. 抄（寫）（动）　chāo(xiě)　to copy

5. 背　　（动）　bèi　　to tell from memory, to recite

6. 起來　（动）　qǐlái　to get up, to rise

7. 句　　（量）　jù　　(a measure word)

8. 青年　（名）　qīngnián　youth

9. 社員　（名）　shèyuán　member of a co-operative

10. 長　　（动）　zhǎng　to grow

11. 感到　（动）　gǎndào　to feel

12. 訪問　（动）　fǎngwèn　to call (on, at), to visit

13. 印象　（名）　yìnxiàng　impression

14. 种　　（动）　zhòng　to engage in agriculture, to sow, to plant, to cultivate

15. 凍　　（动）　dòng　to freeze

16. 手　　（名）　shǒu [只 zhī] hand

17.	收入	(动、名)	shōurù	to get an income, income
18.	热爱	(动)	rèài	to love ardently
19.	永远	(副)	yǒngyuǎn	forever, eternally
20.	跟	(动)	gēn	to follow

語法 Yǔfǎ Grammar

64.1 (連)...也... or (連)...都 Expressing Emphasis   When we wish to emphasize a certain element in a sentence, we may use the construction (連)...也 or (連)...都. The word 連 may often be omitted. Now we will deal with this construction in the following:

(1) When the emphasis is on the subject:

1. 連 七八十岁的 老人 也 参加 遊行 了.

Even seventy- or eighty-year-old people joined the parade.

2. 連 小 学生 都 参加 义务 劳动 了.

Even grade-school students participated in the voluntary labor.

(2) When the emphasis is on the main element of the ver-bal predicate in a sentence:

3. 他 連 默写 都 默写对 了, 抄写 当然 更 沒 有 問题 了.

(Since) he can even write (it) correctly from memory, there is certainly no problem in his copying (it).

4. 我 問 他 去 不 去 颐和园, 他 連 想 也 沒 想 就 说: "去".

I asked him whether he wanted to go to Yiheyuan; without even thinking he immediately said, "Yes."

In emphasizing verbs as shown above, there are two points to be noticed:

a) The verb used after the word 都 or 也 must be reduplicated. The second form of the reduplicated verb can be omitted when there is an optative verb. e. g.

5. 这篇 文章 他 连 念 都 不 会
(念), 怎么 背得出来 呢!

He can't even read that article; how can he say it from memory?

b) The reduplicated verbs are used with complements, adverbial modifiers or other elements, such as the resultative complement, the negative word and the optative verb used in the above sentences.

c) When the emphasis is on the object:

6. 今天 晚上 父亲 连 饭 也 没
有 吃, 就 忙着 去 开 会 了.

Tonight my father went busily to the meeting without even eating his meal.

7. 二年级的 老 同学 连 中文
小说儿 都 看得懂 了.

The second-year old schoolmates can even read (with understanding) Chinese novels.

Note: Since what we wish to emphasize is the object, the word 连 and the object should be placed before the predicate (63.1). This, we have already learned.

64.2 — Expressing Emphasis   In a negative sentence, we often use the word — and a measure word before the noun we wish to emphasize. After the noun the words 都 and 也 are also frequently used. The chief functions of the word — are shown as follows:

(1) When the emphasis is on the subject:

8. 天 还 沒 亮 呢, 一个 人 也 沒 起来 呢.

It hasn't dawned yet. Not a single person has got up.

The above sentence expresses emphatically the thought that "nobody" got up or "none of them got up".

(2) When the emphasis is on the object:

9. 默写 生詞 的 时候兒, 他 一个 汉字 都 沒 有 写錯.

When writing new words from memory, he did not write one single character wrong.

10. 我 到 中国 来 以前, 一句 中国 話 也 不 会 說.

Before I came to China, I could not speak even one word of Chinese.

(3) When the emphasis is on the adverbial modifier:

11. 那个 工人 一分鐘 都 不 停地 工作.

That laborer works without pausing for one minute.

12. 考試 的 时候兒 他 一点兒 也 不 緊張地 把 問題 都 回答对 了.

During the examination, he calmly (not even one bit excited) answered all the questions correctly.

After such adverbial modifiers the structural particle 地 should be used.

64.3 是 Expressing Emphasis We know that in Chinese, the copula 是 is used only in the sentence with a substantive predicate, it is not necessary in the sentence with a verbal predicate and the sentence with a clause predicate. But 是 may also express emphasis when it is used in the predicate of any sentence. 是 here means "indeed" or "really". e. g.

13. 第二頁上的 生詞 是 多, 他 当然 看得 慢 一点兒.

There *were* indeed more new words on the second page, so naturally he read a bit more slowly.

14. 这篇 文章 他 是 看懂 了, 但是 不 会 用 自己的 話 説出来.

He *did* indeed understand this article, but he could not tell it in his own words.

15. 那个 干部 是 經驗 多, 作 这 方面的 工作 已經 作了 十几年 了.

That cadre *is* certainly very experienced. He has done this kind of work for more than ten years.

64.4 就 Expressing Emphasis:

(1) When we wish to emphasize a sentence with a substantive predicate, we put the word 就 before the copula. Here 就是 means "to be just". e. g.

16. 青年 就 是 我們的 希望.

Youth is our hope.

17. 她 就 是 我們的 領导 同志.

She is our comrade leader.

(2) When we wish to emphasize a sentence with a verbal predicate, we may also use the word 就 before the predicate. Here 就 means "decidedly". e. g.

18. 我 就 不 爱 吸 烟, 吸 烟 沒 好处.

I simply don't like smoking. There is no advantage in smoking.

19. 我 就 要 去 遊行, 累 也 不 怕.

I simply want to go traveling. I am not even afraid of fatigue.

課文 Kèwén Text

我們 今天 參观了 胜利 人民 公社.
我們 到 那兒 的 时候兒, 人民公社的
男 女 社員們 正 在 地里 愉快地
勞动. 綠綠的 庄稼 長得 非常 好.
大家 看着 这样的 好 庄稼 都 感到
說不出來的 高兴.

Today we visited the People's Commune "Victory."
When we arrived there the male and female members of
the People's Commune were laboring happily. The
lusciously green crops grew very well. When we saw that
kind of good crops, we all felt unutterably happy.

我 訪問了 一个 老 农民, 他的
談話 給 我的 印象 很 深. 現在 我
把 他的 話 簡單地 記在 下边兒.

We visited one old peasant. What he said gave me a very
deep impression. I shall briefly put down below what he
said:

"我种地种了三十多年了。从前给地主种地，天天早起晚睡，一点儿休息的时间也没有，到最后，地主还要把我们收的粮食都拿去。我们家年年吃不饱、穿不暖。我有一个小女儿就是在冬天冻死的。

"I have been working on the land for more than thirty years. Formerly I used to work for the landlords. Every day I got up early and worked until very late. There was not even one moment of rest. In the end, the landlords even took away the grains we reaped. Each year our family did not have enough to eat or enough clothes to keep us warm. One of my little daughters died of exposure (was frozen to death) in one winter.

"解放了。五〇年春天从地主手里分回来地，生活就一天比一天好起来了。不但吃饱了、穿暖题，连小孩子念书的问题也解决了。五三年我参加了合作社，五八年，组织了人民公社，收入更多了，生活更好了，一点儿困难也没有了。毛主席领导得真好，我们都热爱毛主席、热爱共产党。我们永远跟着毛主席和共产党走！"

"(Then) came the Liberation. In the spring of 1950, we reclaimed our part of the land from the landlords. Ever since, life has been better day by day. Not only have we had enough food and clothing, even the problem of children's education has been solved. I joined the Co-op in 1953. In 1958, we organized the People's Commune. Now our income is even bigger and life is even better. We have no hardship at all. Chairman Mao really leads us well, and we all fervently love Chairman Mao and the Communist Party. We shall forever follow the steps of Chairman Mao and the Communist Party!"

課外練習　Kèwài liànxí　Home Work

1) Re-write the following sentences using 連... 也 or 連... 都 placing emphasis on the words underlined.

(1) 他 不 知道 方向, 怎么 走得到 呢?

(2) 人民 画报 不 是 我 拿走 的.
我 沒 有 看.

(3) 坐在 后排 的 观众 听得清楚
这个 演員 说 的 話.

2) Re-write the following sentences using 一 laying emphasis on the words underlined.

(4) 音乐 会 我 去晚 了, 沒 有
好 座位 了.

(5) 大家 都 去 参加 义务 劳动 了,
我們 宿舍里 沒 有 人 了.

3) Make two sentences using 是 and 就 expressing emphasis.

汉字表　Hànxì biǎo　Chinese Characters

1	連	車
		辶

2	老	土 耂 老
3	默	黑
		犬
4	抄	扌
		少
5	背	北
		月
6	青	
7	感	厂 厂 厄 咸 咸 感 感
8	訪	言
		方
9	印	丿 𠂊 𠂤 印
10	象	
11	冻	冫
		东
12	手	
13	永	丶 丁 永 永 永

Lesson 65

生詞 Shēngcí New Words

1.	被	(介) bèi	by
2.	讓	(介) ràng	by, to let, to yield
3.	叫	(介) jiào	by, to call, to order
4.	杯子	(名) bēizi	cup
5.	選	(动) xuǎn	to elect, to choose, to select
6.	各	(代) gè	every, each
7.	畢業	(动) bìyè	to graduate
8.	派	(动) pài	to appoint, to send
9.	接受	(动) jiēshòu	to accept, to receive
10.	鋼	(名) gāng	steel
11.	鉄	(名) tiě	iron
12.	燒	(动) shāo	to burn
13.	伤	(名) shāng	wound
14.	占	(动) zhàn	to amount to, to take possession of
15.	点	(名) diǎn	point
16.	資本主义	(名) zīběnzhǔyì	capitalism
17.	医学	(名) yīxué	medical science
18.	文献	(名) wénxiàn	literature
19.	救	(动) jiù	to save

20.	活	(动) huó	to be alive, to live
21.	昏迷	(动) hūnmí	to lose consciousness
22.	醒	(动) xǐng	to wake up, to return to consciousness
23.	迷信	(动) míxìn	to believe superstitiously in
24.	办	(动) bàn	to build or run (a factory or school)
25.	思想	(名) sīxiǎng	thought, thinking, mind
26.	共产党員	(名) gòngchǎndǎngyuán	member of the Communist Party
27.	力量	(名) lìliàng	strength
28.	在……下	zài...xià	under

語法   Yǔfǎ   Grammar

65.1 Passive Voice According to the Sense   In Chinese, the subject in the sentence with a verbal predicate is the doer of the action expressed in the predicate. For example: in 他来了, and 我洗衣服, 他 and 我 are subjects or doers of the actions 来 and 洗衣服. But in some sentences the relation between the subject and the predicate is just the opposite. e. g.

1. 这个 意見 提得 很 对.

This opinion is rightly expressed.

2. 衣服 洗好 了.

The clothing has been washed.

In the two examples above, the subjects are all receivers of action. Whether the subject of a sentence represents the doer or the receiver of an action, it does not affect the form of the verb. As we can easily make out the relation between the subject and the predicate from the context, there is no need to indicate such a relation by any special grammatical construction. Such passive voice according to the sense is also one of the characteristics of the Chinese language.

65.2 The Passive Form with the Preposition 被, 讓 or 叫   When we wish to stress the fact that the subject is the receiver of an action, and tell at the same time who the doer is, we may use the passive form with the preprositions 被, 讓 and 叫:

Receiver——被——Doer — Verb — Other Elements.
　　　　　　讓
　　　　　　叫

In other words, the characteristic feature of such kind of sentence lies in that the prepositional construction (the preposition and its object, the doer) is used as adverbial modifier to show the relation between the doer and the receiver. e. g.

3. 那棵 老 树 被 風 刮倒 了.

That old tree was uprooted (blown over) by the wind.

4. 自行車 讓 哥哥 騎到 学校 去 了.

The bicycle has been ridden to the school by (my) elder brother.

5. 紅 旗 叫 我們 得来 了.

The red flag was won (gotten) by us.

老树, 自行車 and 紅旗 are receivers of action, 風, 哥哥 and 我們 are the doers, 倒了, 到学校去了 and 来了 are other elements following the verbs.

There are a few rules for the use of the passive form with 被, 讓 and 叫:

(1) The preposition 被 is more formal, while 叫 and 讓 are more often used in speech. 被 is often used in writing, and its object, the doer, may be understood. e. g.

6. 学習上的 困难 都 被 克服 了.

All the difficulties in studying have been overcome.

7. 父亲 被 請去 看 戏 了.

Father has been invited to go watch a play.

If we use the preposition 叫 or 讓 instead of 被, the object, that is, the doer of action, must be given. e. g.

8. 那个　杯子　讓　他　拿走　了.

That cup has been taken away by him.

9. 我　剛　拿來　的　那杯　茶　叫
妹妹　喝　了.

That cup of tea which I just brought over was drunk up by (my) younger sister.

If it is impossible to tell who the doer is or when the doer is indefinite, we use 人 instead. e. g.

10. 父亲　讓　人　請去　看　戏,　走了
一会兒　了.

Father has been invited by someone to a play. He left quite a while ago.

11. 圖書館的　新　書　都　叫　人　借走
了.

The new books in the library have all been taken out (by people).

(2) If there is an optative verb, it should be placed before the preposition and not before the verb. e. g.

12. 这个　同志　条件　合适,　可以　被
选作　人民　代表.

This comrade's qualifications are suitable. He may be elected to serve as a people's representative.

13. 他　各　方面　都　好,也許　能　被
派到　外国　去　学習.

He is good in every aspect, perhaps he can be sent overseas to study.

(3) The negative adverb must be placed before the preposition and not before the verb. e. g.

14. 我 剛 种 的 那棵 小 树 沒 有 叫 風 刮倒.

That little tree which I just planted was not blown over by the wind.

15. 姐姐 （在） 大学 畢业 了, 要是 不 被 派到 学校 去 教書, 也許 会 到 这兒 来 作 翻譯.

(My) elder sister has graduated from the university. If she is not sent to a school to teach, probably she will come here to do translation.

(4) In general, there must be some other elements after the verb. e. g.

16. 画兒 叫 誰 掛在 这兒 了?

Who hung the painting up here? (By whom was the painting hung up here?)

17. 他 被 朋友 請去 吃 飯 了

He was invited by (a) friend to dinner.

18. 馬車 讓 赶 車 的 赶到 湖 南边兒 去 了.

The horse cart was driven by the driver to the south side of the lake.

But, in formal writing, especially when the verb is dissyllabic, there may be no other elements. e. g.

19. 只要 你的 意見 正确, 就 一定 被 接受.

So long as your views are correct, they will certainly be accepted.

課文 Kèwén Text

一个 鋼鉄 工厂 的 工人 燒伤 了, 叫 人 送到 医院里 来 了. 他的伤 很 重, 占 全身的 百分之 八十九 点 三, 不少 大夫 看着 这个 工人 都 想: 没有 办法 了, 因为 資本主义 国家的 医学 文献 上 説, 燒伤 百分之 七十五 就 不 能 救活. 正 在 这个 时候兒, 工人 从 昏迷 中 醒过来, 他 看着 大夫們 説: "我 要 活下去, 鋼 需要 我……"

A worker in a steel mill was burned, and was brought (by someone) to the hospital (here). His burns were (very) severe. They covered 89.3% of his entire body. Quite a few doctors, upon seeing this man, thought, "This is hopeless! Because in the medical documents of capitalistic countries, it is said that if 75% of a person's body is burned, he cannot be saved." Just at this time, the worker woke up from his unconsciousness. Looking at the doctors, he said, "I want to live on. Iron needs me . . . ."

党一定要救活他，医院里的
领导同志立刻把大夫們找来开
会。会上領导同志说："在资本主义
国家里，燒伤的是誰？当然是劳动
人民，资本主义国家会想出各种
方法来救劳动人民嗎？我們不
能迷信资本主义国家的医学文献，
我們是社会主义国家，一定要救活
这个工人。我們一定能作出资本主义
国家办不到的事情……"。这些话
解放了大夫的思想，提高了他們的
認識。一个青年大夫——共产党員说：
"我們一定要拿出自己所有的力量
来救活建設社会主义的人。"

The Party decidedly wanted to save him. The leading
comrade of the hospital immediately gathered all the
doctors together and had a meeting. At the meeting, the
leading comrade said, "In capitalistic countries who
suffers from burns? Of course, it is the working people.
Would the capitalistic countries think of various ways to
save the working people? We cannot superstitiously
believe the medical documents of capitalistic countries.
We are a socialistic country and certainly must save this
worker. We certainly can do things which the capitalistic
countries cannot do . . . ." These words liberated the
doctors' thoughts, (and) heightened their understanding.
A young doctor — a Communist Party member — said, "We
certainly will use all our own strength to save a person who
builds socialism."

別的 医院里 有名的 大夫 也 被 派到
这里 来 了, 为 救活 这个 工人, 大夫們
开始了 紧張、 困难的 工作. 一个 月
过去 了, 这个 工人 不但 还 活着,
而且 伤 慢慢兒地 好起来 了. 在 党的
領导 下, 他 被 大夫 救活 了.

Famous doctors from other hospitals were also
dispatched to this place. In order to save this worker, the
doctors began a tense and difficult job. A month passed.
Not only was this worker still living but also his wounds
slowly healed. Under the Party's leadership, the doctors
saved him.

課外練習 Kèwài liànxí Home Work

1) Make sentences with each of the following words,
   showing the passive voice according to the sense:

   (1) 抄写

   (2) 改善

   (3) 推

2) Change the following sentences into the passive
   form by using 被, 讓 or 叫:

   (4) 他 把 鋼笔 忘在 教室里 了.

   (5) 我 把 那 两張 戏 票 送給
       他 了.

   (6) 有 人 把 那架 机器 搬走 了.

3) Copy and complete the following sentences in the
   passive voice:

   (7) 上月 他的 手 和 臉 都_____

燒伤 了. 但是 現在 已經————

大夫 治————了.

(8) 喜兒————大春 从 山里 救————

了.

汉字表　Hànzì biǎo　Chinese Characters

1	被	衤
		皮（一 厂 广 皮）
2	选	先
		辶
3	各	
4	畢	曰 昇 昆 昆 畢
5	派	氵
		厎（' 丆 厂 厎 厎 厎）
6	鉄	金
		失（' 失）
7	燒	火
	堯	土
		土
		土
		兀（一 兀）
8	伤	亻 亻 伫 伤
9	占	

10	資	次
		貝
11	獻	南
		犬
12	救	求
		攵
13	昏	
14	迷	米
		辶
15	醒	酉（一 丅 丆 丙 酉 酉）
		星
16	量	旦
		里

Lesson 66

語法复習 Yǔfǎ fùxí Review

66.1 Passive Voice According to the Sense and the Passive Form   In Chinese, the subject always represents the doer of action in the majority of sentences. But in a sentence of the passive voice, the subject becomes the receiver of action. In Chinese, the passive voice may be expressed in two ways:

(1) The passive voice according to the sense:

1. 他的　字　写得　很　好看.

His characters are written beautifully.

2. 劳动　人民的　生活　水平　提高
了.

The living standard of the laboring people has been raised.

3. 他　姐姐　派到　苏联　去　学習　了.

His elder sister was sent to study in the Soviet Union.

Such kind of sentence has three characteristic features:

a) The receiver of action is represented by the subject, but the doer does not appear in the sentence.

b) The subject is a noun representing an inanimate object, such as 字, or an abstract idea, such as 水平, which cannot perform the action expressed by the verb. Although the subject may sometimes be a noun representing a living object or a person such as 他姐姐, it is the receiver of the action and not the doer, for there is and can be no object after the verb; therefore the relation between the subject and the predicate is passive.

c) The verb is transitive, often carrying a complement or some other element. The verb governs the subject according to the sense. We may add the preposition 被 before the verb without affecting the sense, but it is more idiomatic not to use this preposition.

(2) The passive form with 被, 讓 and 叫. e. g.

4. 高　同志　被（我們）选作　大会的
主席　了.

Comrade Gao was elected by us to be the chairman of the general meeting.

5. 那个　工人　讓　大夫　救活　了.

That worker was saved by the doctor.

6. 那本　中国　革命史　叫　人　借走　了.

Someone has borrowed that volume of the History of the Chinese Revolution.

The characteristic features of such kind of sentence are as follows:

a) The subject is the receiver of action. There is a prepositional construction introducing the doer of action (such as 我們, 大夫 or 人). The preposition 被 is rather peculiar, for it is only after this preposition that the object, the doer of action, can be omitted.

b) The subject may denote a person or thing, but it is governed by the verb in sense.

c) The verb is transitive, and it must carry a complement or some other element.

From the above, we may come to the conclusion that there is some similarity between the sentence of the passive voice and that of the passive form composed of a preposition. The difference lies in that in the former the doer is not given, and the whole sentence is chiefly concerned with what has happened to the receiver after receiving an action, but in the latter the doer is expressed, and the whole sentence is chiefly concerned with the effect upon the receiver or how the doer has affected the receiver.

66.2 The Uses of the Word 就   The adverb 就 is a very important word, we use it very often and it appears very often in modern Chinese.   In the previous lessons we have already come across it many times; here we will sum up its various uses as follows:

(1) When it indicates a consequential relation   **When** we wish to express "in such a case... then..." we use the word 就.   This kind of relation is not so clear as that of cause and effect, but it is frequently used. e. g.

7. 他 畢 了 业, 就 到 別的 地方 去 工作 了.

After he graduated, he went to work in some other place.

8. 有 人 送 他 一張 音乐 会的 票, 他 就 去 了.

Someone gave him a ticket to the concert, so he went.

(2) When it is used for emphasis   In the sentence with a substantive predicate or with a verbal predicate, we always use the word 就 before the predicate for emphasis. e. g.

9. 团結 就 是 力量.

Unity is power.

10. 我 就 要 在 今天 写完 这篇 文章, 不 睡 觉 也 可以.

I definitely want to finish writing this article today. I will do so even without sleep.

(3) When it shows the immediate occurrence of something

When we wish to stress the fact that an action or a state is about to take place, we use the construction 要...了; before the word 要 we often use the word 就 as adverbial modifier to give the sense of immediacy. e. g.

11. 要 开 会 了, 代表 就 要 到 了.

The meeting is about to start. The delegates are about to arrive.

12. 就 要 放 假 了, 大家 都 在 计划 旅行的 事.

Vacation will start soon. Everybody is planning for travel.

The word 就 may be used alone, without the construction 要...了, because it possesses in itself the sense of immediacy. e. g.

13. 請 你們 在 門口兒 等 一会兒, 他們 就 来.

Please wait a little while at the gate. They are coming right away.

14. 車 就 开, 快 上来 吧!

The car will start right away; come up quickly.

(4) When it means "only":

15. 他 就 学过 俄文, 别的 語言 都 不 懂.

He has learned only Russian. He does not understand any other language.

16. 这課 語法 我 就 看了 一遍, 没 有 記住.

I have read over the grammar of this lesson only once. I have not committed it to memory.

(5) When it expresses the immediacy or ease of an action:

17. 老 工人 只 用 一会儿 时間 就 把 两架 机器 都 修理好 了.

The old worker repaired both pieces of machinery in only a short while.

18. 他 一天 就 把 那篇 文章 写好 了.

He finished writing that article in only one day.

(6) When it gives the result or consequence in a conditional sentence   We have learned two kinds of composite conditional sentences:

a) Using the construction 要是…就…:

19. 要是 星期日 有 义务 劳动, 我 就 不 进 城.

If there is volunteer labor on Sunday, I shall not go into the city.

The word 就 here is very similar to that indicating a consequential relation explained under point 1.

b) Using the construction 一… 就…   This construction sometimes expresses the time sequence of two related matters, one closely following the other. e. g.

20. 一 解放, 这儿的 地 就 分給 农民 了.

As soon as this place was liberated, the land was divided up and given to the peasants.

21. 汽車 一 到, 我們 就 出發.

We shall start out as soon as the bus (car) arrives.

Here the use of the word 就 may be compared with that explained under point 3. Sometimes this construction also expresses a customary condition. e. g.

22. 他 一 看見 語法 方面的 新 書
    就 想 买.

Whenever he sees any new books on grammar, he wants to buy them.

Here the use of the word 就 may be compared with that explained under point 1.

66.3 The Uses of the Word 还   The adverb 还 is also very common in use. Here we will sum up its various uses as follows:

(1) It means "still" in connection with time:

23. 他 工作 非常 积極, 我們 还 选
    他 作 代表.

He (always) works very enthusiastically. We shall elect him to be our representative again.

24. 她 穿上了 毛衣 还 觉得 有 一
    点兒 冷.

She still felt a little cold even after she had put on a sweater.

When an action is not yet completed, but is about to be completed, we also use the word 还 as an adverbial modifier meaning "yet". In this case, the modal particle 呢 must be added at the end of the sentence. e. g.

25. 这个 計划 我們 还 沒 有 討論
    呢!

We haven't discussed this plan yet.

26. 我們 六十課 語法 还 沒 有
講完 呢!

We haven't yet finished explaining the grammar of Lesson
60.

(2) It expresses addition:
   a) 还 shows some action or some object is added on top
of others. e. g.

27. 他 女兒 喜欢 听 音乐, 还 喜欢
看 小説兒.

His daughter likes to listen to music and also likes to read
novels.

28. 窗戶 前边兒 放着 一張 桌子,
桌子 上边兒 还 有 一架 无綫电.

In front of the window there was a table and on the table
there was a radio.

The construction 除了…以外 is also used in a sentence to
express addition, the word 还 often plays the part of an
adverbial modifier in such a sentence. e. g.

29. 考試 的 时候兒 除了 默写 以外,
还 要 翻譯 几个 句子.

At the examination, besides writing from memory, we also
have to translate a few sentences.

   b) 还 shows an action is repeated or continued:

30. 那个 地方 真 有意思, 去了 一次
还 想 去.

That place is really interesting. After having been there
once, one likes to go again.

31. 那架 机器 还 能 用 十年.

That machine is good for another ten years.

(3) It means moreover:

a) The adverb 还 is often used in the construction 不但...
而且.... e. g.

32. 这个 领导 同志 不但 跟 工人
一起 劳动, 而且 还 跟 工人
住在 一起.

This leading comrade not only labors together with the
workers, but also lives together with them.

b) The adverb 还, meaning "still more", expresses the comparative degree, when it is used in a sentence of comparison. e. g.

33. 这座 山 高, 那座 山 比 这座
还 高.

This mountain is high, but that mountain is even higher.

課文 Kèwén Text

我 十岁 的 时候兒, 我們 家 旁边兒
办了 一个 小学. 学生 差不多 都 是
地主 家的 孩子, 他們 都 穿得好, 吃得好,
天天 到 学校里 去 念 書. 但是 我 家里
生活 非常 困难, 父亲 天天 給 地主
种 地, 我 也 跟着 父亲 去 劳动. 我們

常常 連 飯 都 吃不飽, 哪兒 能 去 念
書 呢.

When I was ten years old, an elementary school was established next to our home (someone ran an elementary school next to our home). Almost all the students were children from landlord families. They were all well-clothed and well-fed. Every day they went to school to study. But life in our family was very difficult. Every day my father cultivated the land for our landlord, and I also worked with my father. We often could not even have enough to eat. How could I go to school to study?

因为 沒有 錢, 不 能 到 学校 去
念 書, 所以 我 常常 在 教室 外边兒
听 先生 講. 有 一天, 我 又 去 了,
看見 先生 正在 提 問題. 先生 問 了
很 多 人, 一个 人 也 回答 不上来. 我
在 窗戶 外边兒 站着 很 着急, 就 替
他們 回答 了. 我 又 想到 自己 不
是 学生, 怕 讓 人 看見, 就 立刻
跑开 了. 第二天, 农民 都 在 談 我
在 窗戶 外边兒 回答 問題 的 事,
沒有 一个 不 这样 說: "这个 孩子
念 不了 書, 就 是 因为 沒有 錢.
要是 能 念 書, 他 一定 比 那些
地主 家的 孩子 好得 多."

Because we had no money and I could not go to school to study, I often listened to the teacher from outside of the classroom. One day, I went again. The teacher was asking questions. He asked many students but none of them could answer. Standing outside the window, I felt very anxious, so I answered for them. Then I realized that I was not a student. I was afraid to be seen by other people. So I ran away immediately. The next day, all the peasants were talking about the incident of my answering a question from outside of the window. Everyone said thus: "This child can't study simply because he has no money. If he could study, he could certainly do much better than the children from the landlord families."

这 是 十几年 以前的 事 了，现在
我 已经 坐在 学校的 窗户 里边儿 了，
要是 没 有 毛 主席的 领导，党的
关心，我 怎么 有 今天！

This event happened more than ten years ago. Now I am already sitting inside of the school windows. Without the leadership of Chairman Mao and the concern of the Party, how could I have this day?

Lesson 67

生詞 Shēngcí New Words

1. 缺点 (名) quēdiǎn defect, shortcoming
2. 願意 (能动) yuànyì will, to be willing
3. 弟弟 (名) dìdi younger brother
4. 風景 (名) fēngjǐng scenery, landscape
5. 展覽 (名、动) zhǎnlǎn exhibition, to exhibit
6. 和平 (名) hépíng peace
7. 反对 (动) fǎnduì to oppose, to stand against
8. 侵略 (动、名) qīnlüè to invade
9. 战争 (名) zhànzhēng war
10. 發明 (动、名) fāmíng to invent, invention
11. 創造 (动、名) chuǎngzào to create, creation
12. 坚持 (动) jiānchí to insist, to maintain, to persist
13. 礼物 (名) lǐwù gift
14. 利用 (动) lìyòng to make use of, to utilize
15. 溜(冰) (动) liū(bīng) to skate
16. 冰 (名) bīng ice
17. 内容 (名) nèiróng contents
18. 散(会) (动) sàn(huì) to dismiss (a meeting)

19. 同意　　(动)　　tóngyì　　to agree, agreement
20. 貢献　　(名、动)　gòngxiàn　　contribution, to contribute to

語　法　Yǔfǎ　Grammar

67.1 The Extended Uses of Interrogative Pronouns Interrogative pronouns are not only used in questions, but may also have other functions, or extended uses, in declarative sentences. In this lesson we will introduce a few common extended uses of interrogative pronouns.

67.2 Interrogative Pronouns of General Denotation An interrogative pronoun is sometimes used to denote "any" person or thing, making no exception to the case. e. g.

1. 在 我們 班上, 誰 都 喜欢 看
这个 話剧.

   In our class, everyone likes to watch this play.

2. 什么 缺点 都 是 可以 克服 的.

   Any defect can be overcome. (One can overcome any defect.)

誰 means "every one", 什么缺点 means "every defect"; in the first example, the interrogative pronoun is the subject; in the second example, the interrogative pronoun is used to modify the subject. The subject in each case is rather stressed.

Sometimes, an interrogative pronoun of general denotation may also be used as the object or the modifier of the object in a sentence. e. g.

3. 只要 是 祖国 需要 的, 他 哪种
工作 都 願意 作.

   As long as it is some work that the fatherland needs, he is willing to do it.

4. 他 最 爱 看 戏, <u>什么</u> 戏 他 都 看.

He likes to watch plays most; he will watch any play.

In example 3 it is emphatically expressed that "he would do any work"; while in example 4 the stress is laid on the fact that "he likes to see every play". Notice, since such expressions are emphatic, the object, formed or modified by an interrogative pronoun, has to be placed before the verb (as in example 3), or before the subject (as in example 4).

Sometimes we may also use an interrogative pronoun as adverbial modifier. e. g.

5. 山上 站着 一个 同学, 我 <u>怎么</u> 看 也 看不出来 他 是 谁.

A schoolmate was standing on the mountain. However hard I looked, I could not tell who he was.

6. 天气 <u>怎么</u> 冷, 弟弟 都 出去 打 球.

No matter how cold the weather is, my younger brother will go out to play ball.

Here the interrogative pronouns are used to stress the manner of "seeing", and the degree of "coldness".

An interrogative pronoun may be any part of a sentence, but the adverb 都 or the adverb 也 is always used in this kind of sentence. 都 is more frequently used, while 也, in general, is more often used in the negative sentence.

67.3   Interrogative Pronouns of Indefinite Denotation

When we refer to indefinite persons, things, qualities, manners, quantities, degrees, actions etc., we may also use interrogative pronouns. e. g.

7. 星期日 我 想 到 <u>哪儿</u> 去 玩儿一玩儿.

I am thinking of going somewhere on Sunday to have fun.

8. 我　希望　誰　能　帮助　我
一下兒.

I hope someone can help me a little.

In the above examples, 哪兒 does not mean "which place" but "any place" or "some place"; 誰 does not mean "which one or who" but "someone". So far as the word order is concerned, this kind of sentence is the same as the general interrogative sentence, but different in tone.

67.4 Interrogative Pronouns of Particular Denotation in the Composite Sentence Sometimes we may use interrogative pronouns in the composite sentence to represent particular persons, things, qualities, manners, quantities. degrees, actions etc. In such a case, we should reduplicate the interrogative pronoun in the second clause, and the adverb 就 has to be used. e. g.

9. 誰　俄文　好,　誰　就　給　參观
的　人　作　翻譯.

Whoever speaks better Russian should serve as interpreter for the visitors.

10. 哪个　小組　团結得　好,　哪个　小組
的工作　就　作得好.

Whichever group is better united will do the work better.

The meaning of example 9 is "whoever is gocd in Russian should interpret for the visitors", and that of example 10 is "whatever are the better organized co-operatives will excel in production." That is to say, we use the first clause to restrict the subject of the second clause. Similarly, we may also use the first clause to restrict the object of the second clause. e. g.

11. 哪兒　風景　最　好,　我們　就　到
哪兒　旅行.

We shall travel to wherever the scenery is best.

12. 你們 那兒的 工作 需要 幾個 干部, 我們 就 派 幾個 干部 去.

We shall send to you as many cadres as your work requires.

The above examples mean "we shall make a trip to the place where the scenery is best", and "we send you enough cadres". Sometimes, we may also use the first clause to restrict the predicate or the adverbial modifier of the second clause. e. g.

13. 大家 決定 怎么样, 就 怎么样.

We shall do whatever way people decide.

14. 什么 时候兒 方便, 我 就 什么 时候兒 来 找 你.

I shall come to visit you whenever it is convenient.

15. 先生 怎么 念, 我 就 怎么 念.

I shall read it whichever way the teacher reads it.

Example 13 means "it should be done in accordance with the wishes of all the people", example 14 means "I shall come whenever you are free" and example 15 means "I shall read as the teacher reads". There are two points to be observed in using interrogative pronouns in the composite sentence:

(1) We use 誰, 什么人 or 哪个人 to stress a sentence element denoting persons, we use 哪兒 or 什么地方 to stress a sentence element denoting place, and we use 怎么 to stress an element expressing way or manner.

(2) In the second clause, 就 has to be placed before the predicate as adverbial modifier (as shown in the above examples). But we can omit the word 就, when the two clauses are simple enough and parallel in construction. e.g.

16. 有 — 什么 意見，(就) 提 什么 意見 吧!

Please express whatever opinion you may have.

17. 先生 怎么 問，学生 (就) 怎么 回答.

The students answered according to the way the teacher asked.

課文 Kèwén Text

I

1. 来 看 农业 展覽 的 人 真 多，什么 地方的 农民 都 有.

There were lots of people who came to see the agricultural exhibition. There were farmers from every place.

2. 哪个 国家的 劳动 人民 都 是 热爱 和平 反对 侵略 战争 的.

The working people of all countries ardently love peace and are opposed to wars of aggression.

3. 多少 困难 他 都 克服 了，从来 也 沒 有 怕过.

He has overcome many, many difficulties. He has never been afraid.

4. 在 社会主义 国家里，誰 都 可以 發明 創造.

In a socialist country, anyone can invent and create.

5. 大家 怎么 劝 他 休息 他 也 不
听, 还是 坚持 工作.

No matter how everyone urged him to rest, he would not listen but (still) insisted on working.

II

6. 我的 朋友 要 結婚, 我 想 买
点兒 什么 礼物 送給 他們.

My friends are going to get married. I want to buy some small gift for them.

7. 我 不 願意 一个 人 去 散
步, 想 找 誰 跟 我 一塊兒 去.

I don't like to go strolling by myself. I want to find someone to go with me.

8. 我 希望 您 哪天 有 時間, 到
我們 宿舍 来 玩兒玩兒.

I hope someday when you have time you'll come to our dormitory to have some fun.

9. 我們 都 应該 利用 放假 的 时
候兒 干 点兒 什么.

We all should utilize vacation time to do a little something.

III

10. 哪兒 最 近, 我們 就 到 哪兒
去 溜 冰.

We shall go ice skating to whichever place is the nearest.

11. 哪本 小說兒 內容 最 好 就
介紹 哪本.

Recommend (Introduce) whichever novel has the best contents.

12. 什么 时候兒 討論完, 什么 时候兒
散 会.

The meeting will be dismissed whenever we finish our discussion.

13. 誰的 意見 正確 大家 就 同意
誰的 意見.

Everyone will agree with whoever has the correct opinion.

14. 我們 有 多少 力量 就 应該 貢献
多少 力量.

We ought to contribute as much manpower as we have.

課外練習　Kèwài liànxí　Home Work

1) Re-write the following sentences by using interrogative pronouns, emphasizing the words underlined:

(1) 所有的 人 都 看 过 这个 展覽.

(2) 这个 宿舍里, 从 早上 到 晚上
都 很 安静.

2) Change the following sentences into composite ones using interrogative pronouns according to the grammar rule of 67.4.

(3) 我們 要 用 能 提高 生产 的
方法.

(4) 他 要 找 个 会 溜 冰 的 人
教 他.

3) Write out the following transcriptions in Chinese:

(5) Dìdi yào bìyè le, wǒ yào sòng tā diǎnr shénmǒ.

(6) Shéi xuéxíde hǎo, shéi jiù xiàng dàjiā jièshào jīng yàn.

4) Make sentences using 哪兒 and 誰 according to the grammar rule of 67.3.

汉字表　Hànzì biǎo　Chinese Characters

1	缺	缶（ノ 𠂉 缶）
		夬
2	願	原 厂
		白
		小
	頁	
3	弟	丶 丷 弟
4	景	
5	覽	一 厂 厂 𠂆 𠂤 𠂤 臣 臣 臥 臥 臨
		見
6	反	
7	战	占
		戈
8	爭	
9	侵	亻
		㑺（⺋ ヨ ヨ 彐 㑺）
10	略	田
		各

11	創	倉 (ノ 𠆢 𠆢 今 今 今 倉 倉)
		刂
12	造	告
		辶
13	堅	収
		土
14	持	扌
		寺
15	物	牛
		勿
16	溜	氵
		留 (ノ 𠂊 𠂉 𠚍 留)
17	氷	冫
		水
18	内	冂 内
19	貢	工
		貝

Lesson 68

1.	对	(介、动) duì	for, to; to face; right
2.	对于	(介) duìyú	as for, as to, to, for
3.	要求	(动、名) yāoqiú	to ask, to demand, demand
4.	具体	(形) jùtǐ	concrete
5.	组长	(名) zǔzhǎng	group-leader
6.	信心	(名) xìnxīn	confidence
7.	政府	(名) zhèngfǔ	government
8.	拥护	(动) yōnghù	to support, to uphold
9.	亲爱	(形) qīn'ài	dear, affectionate
10.	原谅	(动) yuánliàng	to pardon, to excuse
11.	晴	(形) qíng	fine, clear, fair (weather)
12.	阶段	(名) jiēduàn	step, section
13.	语音	(名) yǔyīn	phonetics, speech sound
14.	基本	(形) jīběn	basic, fundamental
15.	认为	(动) rènwéi	to consider
16.	严格	(形) yángé	strict
17.	辅导	(动、名) fǔdǎo	to help...to study, help
18.	基础	(名) jīchǔ	basis, foundation

19. 在...上   zài...shàng   on
20. 将来 (副)   jiānglái   in the future
21. 祝   (动)   zhù   to bless, to pray

語法 Yǔfǎ Grammar

68.1 The Word 有 Used in Comparison   Besides the word 比 and the construction 跟...一樣 used to compare two persons or things, we also use the following sentence pattern to make a comparison:

A — 有 — B — the Quality Compared

A is subject, B is the standard of comparison, and the whole sentence means "A has reached B in the quality compared". e. g.

1. 弟弟 有 我 高 了.

My younger brother is as tall as I am now.

2. 你 跑得 有 他 快 嗎?

Can you run as fast as he does?

Example 1 means: as "I" am taken as the standard of comparison, my "younger brother" has reached my height in stature. Example 2 means: taking "him" as the standard of comparison, "you" are equal to him in "speed".

In such a sentence, we often use 这么 or 那么 as adverbial modifier of degree in the predicate. e. g.

3. 弟弟 有 我 这么 高 了.

My younger brother is as tall as I am now.

4. 你 跑得 有 他 那么 快 嗎?

Can you run as fast as he does?

In example 3, the standard of comparison is 我 , so we use 这么 as adverbial modifier pointing towards an object that is near by. In example 4, 他 is the standard of comparison, so we use 那么 as adverbial modifier, pointing towards an object that is at a distance.

Besides adjectives, a number of verbs and optative verbs, which can be modified by such adverbial modifiers of degree, may also appear in a comparison with the construction 有... e.g.

5. 他 有 你 （这么） 爱 音乐.

He likes music as much as you do.

6. 你 有 他 （那么） 会 唱 歌儿 吗?

Can you sing as well as he does?

In the negative sentence, we use 没有.... e. g.

7. 那棵 树 <u>没 有</u> 这座 楼 （这么） 高.

That tree is not as tall as this building.

8. 这棵 花儿 长得 <u>没 有</u> 那棵 （那么） 好.

This flowering plant does not grow as well as that one.

9. 谁 也 <u>没 有</u> 你 （这么） 爱 溜 冰.

Nobody likes to skate as much as you do.

68.2 没有 and 跟...不一样 (or 不跟...一样)   These two expressions are both used in negative sentences of comparison, but they are different in meaning. 跟...不一样 (or 不跟...一样) is used to show that two persons or things are dissimilar in a certain quality, while 没有... is used to show that there is not only a difference in some quality between two persons or things, but also that one person or thing is greater (or less) in degree in some quality than the other. e. g.

10. 这个 箱子 <u>跟</u> 那个 箱子 <u>不</u> <u>一样</u> 重.

This suitcase (OR: trunk) and that suitcase are not of the same weight (don't weigh the same).

11. 这个　箱子　<u>没 有</u>　那个　箱子　那么　重.

This suitcase is not as heavy as that one.

Example 10 merely shows that these two trunks are not of the same weight. But in example 11, the idea is: the two trunks are not only different in weight, but it is pointed out that one is heavier than the other; in other words, "that trunk is heavier than this one".

68.3　The Prepositions 对 and 对于

(1) 对　　对 may be used as a verb. For example, we may say 他住的地方对着湖, or 前边兒的窗戶和后边兒的对着, 所以屋子的風特別大. But it is more often used as a preposition. e. g.

12. 早上　我　看見　先生　的　时候兒. <u>对</u>　先生　說:　"您 早!"

In the morning when I see the teacher, I say to the teacher, "Good morning."

13. 他　<u>对</u>　每个　同志　都　很　热情.

He is very warm to every comrade.

In the two examples above, the preposition 对 still possesses the definite meaning of the verb 对 to some extent.

(2) 对于　　It is a preposition and not a verb, and it may be shortened as 对. But 对于 is more formal. This preposition has two common uses as follows:

a) 对 (于) forms a prepositional construction used as adjective or adverbial modifier. e. g.

14. 朋友　<u>对(于)</u>　我　的　帮助　很　大.

My friends help me a lot. (My friends' help to me is big.)

15. 先生 对(于) 学生 的 要求 应该 很 具体.

A teacher's demands on his students should be concrete.

In the above examples, the prepositional construction is used as adjective modifier to the subjects 帮助 and 要求. But in most cases the prepositional construction of 对于 is used as adverbial modifier. e. g.

16. 组长 对(于) 同学 的 学习 情况 应该 很 清楚.

A section leader should be very clear about the studying conditions of the students.

17. 我们 对(于) 学好 中文 都 很 有 信心.

We all have great faith in our mastery of Chinese.

Such prepositional constructions are often put at the beginning of a sentence. e. g.

18. 对(于) 同学的 学习 情况, 组长 应该 很 清楚.

A section leader should be very clear about the studying conditions of the students.

19. 对(于) 学好 中文 我们 都 很 有 信心.

We all have great faith in our mastery of Chinese.

b) The preposition 对(于) may be used to transpose the object of a verb to the beginning of a sentence. When the predicate of a sentence is rather complicated or when we wish to stress the subject, we may use the preposition 对于 to transpose the object to the beginning of the sentence. e. g.

20. 对(于) 正确的 意見, 我們 应該 立刻 接受.

As for correct opinions, we should accept them immediately.

21. 对(于) 人民 政府, 誰 都 非常 拥护.

Everyone gives strong support to the People's government. (As for the People's government, everyone supports it strongly.)

課文 Kèwén Text

亲爱的 ××:

Dear ――:

你的 信 收到 了. 因为. 准备 考試, 沒 有 立刻 回 信, 請 原諒.

I have received your letter. Because I had to prepare for the examination, I did not write back right away. Please excuse me.

時間 过得 真 快, 到 中国 已經 三个多 月 了. 現在 正 是 冬天, 北京 的 天气 跟 祖国 不 一样, 沒 有 祖国

那么 冷. 除了 下 雪 以外, 差不多
都 是 晴天, 讓 人 感到 很 舒服.

Time goes by really fast. It has been already three
months since I arrived in China. It's winter now. The
weather in Peking is not the same as our own country
(fatherland). It is not as cold. Except when it snows, the
days are always sunny and make one feel very
comfortable.

我們 学習 中文 的 第一 阶段 是
語音 和 基本 語法, 在 这个 阶段里
語音 跟 基本 語法 一样地 重要. 我
認为 語法 沒 有 語音 那么 难. 先生
不但 对于 我們 的 要求 很 严格,
而且 給 我們 的 帮助 也 很 具体.
除了 上課 以外, 每星期 都 有 几次
輔导, 所以 我們的 进步 都 很 快.
有些 老 同学 說 中文 說得 有
中国 人 那么 流利 了, 我 也 有 信心
在 现在的 基础上 繼續 提高, 将来
說得 跟 他們 一样 好.

Our first stage in learing Chinese is pronunciation and
basic grammar. In this stage, pronunciation and basic
grammar are equally important. I feel that grammar is not
as hard as pronunciation. The teacher not only makes

strict demands upon us but also gives us concrete help.
Besides having classes, every week we also have several
sessions of studying with assistance. So we all make rapid
progress. Some old schoolmates can now speak Chinese as
fluently as the Chinese. I also have confidence that I can
continually raise my level of achievement on the present
basis and speak as well as they do in the future.

在 生活 上, 先生 和 中国 朋友
对 我們 也 很 关心. 虽然 住在
外国, 也 跟 在 自己的 家里 一样.
昨天 北京 下 雪 了, 我 跟 先生
和 中国 朋友 照了 几張 像片兒, 下次
写 信 再 給 你 寄去. 我 要 到
先生那兒 去 了. 再 談 吧! 希望 你
常常 来 信. 祝 你
快乐!

In daily life, both the teachers and the Chinese friends
are very concerned about us. Although I am now staying in
a foreign land, I feel very much at home. It snowed in
Peking yesterday. My teachers, my Chinese friends and I
took a few pictures. I will send them to you when I write
again next time. Now I have to go to the teacher. I shall
write again. (Let's talk again.) I hope you write often.
With best wishes for your happiness.

× ×

十二月五日

— —

December 5th

課外練習　Kèwài liànxí　Home Work

1) Re-write the following comparative sentences using 有...:

(1) 这次　考試　我　考得　跟　上次　一样　好.

(2) 您　爱　照　像,　我　同屋　也　像　您　一样　爱　照　像.

2) Re-write the following sentences using 沒有...:

(3) 汽車　比　船　走得　快.

(4) 今天的　节目　比　前天的　有意思.

(5) 这間　屋子　比　那間　亮.

3) Copy the following sentences and fill the blanks with 对 or 对(于):

(6) 和平 ＿＿＿＿ 我們的　建設　很　重要.

(7) ＿＿＿＿ 这个　問題,　我們　应該　好好兒地　研究　一下兒.

(8) 先生 ＿＿＿＿ 大家　説:　"請　你們　繼續　抄写　下去."

汉字表　Hànzì biǎo　Chinese Characters

1	于	二 于
2	求	
3	具	丨 冂 冂 月 目 且 具

4	政	正	
		攵	
5	府	广	
		付	亻
			寸
6	拥	扌	
		用	
7	护	扌	
		户	
8	原		
9	谅	言	
		京	
10	晴	日	
		青	
11	阶	阝	
		介	
12	段		
13	基	一 十 卄 艹 甘 甘 其 其 其 基	
14	严	一 丆 亚 亚 亚 严	
15	格	木	
		各	

16	輔	車
		甫（一 丆 丏 甶 甫 甫）
17	础	石
		出
18	祝	礻
		兄（口 兄）

Lesson 69

生詞　Shēngcí　New Words

1. 多（么）　(副)　duó(mð)　how
2. 唉　(嘆)　āi　(an interjection)
3. 斤　(量)　jīn　catty
4. 公斤　(量)　gōngjīn　kilogram
5. 里　(量)　lǐ　lǐ
6. 公里　(量)　gōnglǐ　kilometre
7. 尺　(量、名)　chǐ　foot
8. 公尺　(量)　gōngchǐ　metre
9. 可爱　(形)　kěài　lovable, lovely
10. 城市　(名)　chéngshì〔座〕　city, town
11. 留学生　(名)　liúxuéshēng　student from abroad
12. 輕　(形)　qīng　light
13. 收拾　(动)　shōushí　to put in order, to tidy up
14. 領袖　(名)　língxiù　leader
15. 修　(动)　xiū　to build, to repair
16. 群众　(名)　qúnzhòng　the masses
17. 重视　(动)　zhòngshì　to attach importance to, to respéct highly
18. 光荣　(形、名)　guāngróng　glorious, glory
19. 检查　(动、名)　jiǎnchá　to examine, examination

20.	大概	(副)	dàgài	probably
21.	瘦	(形)	shòu	thin, lean
22.	胖	(形)	pàng	fat
23.	經常	(形)	jīngcháng	frequent, constant

語法 Yǔfǎ Grammar

69.1 **The Exclamatory Sentence** The exclamatory sentence is used to express strong emotions and feelings. In general the exclamatory sentence is formed by putting the adverb 多么 (as adverbial modifier) before the adjective or the verb (or optative verb) in the predicate. e. g.

1. 新 中国 建設得 多么 快 啊!

How quickly the new China has been constructed!

2. 今天 孩子們的 生活 多么 幸福 啊!

How fortunate is the life of today's children!

3. 他 多么 喜欢 音乐 啊!

How he likes music!

4. 他 多么 会 溜 冰 啊!

How well he can ice skate!

There are three points to be noticed concerning the exclamatory sentence:

(1) The word 多 in the bound-form 多么 is pronounced in the second tone in the spoken language, moreover, 多么 is always shortened as 多.

(2) The modal particle 啊 may be omitted, but when it is used, the sentence mood of exclamation is much stronger.

(3) The exclamatory sentence is always used together with the interjection. An interjection represents a sound of joy or grief, or an answer, and it may be used alone or in a sentence. e. g.

5. 唉! 解放 以前 中国 工人 受 的
   压迫 多么 重 啊!

Alas! Before the Liberation how badly the Chinese workers were oppressed!

唉 in the above sentence expresses disappointment or dissatisfaction.

69.2   The Word 多 in a Question of Degree

When we wish to ask about the degree of a certain quality, we put the word 多 (duó or duō) before the predicative adjective expressing such a quality. e. g.

6. 这个 孩子 多 大 了? 十岁.

How old is this child? (He is) ten.

7. 那个 箱子 多 重? 二十斤 (十公斤).

How heavy is that trunk? (It is) twenty catties (ten kilograms).

8. 这条 路 多 长? 三十里 (十五公里).

How long is this road? (It is) thirty li (15 kilometers).

In such a sentence pattern, we often use the word 有 in the predicate, meaning "reaching" or "up to". e. g.

9. 这个 湖 有 多 深?

How deep is this lake?

10. 很 浅, 只 有 五尺 (深).

It is very shallow, only five feet (deep).

11. 那座 楼 有 多 高?

How high is that (multi-storied) building?

12. 有 一百多 公尺 (高).

It is more than a hundred meters (high).

Notice that after the numeral and the measure word, we may use an adjective of quality (such as in the above examples: 五尺深 and 一百多尺高).

69.3 Appositives and Extra-positional Words   We have already learned the following elements of a sentence: the subject, the predicate, the adjective modifier, the adverbial modifier, the object and the complement. There may also be an element of re-designation in a sentence, that is to say, there may be two elements in a sentence, serving to designate the same person or thing, and they are of the same grammatical importance (both are used as the subject or object in a sentence). The use of an element of re-designation will sometimes make our expression much more accurate and lively. Here we will introduce two such elements of re-designation in the following, classified according to their grammatical relation:

(1) The appositive   When there are two elements used in a sentence to suggest the same person or thing, and considered as one sentence element, we take one of these as the basic word and the other as an appositive used to explain the basic word. e. g.

13. 北京, 中国的 首都, 是 一个 非常 可爱的 城市.

Peking, China's capital, is an exceptionally lovely city.

14. 我們, 外国 留学生 都 喜欢 在 北京 住.

We, the foreign students, all like to live in Peking.

In the above sentences, the subjects 北京 and 我們 are basic words; 中国的首都 is the appositive of 北京 and 外国留学生 is the appositive of 我們. When a pronoun is used as the basic word (such as 我們 in example 14), the positions of the basic word and the appositive are somewhat fixed; but when a noun is used as the basic word, the position of the basic word and that of the appositive can be interchanged, and so, we may change example 13 into the following:

15. 中国的 首都, 北京 是 一个 非常 可爱的 城市.

China's capital, Peking, is an exceptionally lovely city.

Besides the subject, other elements of a sentence may also be followed by an appositive. e. g.

16. 前天　我們　一天　看了　两个　展覽
　　—— 一个　农业．展覽，一个　輕
工业　展覽．

Day before yesterday, we saw two exhibitions in one day —an agricultural exhibition and a light-industry exhibition.

17. 連　农民，馬老庄的　女兒　也　会
开　机器　了．

Even the daughter of a peasant, Ma Lao-zhuang, knows how to operate the machinery now.

18. 他們　都　在　給　新　来　的　同志，
老張　和　小黄　收拾　宿舍．

They are all tidying up the dormitory for the newly arrived comrades, old Zhang and little Huang.

(2) The extra-positional word　Sometimes in a sentence, there are two elements also used to denote the same person or thing, only they do not stand together; one of them is at the beginning of the sentence and outside of the sentence structure. This is called the extra-positional word. The other is the basic word, which stands in its proper place within the sentence. e. g.

19. 掌握　中文、学好　專业，这　是
我　努力　的　方向．

To master Chinese and to successfully learn a special field —this is the direction of my efforts.

20. 对　工作　热情、对　同志　关心，
那　是　他的　特点．

Being enthusiastic toward his work and concerned about the comrades — those are his characteristics (special attributes).

In the above examples, the subjects composed of demonstrative pronouns are preceded by extra-positional words. But the other elements of a sentence (such as the object, the double-function word, the adjective modifier etc.) may also take extra-positional words. e. g.

21. 那个 劳动得 最 好的 女 同志,
大家 都 要 选 她 作 小 组长.

Everyone wants to elect that female comrade, who works the best, to be the group leader. (As for that female comrade who works so well, every one wants to elect her to be the group leader.)

22. 水平 高、条件 好 的 同志, 可以
派 他们 去 帮助 新 工厂 建设.

(We) can send those comrades with high levels and good qualifications to go and help construct new factories.

23. 發音 还 不 正确 的 同学, 这些
人 的 课外 辅导 还 需要 增加
一些.

As for students whose pronunciation is still not accurate, we need to somewhat increase their extracurricular guidance.

24. 要 去 参观 的 同学, 張 同志
已经 替 他们 买好 船票 了.

Comrade Zhang has bought boat tickets for those schoolmates who want to go on the tour.

課文 Kèwén Text

I

1. 中国 人民 都 热爱 自己的 領袖 ＿＿＿＿ 毛澤东 主席.

The Chinese people all ardently love their own leader—
Chairman Mao Tse-tung.

2. 学校里 新 修了 两个 宿舍 ＿＿＿＿ 一个 中国 学生的, 一个 外国 留学生的.

In our school two dormitories have been newly built—a
Chinese students' (dormitory) and a foreign students'
(dormitory).

3. 关心 群众 生活、重視 群众 意見, 这 是 作好 領导 工作 的 重要 条件.

To be concerned with the life of the masses and to value
the opinions of the masses—these are important
qualifications for doing well the work of a leader.

4. 她 認为 参加 工作、为 人民 服务, 那 是 她 最 大的 光荣 和 快乐.

She considers that participating in work and serving the
people are her greatest glory and happiness.

5. 学習 好 的 同学, 先生 应該 組織 他們 把 經驗 給 大家 介紹 一下兒.

The teacher should organize the students who have learned well so that they can introduce a little of their experience to everyone.

II

(a₁) 你 檢查完 身体 了 嗎?

Have you finished (your) medical examination?

(b₁) 檢查完 了. 你 知道 我 有 多 重?

Yes. Do you know much I weigh?

(a₂) 大概 五十几 公斤 吧?

Probably fifty-odd kilograms.

(b₂) 不, 六十 公斤. 这 半年 又 增加了 四公斤. 你 看过 我 两年前 照 的 像片兒 吧? 那 时候兒 我 多么 瘦 啊!

No. Sixty kilograms. This past half-year I have gained four kilograms. You have seen my picture taken two years ago, haven't you? At that time, how skinny I was (or: I was so skinny)!

(a₃) 对了, 你 现在 胖 多 了. 我 虽然 长得 比 你 高, 但是 只 有 五十几 公斤 重.

Right, you have put on a lot of weight since (you are much fatter now). Although I am taller than you, I weigh only fifty-some kilograms.

(b₃) 你 有 多 高?

How tall are you?

(a₄) 一公尺七.

One meter point seven.

(b₄) 你是比我高一点兒, 我只有一公尺六.

You are a little bit taller than I am. I am only one meter point six.

(a₅) 但是你的身体多好啊!

But how healthy you are!

(b₅) 要想身体好, 必須經常鍛鍊. 我和班上的几个同学組織了一个鍛鍊小組. 你願意參加不願意參加?

If one wants to have good health, one must exercise constantly. Several schoolmates in (our) class and I have organized an exercising group. Do you wish to join us?

(a₆) 願意參加. 从什么时候兒起开始鍛鍊呢?

Yes. When should I start exercising?

(b₆) 明天你就来吧!

Come tomorrow.

課外練習   Kèwài liànxí   Home Work

1) Change the following into exclamatory sentences using the word 多么, emphasizing the words underlined:

(1) 庄稼 長得 <u>真 快</u>.

(2) 唉! 这間 屋子 <u>太 髒 了</u>, 快 收拾收拾 吧!

(3) 領导上 <u>很 重視</u> 群众的 創造 發明.

2) Write down questions for the following sentences using the word 多:

(4) 我 弟弟 剛 十岁.

(5) 这包 棉 衣服 有 两公斤 重.

(6) 外边兒的 雪 有 半尺 深.

3) Make two sentences one using an appositive, the other using an extra-positional word:

(7) 有同位語的

(8) 有外位語的

汉字表　Hànzì biǎo　Chinese Characters

1	唉	口	
		矣	厶
			矢
2	斤		
3	公	八	
		厶	
4	尺	尸	尺
5	市	丶 亠	市
6	留		
7	輕	車	
		巠	

8	拾	扌	
		合	
9	袖		
10	群	君	尹 (ㄱ ⺕ ⺕ 尹)
			口
		羊	
11	視	礻	
		見	
12	光	丨 丨 ⺌ 光	
13	荣	一 十 卄 龷 荣	
14	檢	木	
		僉	
15	概	木	
		既 (ㄱ ⺕ ヨ 目 艮 艮 艮 既 既)	
16	瘦	疒	
		叟 (丿 ㇄ 亻 亻 彳 臼 臼 叟)	
17	胖	月	
		半	

Lesson 70

生詞　Shēngcí　New Words

1.	健康	(形、名)	jiànkāng	healthy, health
2.	超額	(动)	chāoé	over-production over-fulfilment
3.	棉	(形)	mián	cotton
4.	……上		…shàng	on, on the side of
5.	交流	(动)	jiāoliú	to exchange
6.	領导上	(名)	lǐngdǎoshàng	leading personnel, superiors
7.	边兒	(名)	biānr	side, border
8.	部分	(名)	bùfēn	part, portion
9.	公园	(名)	gōngyuán	park
10.	傳統	(名)	chuántǒng	tradition
11.	教师	(名)	jiàoshī	teacher
12.	英勇	(形)	yīngyǒng	heroic, brave
13.	民主	(形、名)	mínzhǔ	democratic, democracy
14.	运动	(名、动)	yùndòng	movement, physical exercise, sport; to move, to take physical exercise
15.	五四	(名)	Wǔsì	May 4th (Movement)
16.	培养	(动)	péiyǎng	to educate, to cherish

17. 觉悟　(名、动) juéwù　　consciousness, awakening, to awake

18. (劳动)者(尾) (láodòng)zhě　(labour)er

19. 民族　(名)　mínzú　　nation

20. 操场　(名)　cāochǎng　playground

21. 当　　(动)　dāng　　to become, to act as

22. 主任　(名)　zhǔrèn　head (of an organization)

語法　Yǔfǎ　Grammar

70.1　The Complex Sentence　A sentence may be very simple. A subject and a predicate can form a complete sentence, e. g. 他来，那是合作社 etc. But, if we wish to express a rather complex thought, we cannot use only simple sentences, for they seem isolated, detached and even confused. So in practical use, we always prefer to use complex sentences. Furthermore, sentences in writing are generally more complicated in structure than those of oral speech. Under the following three points, we shall discuss how a complex thought is expressed in a complex sentence:

(1) The elements of a complex sentence　The subject and the predicate are the fundamental elements of a sentence, either of which may be made up of a single word or a construction. If a construction is used instead of a single word, the sentence is complex. e. g.

1. 学好　中文　是　我的　任务.

It is my task to successfully learn Chinese.

2. 身体　健康　很　重要.

It is very important to be in good health.

Co-ordinate elements are also a characteristic of complex sentence. e. g.

3. 哥哥 姐姐 和 我 都 （是） 在 这个 学校 畢业 的.

My elder brother, my elder sister and I all graduated from this school.

4. 那篇 文章 又 長 又 深.

That article is both long and deep in meaning.

(2) The subordinate elements in a sentence   The subject and the predicate are the basic elements of a sentence, and both may take other elements. e. g.

5. 到 中国 来 訪問过 的 外国 朋友 都 很 喜欢 北京.

Foreign friends who have visited China all like Peking a lot.

6. 他 是 一个 月月 都 超额 完成 生产 計划 的 工人.

He is a worker who exceeds the production quota month after month.

Thus, an adjective modifier may make a sentence complex. More examples are:

7. 那个 合作社 从 早上 七点 起 卖 东西.

That cooperative store starts to sell things at 7:00 in the morning.

8. 这次 語法 檢查 比 上次 檢查 难 一点兒.

This grammar examination is a little more difficult than the last examination.

In the above, the two sentences are complex because of adverbial modifiers. More examples are:

9. 屋子里 热得 穿不住 棉 衣服.

The room was so hot that one could not keep wearing the cotton padded garment.

10. 他 讲 故事 讲得 大家 都 忘了 睡 觉 了.

He told the story so well that everyone forgot to go to bed.

In the above examples, complements make the sentences complex.

Besides the adjective modifier, the adverbial modifier and the complement, we may also use the element of re-designation in a complex sentence. e. g.

11. 最 受 观众 欢迎 的 电影 又 要 演 了.

The movie most well-received by audiences, "The Revolutionary Family," is going to be shown again.

12. 那个 非常 关心 群众 的 干部 大家 都 拥护 他!

Everyone supports that cadre who (always) has great concern for the masses.

(3) A composite sentence instead of a simple sentence
When we wish to express a complex thought, we may use a composite sentence formed by joining two (or more) clauses. e. g

13. 他 要 去 参加 讨论 会.

He wants to participate in the discussion meeting (conference).

14. 他 五点半 就 吃 晚飯 了

He ate supper as early as 5:30.

These two sentences may be re-written as follows:

15. 他 因为 要 参加 讨论 会，五点半
    就 吃 晚饭 了.

Because he wanted to participate in the conference, he had supper as early as 5:30.

More examples are:

16. 这个 农民 文化 水平 不 高.

This peasant's cultural level is not high.

17. 这个 农民 解决了 很 多 生产上
    的 具体 问题.

This peasant solved many concrete problems of production.

These two sentences may be re-written as follows:

18. 这个 农民 虽然 文化 水平 不
    高，但是 他 解决了 很 多 生产
    上的 具体 问题.

Even though this peasant's cultural level is not high, he has nevertheless solved many concrete problems of production.

70.2 **From Simple to Complex**   Suppose we have a number of thoughts, and they are expressed by the following sentences:

(1) 我 有 一个 朋友.

I have a friend.

(2) 这个 同志的 名字 是 马政.

This comrade's name is Ma Zheng.

(3) 他 在 学校里 工作.

He works at (a) school.

(4) 他 教 俄文.

He teaches Russian.

(5) 他的 俄文 水平 很 高.

His Russian ability (level) is very good (high).

(6) 他的 工作 态度 很 好.

His working attitude is very good.

(7) 他 要 帮助 学生 学习.

He wants to help students to study.

(8) 他 想出来 很 多 办法.

He figured out many methods.

(9) 最近 他們 学校 組織了 一个 經驗 交流 会.

Recently their school organized a meeting to exchange experiences.

(10) 馬政 同志 在 会上 作了 报告.

Comrade Ma Zheng gave a report at the meeting.

(11) 領导上 重視 他的 报告.

The leadership paid close attention to his report.

(12) 同志們 也 重視 他的 报告.

(His) comrades also paid close attention to his report.

These twelve sentences are rather simple. We can combine them into six sentences using the methods shown above. (The numbers at the end of each new sentence **are** the numbers of the original sentences given above, showing that the new sentence is composed of the same simple sentences.)

(1) 我 有 一个 朋友 馬政 同志. (1,2)

I have a friend, comrade Ma Zheng. (1, 2)

(2) 他 在 学校里 教 俄文. (3,4)

He teaches Russian at a school. (3, 4)

(3) 他 俄文 水平 高、 工作 态度 好. (5,6)

His Russian ability (level) is very good (high), (and his) working attitude is very good. (5, 6)

(4) 为 帮助 学生 学習, 他 想出来 很 多 办法. (7,8)

He has thought of many ways to help students study. (7, 8)

(5) 馬政 同志 最近 在 他們 学校 組織 的 經驗 交流 会上 作了 报告. (9,10)

Comrade Ma Zheng recently made a report at the meeting their school organized for the exchange of experiences. (9, 10)

(6) 領导上 和 同志們 都 很 重視 他的 报告.(11,12)

The leadership and (his) comrades all paid close attention to his report. (11, 12)

We can re-organize them further into three sentences:

(1) 我的　朋友　馬政　同志　在　学校里
教　俄文. (1, 2, 3, 4)

My friend, comrade Ma Zheng, teaches Russian at a
school. (1, 2, 3, 4)

(2) 他　俄文　水平　高、工作　态度
好, 为　帮助　学生　想出来　很　多
办法. (5, 6, 7, 8)

His Russian ability (level) is very good (high), (his)
working attitude is good, (and he) has thought of many
ways to help students. (5, 6, 7, 8)

(3). 最近. 在　学校　組織　的　經驗
交流　会上, 他的　报告. 受到
領导上　和　同志們的　重視. (9,10,11,12)

Recently, at a meeting the school organized for the
exchange of experiences, his report received the
leadership's and (his) comrades' close attention. (9, 10, 11,
12)

課文　Kèwén　Text

我們的　学校, 北京　大学, 在　北京
城外. 从　城里　到　頤和园　的　路上,
两边兒　有　很　多　学校, 北京　大学
也. 在　这条　路上.

Our school, Peking University, is on the outskirts of the
city of Peking. Along the road from the city to Yiheyuan
there are many schools. Peking University is also on this
road.

走进 学校 就 可以 看見 一座(一)座的
大楼. 这些 大 楼 大 部分 都 是 解放
后 新 修 的. 这里 有 礼堂、教室、圖書館、
宿舍 和 食堂. 我們的 校园里, 有 山、
有 水、有 树、有 花兒, 像 公园 一样.

As soon as one enters the school, one can see many big
buildings, one after another. Most of these buildings were
rebuilt after the Liberation. There are auditoriums,
classrooms, libraries, dormitories and dining halls here.
Our campus has hills, waterways, trees and flowers, just
like a park.

北京 大学 是 中国 最 有名的 一个
大学, 她 有 光荣的 革命 傳統. 三十多
年 以前, 北京 大学的 教师 和 学生 就
英勇地 参加了 中国 民主 革命 运动
———"五四 运动". 中国 人民的 領袖
毛澤东 主席 也 在 北京 大学 工作过.
現在 北京 大学 正 在 为 新 中国
培养 有 社会主义 觉悟 的、有
文化 的 劳动者. 在 这兒 学習的 有
中国 各 民族的 青年, 也 有 我們
外国 留学生.

Peking University is one of the most famous universities
in China. It has a glorious revolutionary tradition. Even as

far back as more than thirty years ago, the teachers and students of Peking University had bravely joined the Chinese democratic revolutionary movement—the May 4th movement. The Chinese people's leader, Chairman Mao Tse-tung, also worked at Peking University before. Right now, Peking University is educating laborers with socialist consciousness and culture for the new China. Among those who study here are youths from the various ethnic groups in China as well as we foreign students.

我們 在 北京 大学 每天 除了 上 課 和 自学 以外, 还 在 操場上 鍛鍊, 湖 边兒上 散 步. 我們 有 不 少 机会 和 中国 同学 在 一起. 这些 中国 青年 都 很 热情, 非常 可爱. 他們 除了 帮助 我們 学習 以外, 还 給 我們 介紹 新 中国 各 方面的 情况, 帮助 我們 認識 中国. 我 觉得 能 在 这兒 学習 是 很 幸福 的, 我 一天 比 一天 更 爱 我們的 学校 了.

At Peking University, besides going to classes and studying by ourselves every day, we also do physical exercises in the playground and take walks along the lake. We have many opportunities to mix with Chinese schoolmates. These Chinese youths are all very warm and nice. Besides helping us study, they also introduce the (conditions of) various aspects of the new China to us, thus helping us to understand China. I feel it is very fortunate to be able to study here. I like our school more and more each day.

課外練習 Kèwài liànxí Home Work

Write a comparatively complex sentence from each group of sentences given below

(1) ① 第三 車間的 任務 是 一个月
生产 五百架 农业 机器.

② 第三 車間的 工人 都 有 信心
超額 完成 生产 任务.

(2) ① 学校 給 学生 修 新 宿舍.

② 那些 新 宿舍 已經 修好 了.

③ 宿舍 修好 的 时候兒, 新 学生
还 沒 有 来.

(3) ① 她 作了 一件 棉 衣服.

② 那件 棉 衣服 又 輕、 又
暖(和)、 又 合适.

③ 她--用了 七八塊 錢 作 这件
棉 衣服.

(4) ① 那个 农民 給 地主 种 地
种过 三十年.

② 现在 那个 农民 当了 人民
公社的 主任 了.

③ 他的 名字 叫 黃 老九.

汉字表 Hànzì biǎo Chinese Characters

1	健	亻
		建
2	康	广

		隶(フ ヨ ⺕ 聿 聿 隶 隶 隶)	
3	超	走	
		召	
4	額	客	
		頁	
5	棉	木	
		帛	白
			巾
6	統	糸	
		充(丶 亠 云 充)	
7	师	丨 刂 刂一 师	
8	英	艹	
		央(丨 冂 口 央 央)	
9	勇	甬	
		力	
10	运	云	
		辶	
11	培	土	
		咅	
12	养	丶 丷 兰 养	
13	悟	忄	

		呑
14	族	方 方 方 族
15	操	扌
		品 (口 品)
		朮

Lesson 71

生詞 Shēngcí New Words

1.	根据	(介、名) gēnjù	according to, evidence, authority
2.	海	(名) hǎi	sea
3.	石头	(名) shítóu〔塊〕	stone
4.	黑	(形) hēi	black
5.	扔	(动) rēng	to throw
6.	赞成	(动) zànchéng	to approve
7.	世界	(名) shìjiè	world
8.	班	(量) bān	(a measure word), class
9.	号召	(动、名) hàozhāo	to call on, summons
10.	上海	(名) Shànghǎi	Shanghai
11.	日记	(名) rìjì	diary
12.	火車	(名) huǒchē	train
13.	心	(名) xīn	heart
14.	跳	(动) tiào	to pulsate, to jump
15.	终于	(副) zhōngyú	at last, eventually
16.	天安門	(名) Tiān'ānmén	Tien-An-Men
17.	广場	(名) guǎngchǎng	square
18.	过去	(名) guòqù	the past
19.	美	(形) měi	beautiful

20.	英雄	(名) yīngxióng	hero
21.	紀念	(动、名) jìniàn	to commemorate, commemoration
22.	碑	(名) bēi	monument
23.	牺牲	(动、名) xīshēng	to sacrifice, sacrifice
24.	敬爱	(动) jìng'ài	to revere and love
25.	向	(介) xiàng	from, towards

語法 Yǔfǎ Grammar

71.1 **Punctuation** There are altogether eleven kinds of punctuation marks frequently used in the Chinese written language. Here in this lesson, we shall introduce their chief uses in the following:

(1) Period or full stop "." indicates the pause after the completion of a sentence. e. g.

1. 他的 爱人 是 一个 小学 教师.

His wife is a primary-school teacher.

(2) Comma "," indicates a slight pause within a sentence. e. g.

2. 根据 我們的 了解, 他 的 学習 态度 很 好.

According to our understanding, his studying attitude is very good.

When the subject is comparatively long, we may use a comma to separate the subject from the predicate, e. g.

3. 那張 掛在 窗戶 旁边兒 的 像片兒, 就 是 我 在 校园里 照 的.

That photograph hanging next to the window is exactly the one that I took on campus.

(3) The pause mark " " indicates the pause betwen co-ordinate elements in a sentence. e. g.

4. 海边兒 有 很多 好看的 小 石头兒——红的、綠的、黑的、白的…… 都 有.

By the seashore there are very many beautiful small pebbles — red ones, green ones, black ones, white ones . . . all kinds.

5. 先生 对 学生 的 要求 应该 严格、具体.

Teachers' demands on students should be strict and concrete.

But, when the co-ordinate elements are closely related and clear enough in meaning, we may not use the pause mark. e. g.

6. 高 同志 和 他的 父母 都 到 海 边兒 休息 去 了.

Comrade Gao and his parents have all gone to the seashore to rest.

7. 把 这 两三天的 报 收起来, 别 扔在 桌子上.

Gather together the newspapers of these (last) two or three days, (and) don't strew them on the table.

(4) The question mark "?" is put after an interrogative sentence, indicating interrogation. e. g.

8. 你 知道 "五四 运动" 的 經过 嗎?

Do you know the history of the "May 4th Movement"?

9. 你 贊成 不 贊成 今天 下午
去 公园?

Do you agree (or not agree) to go to the park this afternoon?

(5) The semicolon ";" marks a pause in a sentence, greater than that of a comma and not as great as that of a full stop. e. g.

10. 他 剛 开始 工作, 就 接受了 这个
任务; 虽然 經驗 不 多, 但是 他
完全 有 信心 完成 这个 任务.

As soon as he began to work, (he) received this task; although he is not very experienced, he is nevertheless completely confident that he can complete this task.

It is more often used to separate co-ordinate clauses. e. g.

11. 我們 家 門口兒 是 一个 湖,
湖里 有 船; 湖 旁边兒 是 一
座 小 山, 山上 有 很 多 树.

In front of the door of our house is a lake; there are boats in the lake. Beside the lake is a small hill; on the hill are many trees.

(5) The colon ":" is chiefly used to show that an explanation is following. e. g.

12. 我們 認为: 只要 努力 学習, 就
一定 能 克服 困难, 学好 中文.

We feel: as long as we study hard, we definitely can overcome difficulties and be successful in learning Chinese.

Since it has the function of introducing an explanation, it is also used before a direct quotation, or after the salutation preceding a letter or an address.

(7) The exclamatory point "!" is used after interjections or exclamatory sentences to express strong emotions. e. g.

13. 坏 了! 最后的 一班 车 已經 过去 了!

Alas! The last train (OR: bus) has left.

14. 啊! 今天的 天气 多么 好 啊! 連 一点兒 風 都 沒 有!

Ah! Today's weather is so nice! There isn't even a tiny bit of wind!

The exclamatory point is also often used after an imperative sentence. e. g.

15. 快 上来! 汽車 要 开 了.

Come up quickly! The bus is about to leave!

16. 别 开 无綫电 了! 大家 都 睡了.

Don't turn on the radio! Everyone has gone to sleep.

(8) The quotation marks are of two kinds, the double quotation marks " " and the single quotation marks ' '. The double quotation marks are used to inclose a quotation. e. g.

17. 毛 主席 号召 中国 青年 要 "身体 好、 学習 好、 工作 好."

Chairman Mao calls on Chinese youth "to keep in good health, to study well and to work well."

The single quotation marks are used to inclose a quotation within a quotation, e. g.

18. 弟弟 写 信 来 說: "我 一定 努力作 一个 身体 好、学習 好、工作好 全 面 發展 的 好 青年."

(My) younger brother wrote a letter saying: "I am determined to do my best to become an all-round good youth who 'has good health, studies well and works well.'"

(9) The parenthesis "( )" shows that a word or words are inserted in a sentence as explanation. e. g.

19. 他們 是 上星期六 (九月 二十九日) 在 城里 結 的 婚.

They were married in the city last Saturday (September 29th).

(10) The dashes "——": We use two dashes to indicate a suspension in thought and an insertion of words as explanation. e. g.

20. 他 生在 上海——那时候兒 他 父亲 在 上海 工作——十几岁 才 到 北京 来.

He was born in Shanghai—at that time his father was working in Shanghai—(and) didn't come to Peking until he was more than ten years old.

If the insertion is placed at the end of a sentence, we use one dash only. e. g.

21. 我 一 看 就 知道 这 是 北京 大学的 遊行 队伍, —— 我的 朋友 都 在 里边兒 呢.

As soon as I looked (At a single glance) I knew these were

the paraders from Peking University — all my friends were there.

(11) The dotted line "..." or "......" is used to indicate that a part of the sentence has been omitted. e. g.

22. 他 在 百貨 大 楼里 看見 很
多 作好了 的 棉 衣服 —— 深
顏色的、淺 顏色的 大的、小的
…… 都 有.

Inside the department store he saw many ready-made cotton padded clothes — dark-colored ones, light-colored ones, big ones, small ones . . . all kinds.

課文 Kèwén Text

日記 ×月×日 星期× (晴)

Diary   X month X day X day of the week (weather clear)

火車 慢慢兒地 停下来 了, 我的 心
跳得 更 快 了; 終于 到了 新 中国的
首都 —— 北京 了. 我 对 北京的 情况
虽然 知道得 不 多, 但是 我 早 就
爱上 她 了. 有 机会 到 这兒 来
学習, 我 感到 非常 高兴.

The train slowly came to a stop. My heart beat even more quickly; (I) had finally arrived at the capital of new China — Peking. Although I did not know much about the situation in Peking, I had long ago fallen in love with it. Having the opportunity to come here to study, I felt extraordinarily happy.

一下 火車, 我們 就 受到了 中国
朋友的 热烈 欢迎. 有 人 还 用
我們 祖国的 語言 跟 我們 談 話:
"欢迎 你們 到 这兒 来 学習." 并且
問 我們: "累不累? 在 路上 走了
几天?……"

As soon as (we) got off the train, we received the enthusiastic welcome of our Chinese friends. Some people even used the language of our fatherland to converse with us, "(We) welcome you to come here to study." They asked further, "Are you tired? How many days have you been traveling?"

我們的 汽車 經过 天安門 广場 的
时候兒, 中国 朋友 問 我: "你 認識
这个 地方 嗎?" 我 一 看 就 喊了 出来:
"啊! 天安門!" 过去 在 画报、 电影上
你 給了 我 很 深的 印象, 但是 今天
我 覺得 你 更 美、 更 偉大 了. 我
多么 想 下車 好好兒地 看看 啊!

When our automobile passed Tian-An-Men (Gate of Heavenly Peace) Square, our Chinese friends asked me, "Do you recognize this place?" As soon as I looked I shouted, "Oh! the Gate of Heavenly Peace! In the past, in pictorials and in movies you gave me a very deep impression, but today I feel that you are even more beautiful and magnificent." How I wished to get out of the car to take a good look!

这时候兒 中国 朋友 告訴 我: "那 就 是
人民 英雄 紀念 碑. 上边兒的 字 是
毛 主席 写 的." 因为 汽車 走得 很
快, 我 沒 看清楚 就 过去 了. 我 想
那些 牺牲了 的 英雄 是 会 永远 活在
人民 心里 的; 我 也 跟 中国 人民
一样地 敬爱 他們. 从 今天 起, 我 就
要 跟 中国 人民 生活在 一起 了; 我
不但 要 跟 他們 作 最 好的 朋友, 还
要 向 他們 学习.

At this moment, (our) Chinese friends said to me, "That is the Commemorative Monument to the Heroes of the People. The words on it were written by Chairman Mao." Because the automobile was going very quickly, we passed by before I (could) see it clearly. I think those heroes who sacrificed themselves will live forever in the people's hearts. I (too) respectfully love them as the Chinese people do. Starting from today I shall live together with the Chinese people. I not only want to be their best friend but also want to learn from them.

課外練習 Kèwài liànxí Home Work

Learn the following short story, copy it and put in the punctuation marks:

記 日記 就 是 把 每天 自己 作
的 看 的 听 的 想 的 选 重要 的 記
下来 記 日記 有 下边兒 三个 好处

¹ 能 帮助 进步 可以 把 一天
工作上 和 学習上的 好 經驗 記下来
讓 自己 更 有 信心 要是 有 什么
缺点 也 可以 檢查 一下兒 立刻 改正
这样 自己 就 能 进步 得 更 快

² 一天 工作 很 多 学習 很 忙
要是 有 什么 事情 想不起来 怎么
办 呢 就 可以 查一查 日記

³ 記 日記 还 有 一个 好处 就
是 可以 練習 写 文章 有 人 説
記 日記 就 跟 写 文章 一样 我
觉得 很 对 因为 写得多 了 就 能
想 什么 写 什么 写 文章 的 能力
也 就 提高 了

　記 日記 的 好处 这么 多 我 一定
每天 記 日記

汉字表　Hànzì biǎo　Chinese Characters

1	根	木
		艮
2	据	扌
		居
3	海	氵
		每

4	石	
5	扔	扌
		乃（乛 彐 乃）
6	贊	先
		先
		貝
7	世	一 十 卄 卅 世
8	界	田
		介
9	火	
10	終	糸
		冬
11	广	
12	美	丶 丷 羊 美
13	雄	左（一 ナ 左）
		佳
14	紀	糸
		己
15	碑	石
		卑（白 甶 卑）
16	牺	牜
		西

17	牲	牛	
		生	
18	敬	苟	艹
			句
		攵	

Lesson 72

語法复習　yǔfǎ fùxí　Review

72.1 Four Kinds of Sentences, Classified According to
Their Different Uses　Sentences, according to their different
uses, may be divided into four kinds, here let us sum them
up as follows:

(1) The declarative sentence　Whenever we want to tell
something as a fact, we use the declarative sentence. e. g.

1. 我　認为　常常　开　經驗　交流
　　会　对　提高　生产　有　好处.

   I consider that having frequent meetings to exchange
   experiences is good for increasing production.

At the end of each declarative sentence, a full stop should
be used.

(2) The interrogative sentence　Whenever we wish to ask
a question, we use the interrogative sentence. e. g.

2. 先生　每　星期　輔导　你　几次?

   How many times a week does the teacher help you in your
   studies?

3. 那　两个　同志, 誰　是　你們的
　　小組　长——那个　男的, 还是
　　那个　女的?

   Of those two comrades, which one is your section leader—
   the man or the woman?

We have to put a question mark at the end of an interrogative sentence. We have learned five kinds of interrogative sentences, it is not necessary to sum them up here.

(3) The imperative sentence   When we wish to command or request someone to do something, we use the imperative sentence. A full stop or an exclamatory point must be put at the end of each imperative sentence. e. g.

4. 把 这个 問題 好好兒地 研究研究.

Study this problem thoroughly.

5. 明天 上 課 的 时候兒, 別 忘 了 把 本子 交給 先生.

Tomorrow, during class, do not forget to hand the notebook in to the teacher.

(4) The exclamatory sentence   When we wish to express strong emotions or feelings, we use the exclamatory sentence. After the exclamatory sentence we must put the exclamatory point. e. g.

6. 中国 解放 以后, 劳动 人民的 生活 改善得 多么 快 啊!

Since China's Liberation, the laborer's life has improved so rapidly!

7. 贊成! 贊成! 我 也 要 选 他 作 代表.

(I) agree! (I) agree! I, too, agree to elect him as representative.

72.2   Three Kinds of Comparison   We have learned three kinds of comparison:

(1) The use of the construction 跟...一样 (51.3). e. g.

8. 这篇 文章 跟 那篇 文章 一样 深, 哪篇 都 不 容易.

This article is as deep in meaning as that article; neither is easy.

9. 馬車 跟 汽車 走得 不 一樣 快.

Horse carts and automobiles do not move at the same speed.

(2) The use of 有 (68.1). e. g.

10. 这篇 文章 有 那篇 文章 (那么) 深, 也 不 容易.

This article is as deep in meaning as that article; it also is not easy.

11. 馬車 沒 有 汽車 走得 (那么) 快.

Horse carts do not go as fast as automobiles.

(3) The use of 比 (62.1). e. g.

12. 这篇 文章 比 那篇 深, 先 学 那篇 再 学 这篇.

This article is deeper in meaning than that article; first study that article and then study this article.

13. 馬車 比 汽車 走得 慢.

Horse carts move more slowly than automobiles.

In most cases, we may use any of these three kinds of comparison; but they are different in use, so in choosing the best form of comparison, one must pay special attention to the context.

(1) When we wish to show that two persons or things are similar to each other in comparison, we use either the first or the second form. e. g.

14. 这课的 汉字 跟 那課的 汉字 一样 多.

This lesson's Chinese characters are as numerous as that lesson's Chinese characters.

15. 这課的　汉字　有　那課的　那么
多 ＿＿＿＿ 也　快　三十个　了.

This lesson's Chinese characters are as numerous as that lesson's; there are also about 30.

The above are two affirmative sentences. There is little difference between the first kind and the second kind, except that the first kind is clearer in expression. In negative forms the two sentences will be:

16. 这課的　汉字　不　跟　那課的　一
样　多＿＿＿＿这課　多,　那課　少.

The number of Chinese characters in this lesson is not the same as in that lesson—this lesson has more, that lesson has fewer.

17. 那課的　汉字　沒　有　这課的　这么
多＿＿＿＿那課　二十八个,　这課　三十
个.

That lesson's Chinese characters are not as numerous as this lesson's—that lesson has 28, this lesson 30.

The first kind is not as clear as the second kind: because the first only expresses that the two things are different, while the second shows what the difference is. The third kind of comparison indicates the difference in a clearly-defined way, hence, we can re-write the second sentence as follows:

18. 这課的　汉字　比　那課的　多.

This lesson's Chinese characters are more numerous than that lesson's.

19. 那課的　汉字　比　这課的　少.

That lesson's Chinese characters are fewer than this lesson's.

(2) When we wish to show the difference in comparison clearly, especially the difference of quality or quantity, the third kind should be used. e. g.

20. 这課的　汉字　比　那課的　多得　多

This lesson has many more Chinese characters than that lesson.

21. 这課的　汉字　比　那課的　多　一点兒.

This lesson has a few more Chinese characters than that lesson.

22. 这課的　汉字　比　那課的　多　两个.

There are two more Chinese characters in this lesson than in that lesson.

23. 那課的　汉字　比　这課的　少　两个.

There are two fewer Chinese characters in that lesson than in this lesson.

Before we conclude, there are still two points to be noticed:

a) 跟… 一样 and 比… are two different forms of comparison, and should not be combined into 比…一样…, because 比…, as shown above, indicates a rather concrete difference, and not only whether there is a difference or not.

b) When we use 比…, the difference in comparison is indicated by a complement, and in general, not by an adverbial modifier.   Therefore, we say:

24. 那課的　汉字　比　这課的　少得　多
　　　　　　少　七八个　呢.

That lesson's Chinese characters are a lot fewer than this lesson's—seven or eight fewer.

But we cannot say: 那課的汉字比这課的汉字很少.

72.3 Ways of Emphasis   Up to the present, we have already learned many ways of emphasis, now let us sum them up as follows:

(1) By transposing the object   The change of word order indicates emphasis. The object can be brought before the verb or the subject. e. g.

25. 她 俄文报 看得懂, 中文报 也 看得懂.

She can read Russian newspapers and can also read Chinese newspapers.

26. 給 朋友 买 的 礼物, 我 已經 送去 了.

I have already sent over the gifts I bought for a friend.

(2) By means of reduplication   When we wish to emphasize each individual of a group of persons or things, we reduplicate the measure word. e. g.

27. 他 提了 很多 条 意見, 条条 都 很 重要.

He made many suggestions; every one was important.

There are some· nouns which possess in themselves the character of the measure word, they can also be used reduplicatively. e. g.

28. 人人 都 説 今年 不 冷.

Everybody says it is not cold this year.

If we wish to emphasize a certain quality of a thing, we may reduplicate the adjective. e. g.

29. 我 剛 喝 了 热热的 一杯 茶, 不 能 再 喝 了.

I have just drunk a cup of hot tea; I cannot drink any more.

(3) By using the rhetorical question   When we wish to emphasize an affirmation, we use 不是…嗎. e. g.

30. 你 不是 坐 十点多的 火車 走 嗎?
为 什么 現在 还 沒 准备好 呢?

Aren't you taking the train that leaves (shortly) after ten? Why aren't you ready yet?

When we emphasize a negation, we put 哪兒 into the declarative sentence, changing it into an interrogative sentence. e. g.

31. 这个 礼堂 哪兒 大 啊? 只 能 坐 四五百 人.

How could one say that this auditorium is big? (It) can seat only four or five hundred people.

(4) By using the double negative   The double negative is equal to an affirmative, but it is more forcible than a general affirmative.

32. 不 学好 中文, 就 不 能 学習 专业.

(If one) does not learn Chinese well, then (one) will not be able to study a special field.

(5) By using an interrogative word in the declarative sentence. e. g.

33. 那箱 书 真 重, 我 怎么 也 搬不动.

That box of books is really heavy. I can't lift it no matter how I try.

(6) By using 連…都 (也)   When we wish to emphasize a certain element of a sentence; we use this construction. e. g.

34. 我們的 工业 發展得 真 快, 連 农村 都 办起 工厂 来 了.

Our industry is developing really fast. Even the villages are building factories.

35. 雪下大了, 連路都看不出来了.

The snow is falling more heavily now and even the roads have become invisible.

36. 他第一次学溜冰, 到了冰上連站也站不住.

The first time he learned to skate he could not even stand up (on the ice).

(7) By using the word 一 In the negative sentence the word 一 is often used for emphasis. e. g.

37. 真好! 十个句子, 一句也沒有錯!

Really well done! Of the ten sentences, not even a single one is wrong.

(8) By using the word 是 All the sentences without the copula, 是 may be used before the predicate for emphasis. e. g.

38. 这课他是念熟了, 先生問了他几个問題, 他都答对了.

He has indeed learned this lesson well. The teacher asked him several questions and he answered all of them correctly.

39. 这个地方是安静, 我在这兒看了半天書, 也沒走过来一个人.

This place is indeed quiet. I have been reading here for quite a while, and not even a single soul has walked by.

(9) By using the word 就   In the sentence with a substantive predicate or a verbal predicate, we may use the word 就 as adverbial modifier for emphasis. e. g.

40. 共产党員 就 是 不 怕 困难,
什么 困难 他 都 能 克服.

A Communist Party member is simply not afraid of difficulties. He can overcome any difficulty.

課文 Kèwén Text

从前 有 一个 名字 叫 愚公 (Yúgōng)
的 老人, 快 九十岁 了. 他 住在
两座 大 山的 北边兒. 这 两座 山
有 七万尺 高, 他 出来 进去 感到
很 不 方便.

Once there was an old man, almost ninety years old, whose name was Yugong. He lived to the north of two large mountains. These two mountains were seventy thousand chi tall. He felt it was very inconvenient to come to and from (his home).

有 一天 他 把 家里 人 都 叫到
一起, 对 大家 說:"这 两座 大
山, 正 对着 我們 家的 門口兒; 多么
不 方便 啊! 我 想 把 山 搬开,
以后 就 好 了."

One day he called his family members together and said
to them: "These two large mountains are right in front of
the door of our house, how inconvenient! I want to move
away the mountains, and after that everything will be all
right."

大家 都 很 贊成, 只 有 他的 爱人
信心 有点兒 不 夠. 她 說: "別 忘了
这 两座 山 是 又 高 又 大 啊!
山上的 石头, 都 搬到 哪兒 去 啊?"
愚公 說: "山 大, 海 更 大; 把 石头
扔进 海里 去".

Everybody was agreeable except his wife, who was
somewhat lacking in confidence. She said, "Don't forget
that these two mountains are both tall and big! The rocks
on the mountains, where can they all be moved to?"
Yugong said, "The mountains are big, but the sea is bigger.
(Let us) throw the rocks into the sea."

他們 开始 搬 山 了. 大家 很
有 信心地、 一年一年地 工作下去.

They (then) began to move the mountains. Everybody
worked on, very confidently, year after year.

愚公 有 个 朋友 知道了 这件 事,
就 来 找 他. 那个 朋友 說: "你 已經
九十多 了, 还 想 搬 山 嗎? 你
連 一块 小 石头兒 也 拿不动 啊!
我們 都 是 快 死 的 人 了."

Yugong had a friend who, learning of this matter, came to visit him. The friend said, "You are already over ninety, (and you are) still thinking of moving the mountains? You cannot move even a small rock! We are both persons about to die."

愚公 說: "我 雖然 老 了, 我 还
有 孩子; 将来 我的 孩子 也 要 生
孩子. 我們 人 越 生 越 多, 山上的
石头 越 搬 越 少. 我們 一定 能 把
山 搬开 的......"

Yugong said, "Although I am old, I still have children. In the future, my children will also bear children. Our people will become increasingly more numerous with these births, (but) the rocks on the mountains will diminish as they are moved away. We will definitely be able to move away the mountains . . . ."

他的 朋友 沒 有 話 說, 就
走 了.

Having nothing more to say, his friend left.

A General Review of the Basic Grammar

A. Parts of speech

The noun:

1) 中国　　北京　　毛澤东
2) 同志　　学校　　書
3) 思想　　經驗　　条件
4) 今天　　去年　　上边兒　　中間兒

們 (15.4)　　It is a plural suffix used for nouns denoting persons. e. g.

同志們　　朋友們

But the suffix is not used, when the plural number of a noun is shown clearly by context. e. g.

二百多个留学生
全世界热爱和平的人民

Reduplication of nouns (49.2) Some nouns possessing in themselves the nature of the measure word may be reduplicated with the implication of "each" or "every". e. g.

人人　　天天

The pronoun　　There are three kinds of pronouns:

The personal pronoun:

我　　你　　他
我們

The interrogative pronoun:

誰　什么　哪兒　怎么

The demonstrative pronoun:

这　那

这些

The verb:

坐　躺　培养

在　有　觉得

There are two supplementary kinds of verbs:

The copula (13.1):

是

The optative verb (26.1):

应該　必須　会

Reduplication of verbs (38.2) The action expressed by a reduplicated verb is short and brief. Attention should be paid to the following:

When a monosyllabic verb is reduplicated, the numeral 一 may be added between the two forms of the verb. e. g.

看一看　想一想

A dissyllabic verb is reduplicated by its bound-form. e. g.

討論討論　收拾收拾

In the case of a verb-object construction, whether it is a common construction or a particular one, only the verb is reduplicated. e. g.

看看小説兒　説説話

The adjective.

高　低　流利　热情

Reduplication of adjectives (20.2) Attention should be paid to the following:

When a monosyllabic adjective is reduplicated, the second syllable is often pronounced in the first tone with retroflex ending. e. g.

好好兒　快快兒

A dissyllabic adjective is reduplicated by the syllable. e.g.

干干淨淨　高高兴兴

The numeral　　There are three kinds of numerals:

The cardinal numeral (22.1, 56.1):

一　两　半　万　亿　零

The ordinal numeral (37.1):

第二　第二百三十四

一年級　二月三日

The approximate number (37.2)　It may be expressed in three ways. e. g.

1) 三十几　几百　两万几千

2) 两三　十七八　八九十　一两万

3) 二十多　三百多万

The measure word:

个　張　把　只

遍　次

The nominal measure word (14.1)　It is used before the noun. e. g.

两件衣服　　三个小組

一枝烟

The verbal measure word (40.2)　It is used before the verb. e. g.

去一<u>次</u>　抄写三<u>遍</u>　敲五<u>下</u>兒

Reduplication of the nominal measure word (49.2)　It has the meaning of "each" or "every". e. g.

条条大路　篇篇文章

The preposition:

从　为　跟　对于

The adverb:

很　都　常常　不

The conjunction:

和　或者　所以　但是

The particle:

The structural particle:

的　地　得

The modal particle:

吗　呢　吧　啊　了

The interjection:

啊　唉

B.　The sentence

The classification of sentence:

Sentences may be classified into two kinds according to their structure:

The sentence composed of two parts It may be subdivided into four kinds (a summary of which is to be found in 42.1):

The sentence with a substantive predicate (13.1, 17.1, 19.2):

1) 那是夏天穿的衣服.

2) 这个公园叫北海公园.

3) 那辆很漂亮的汽车是中国第一汽车厂生产的.

The sentence with an adjectival predicate (14.3):

4) 綠綠的庄稼真可爱.

The sentence with a verbal predicate (16.1):

5) 每个人都劳动.

6) 我們要永远記着那些为革命牺牲
   了的英雄.

7) 我送他一个日記本.

The sentence with a clause predicate (39.1):

8) 这間屋子空气好.

The sentence composed of one part It consists of two kinds:

The sentence with an indeterminate subject (55.1):

9) 下雨了!

10) 現在散会.

The sentence composed of a single word (50.3):

11) 他要去溜冰, 你呢?

12) 这是他訂的学習計划, 你的呢?

Sentences may be classified into four kinds according to their uses:

The declarative sentence It is used for telling something, and the examples 1—10 given above are declarative sentences.

The interrogative sentence It consists of five kinds (36.1):

The interrogative sentence with 嗎 (13.3):

13) 你复習課文了嗎?

The alternative interrogative sentence (15.3):

14) 今天你有沒有課外練習?

15) 那篇文章容易不容易?

The interrogative sentence with an interrogative pronoun (19.1):

16) 你要給誰买火車票?

17) 檢查身体的結果怎么样?

The interrogative sentence with (还是)…还是… (29.2):

18) 上次的紅旗（还）是你們得了还是他們得了？

19) （还是）首都劇場大，还是人民劇場大？

The interrogative sentence with 是不是 (35.4):

20) 是不是她默寫得最好？

21) 那封信是不是寄走了？

22) 最近他們又發明了一种新机器，是不是？

The imperative sentence (55-3):

23) 請您在这兒等一会兒．

24) 別在車上吸烟！

25) 讓世界上的劳动人民都团結起来！

The exclamatory sentence (69.1):

26) 这个地方多么美啊！

27) 他多么关心同志啊！

28) 他的病好得多么快啊！

Sentence elements not including the subject, the predicate and the object:

The adjective modifier:

The noun used as adjective modifier (15.1):

29) 星期六的会改到下星期去了．

30) 中間兒的座位好．

31) 湖旁边兒的楼是宿舍和食堂．

The pronoun used as adjective modifier (15.1):

32) 我們的中文水平提高了．

The adjective used as adjective modifier (15.1):

33) 勞駕，給我一杯热茶.

34) 我要找一个安静的地方休息一下.

The verbal construction used as adjective modifier (28.1):

35) 去参观的人就要出發了.

36) 1953 年来的学生已經畢业了.

37) 給母亲写的信在桌子上呢!

The subject-predicate construction used as adjective modifier (28.1):

38) 这是工人休息的地方.

39) 他提的意見很正确.

40) 觉悟高的人工作一定积極.

The verb-object construction used as adjective modifier (28.1).

41) 参加晚会的人都来了.

The verb-complement construction used as adjective modifier (28.1):

42) 那个穿得很漂亮的同志是去参加联欢晚会的.

43) 快把洗干淨了的衣服收起来.

The reduplicated measure word or the reduplicated numeral and measure word used as adjective modifier (49.3):

44) 个个干部的工作热情都很高.

45) 一件一件的礼物都放在桌子上了.

The adverbial modifier:

The adverb used as adverbial modifier:

46) 我們都是外国留学生.

The adjective used as adverbial modifier (20.1):

47) 我們应該<u>严格</u>地要求自己.

48) 我<u>輕輕</u>地走进了圖書館.

49) 他把这件事<u>簡簡單單</u>地說了一遍.

The noun used as adverbial modifier:

50) <u>桌子上</u>放着一本字典.

51) 我<u>下午</u>在<u>操場上</u>鍛鍊.

The prepositional construction used as adverbial modifier (20.1):

52) 他<u>在人民医院</u>工作.

53) 我們<u>跟中国各民族的青年</u>一起学習.

54) <u>对(于)群众的發明創造</u>, 領导上非常重視.

The reduplicated mumeral and measure word used as adverbial modifier (49.3):

55) 先生把同学的練習本子<u>一本一本</u>地改完了.

The complement

The complement of degree (21.2):

56) 在党的培养下, 他的工作能力提高<u>得非常快</u>.

57) 那个农民給我們講他們提高生产的經过, 講<u>得我們都兴奋極了</u>.

The directional complement (34.1, 52.1, 53.1):

58) 一輛車从湖那边兒过<u>来</u>了.

59) 人民代表来了, 我們都立刻跑<u>出来</u>欢迎.

60) 我准备得不夠, 也許有的問題回
答不出来.

The resultative complement (32.1):

61) 山上山下都种上了菓树.

62) 老同学把新同学带到公园去了

The potential complement (57.1):

63) 我們礼堂只坐得下一千多人.

64) 这件衣服太瘦, 我穿不进去.

65) 我的中文水平不夠高, 看不懂这本
小説兒.

Complements of other kinds:

66) 他記日記記了七八年了.

67) 被选作代表, 他感到光荣極了.

68) 这个小組比第一組少两个学生.

The appositive (69.3):

69) "留学生食堂," 我們吃飯的地方,
就在宿舍旁边兒.

70) 他是七年前在那个有名的大学——
北京大学——畢业的.

The extra-positional word (69.3):

71) 掌握中文, 学好專业, 这是我們的
重要任务.

72) 那个公社主任, 以前我們訪問过
他.

Time and aspect

Time

The adverbial modifier of time expresses at what time

or in what period of time an action takes place (25.3):

73) 后天下午三点开經驗交流会.

74) <u>我們从星期一到星期六每天上午</u>
都有課.

75) 先生<u>每星期</u>輔导我三次.

The complement of time expresses how much time an action lasts (46.1):

76) 我学習一課, 要預習<u>三刻鐘</u>, 复習
<u>两个半小时</u>.

77) 他抄(写)生詞, 抄(写)了<u>半点鐘</u>.

78) 我同屋每天念<u>半个鐘头</u>(的)課文.

Aspect

Expressing the completion of action (27.1):

79) 昨天下午, 我接到<u>了</u>两封信.

80) 主席講<u>了</u>話, 节目就开始了.

81) 今天起来得早, 我六点半就吃<u>了</u>
早飯了.

82) 弟弟在小学只念<u>了</u>五年, 还没有
畢业呢!

Expressing the progress of action (44.1):

83) 領导上<u>正</u>研究这个問題呢!

84) 我朋友<u>在</u>研究中国人民反帝 (dì) 斗
爭 (dòuzhēng) 的历史.

Expressing the continuation of action (45.1):

85) 无綫电播送重要新聞, 我們都注意
地听<u>着</u>.

86) 机器旁边兒掛<u>着</u>紅旗.

87) 他拿<u>着</u>一本新出来的人民画报.

Expressing the immediate happening of action (49.1):

88) 船要开了, 快上来吧.

89) 湖里的水冻上了, 就要能溜冰了!

90) 我的朋友将要来中国学习。

Expressing past experience (40.1):

91) 我們班有几个同学作过工人.

92) 这个农民从前給地主种过地.

93) 我在祖国看过"白毛女".

The various forms of the sentence with a verbal predicate:

The telescopic form (38.1):

94) 每个小組都要派一个代表参加那个会.

95) 这个新聞讓我們非常兴奋.

The multi-verbal form (43,45.3):

96) 他要到合作社去买水菓.

97) 我們要用最大的努力来学好中文.

98) 解放以前, 农民起早睡晚地劳动, 还是沒有粮食吃.

99) 他經常騎着自行車送通知.

The disposal form (47.1):

100) 我已經把买来的礼物包好了.

The passive form (65.2):

101) 他被选作学生会主席了.

102) 无綫电讓人借走了.

103) 很多生产上的复杂問題都叫这些青年工人解决了.

The form of indicating existence, appearance or disappearance (61.1):

104) 船上坐着几个孩子.

105) 南边兒开过来一辆汽車.

106) 楼下搬走了一个同学.

The form of stressing the time, place or manner of action (35.1):

107) 他(是)在报上看見的这篇文章.

108) 他們(是)坐飞机来的.

109) "五四运动"是在一九一九年發生的.

Negation

Expressed by the adverb 不:

110) 他过去不吸烟. (A past habitual action)

111) 我們现在不学别的, 只学中文. (A present action)

112) 我从来不关着窗戶睡觉. (A habitual action)

113) 明天我們不放假. (A future action)

114) 昨天我劝他跟我一起去听听音乐, 他不去. (willingness)

115) 我們不应該在汽車上或者剧場里吸烟. (An optative verb)

116) 去年这个时候兒, 我还不認識你呢! (A verb of mental action)

117) 这个节目很長, 十一点以前演不完. (A negative potential complement)

Expressed by the adverb 沒(有) (which is used for completed actions):

118) 我起来的时候兒，天还黑着呢，大家都沒有醒呢．

119) 他沒有念完大学，十九岁就参加工作了．

Ways of emphasis

By transposing the object before the verb or before the subject (29.1, 63.1):

120) 中国戏和中国画兒我都很喜欢．

121) 我中国新小説兒看过不少，旧小説兒还沒看过．

By using the rhetorical question (**63.2**):

122) 他不是在操場上嗎？怎么你沒找着他？

123) 他哪兒在操場上，他一鍛錬完就走了．

By using the double negative (63.3):

124) 我們班的同学，沒有一个人不努力．

125) 不克服缺点，就不能进步．

By using 連…都(也) (64.1):

126) 連小学生也来参加义务劳动了．

127) 上午他刚完成这件工作，連休息也沒休息，下午又接受了一个新的任务．

128) 哥哥連字典也沒有用，很快地就
把那篇文章翻譯出来了.

By using the numeral 一 (64.2):

129) 家里人都出去遊行了，一个人也
沒有了.

130) 這課書他背得熟極了，一句也沒
有錯.

By using the word 是 (64.3):

131) 那輛汽車跑得是快，一小时可以
跑五、六十公里.

132) 今天是不太冷，可以不穿棉衣服.

By using the word 就 (64.4):

133) 最高的那座大楼就是百貨大楼.

134) 這个医学上的問題虽然从来沒有
解決过，我們就要研究出一个結
果来.

By the extended uses of interrogative pronouns (67.1):

135) 要是选他作代表，誰都会举手贊
成.

136) 那个先生經驗多，哪国学生都教
过.

By reduplicating the word:

137) 他照了十几張像，張張像片兒都
很清楚.

138) 人人都說那个地方風景好，我一
定要去一次.

The composite sentence:

"because...(so)" (31.1):

139) 因为他經常練習說中文，所以説
得很流利．

"although...(yet)..." (31.1):

140) 語音阶段虽然早就过去了，但是
我們一直还注意着發音．

"if...(then)..." (31.1):

141) 要是語法的基础好，以后的学習
困难就不大了．

"not only... but also..." (59.1):

142) 一个革命的領导者不但要作群众
的先生，而且要作群众的学生．

143) 他不但自己重視学習，而且也很
关心别人的学習．

"if only... (then)..." (59.4):

144) 你只要把学習方法改一改，就可
以学得更好！

"on one side ... and on the other ...", "both ... and"
(38.3):

145) 他又是工人，又是学生．

"if ... (then) ..." (59.2):

146) 我一买着火車票，就給你送来

"the more ... the more..." (59.3):

147) 准备得越好，就回答得越好．

Interrogative pronouns used for particular denotation
(67.4):

148) 哪兒的工作需要我，我就到哪兒
去．

Vocabulary (Appendix 1)

(The words are arranged in the order of the phonetic alphabet, and the number after each word represents the number of the lesson in which the word appears.)

A

ā	啊	(助、叹)	ā	(a particle and an interjection)	63
āi	唉	(叹)	āi	(an interjection)	69
ài	爱	(动)	ài	to love	53
	爱人	(名)	àirén	lover, sweetheart, (also denoting husband or wife)	58
ān	安静	(形)	ānjìng	quiet, silent	55

B

bā	八	(数)	bā	eight	22
	吧	(助)	bā	(a particle)	50
bá	八路軍	(名)	Bálùjūn	Eighth Route Army	58
bǎ	把	(量)	bǎ	(a measure word)	17
	把	(介)	bǎ	(a preposition)	47
bái	白	(形)	bái	white	45
	白毛女	(名)	Báimáonǚ	a white-haired girl	58
bǎi	百货大楼	(名)	bǎihuò-dàlóu	department store	49
	百	(数)	bǎi	hundred	56
bān	搬	(动)	bān	to move	33

	班	(名)	bān	class	35
	班	(量)	bān	(a measure word), class	71
bàn	半	(数)	bàn	half	22
	办法	(名)	bànfǎ	method, way	59
	办	(动)	bàn	to manage, to build or run (a factory or school)	65
bāng	帮助	(动)	bāngzhù	to help	28
bāo	包	(量)	bāo	pack, parcel, (a measure word)	49
	包	(动)	bāo	to pack, to wrap	53
bǎo	饱	(形)	bǎo	having eaten to the full, enough	62
bào	报	(名)	bào	newspaper	13
	报告	(名、动)	bàogào	report, to make a report	34
bēi	杯	(量)	bēi	(a measure word), cup	63
	杯子	(名)	bēizi	cup	65
	碑	(名)	bēi	monument	71
běi	北京	(名)	Běijīng	Peking	14
	北京大学	(名)	Běijīng-dàxué	Peking University	17
	北	(名)	běi	north	61
bèi	倍	(量)	bèi	times	56
	背	(动)	bèi	to tell from memory, to recite	64
	被	(介)	bèi	by	65
běn	本	(量)	běn	(a measure word)	14
	本子	(名)	běnzi [本]	note-book	16
bǐ	比较	(动、副)	bǐjiǎo	to compare, comparatively	51
	比	(介)	bǐ	than, to compare	62
bì	必须	(能动)	bìxū	must, have to	29
	毕业	(动)	bìyè	to graduate; graduation	65
biān	边儿	(名)	biānr	side, border	70
biàn	遍	(量)	biàn	(a measure word)	52
biǎo	表	(名)	biǎo	watch	40

	表演	(名、动)	biǎoyǎn	performance, to perform	46
bié	别的	(代)	biédě	other, others	45
	别	(副)	bié	don't	55
bīng	冰	(名)	bīng	ice	67
bìng	病	(名、动)	bìng	disease, illness, to fall ill	39
	并且	(連)	bìngqiě	moreover, and	43
bō	播送	(动)	bōsòng	to broadcast	53
bú	不但...		búdàn...	not only...but also	59
	而且...		érqiě...		
	不断	(副)	búduàn	incessantly	63
bù	不	(副)	bù	not, no	13
	部分	(名)	bùfén	part, portion	70

C

cái	才	(副)	cái	(a word expressing delay), just	44
cān	参加	(动)	cānjiā	to take part, to join	40
	参观	(动)	cānguān	to visit	47
cāo	操场	(名)	cāochǎng	playground	70
chá	查	(动)	chá	to look up (word in dictionary)	40
	茶	(名)	chá	tea·	55
chà	差	(动)	chà	less	25
	差不多	(副)	chàbùduō	more or less, almost	35
cháng	長	(形)	cháng	long	15
	常常	(副)	chángcháng	often	21
chàng	唱(歌兒)	(动)	chàng(gēr)	to sing (song)	21
chāo	抄(写)	(动)	chāo(xiě)	to copy	64
	超额	(副)	chāoé	over-production, over-fulfilment	70
chē	車間	(名)	chējiān	workshop	47
	車	(名)	chē〔輛〕	vehicle	61
chéng	城	(名)	chéng	city, town	27

	成	(动)	chéng	to become	39
	城市	(名)	chéngshì〔座〕	city, town	69
chī	吃	(动)	chī	to eat	35
chǐ	尺	(量、名)	chǐ	foot	69
chū	出發	(动)	chūfā	to start, to set out	35
	出	(动)	chū	to go (come) out	37
chú	除了...以外...		chúlě...yǐwài...	in addition to, except, besides	61
chǔ	楚国	(名)	Chǔguó	Ch'u state (kingdom)	61
chuān	穿	(动)	chuān	to put on, to wear	43
chuán	傳說	(名、动)	chuánshuō	legend	61
	船	(名)	chuán〔只〕	boat, ship	63
	傳統	(名)	chuántǒng	tradition	70
chuāng	窗戶	(名)	chuānghǔ	window	33
chuáng	床	(名)	chuáng〔張〕	bed	45
chuàng	創造	(动、名)	chuàngzào	to create, creation	67
chūn	春天	(名)	chūntiān	spring	50
cí	詞彙	(名)	cíhuì	vocabulary	27
	詞	(名)	cí	word	49
cì	次	(量)	cì	times	40
cóng	从	(介)	cóng	from	20
	从前	(副)	cóngqián	in the past, formerly	27
	从...起		cóng...qǐ	since, from the time of	28
	从...到...		cóng...dào...	from... to...	28
	从来	(副)	cónglái	since, hitherto	63
cuò	錯	(形)	cuò	wrong, incorrect, mistaken	33
	錯誤	(名、形)	cuòwǒ	mistake, mistaken	44

D

| dǎ | 打（球） | (动) | dǎ(qiú) | to play (ball) | 46 |
| dà | 大 | (形) | dà | big, large | 14 |

	大家	(代)	dàjiā	all	35
	大声儿	(形)	dàshēngr	loud, loudly	44
	大春	(名)	Dàchūn	(a proper name)	58
	大禹	(名)	Dàyǔ	(a proper name)	59
	大概	(副)	dàgài	probably	69
dài	带	(动)	dài	to bring, to carry	34
	大夫	(名)	dàifù	doctor, physician	39
	带	(动)	dài	to wear, to put on	40
	代表	(名、动)	dàibiǎo	to represent, representative, delegate	53
dāng	当然	(副)	dāngrán	of course	46
	当	(动)	dāng	to become, to act as	70
dǎo	倒	(动)	dǎo	to fall down	55
dào	到	(动)	dào	to reach, to arrive	33
	倒	(动)	dào	to pour	55
dē	的	(助)	dē	(a structural particle)	15
	地	(助)	dē	(a structural particle)	20
	得	(助)	dē	(a structural particle)	21
	...的时候儿		...dēshíhóur	when, at the time of	28
dé	得	(动)	dé	to get	62
děng	等	(动)	děng	to wait	63
dī	低	(形)	dī	low	57
dì	地方	(名)	dìfāng	place	23
	第	(头)	dì	(a prefix)	37
	地主	(名)	dìzhǔ	landlord	58
	地	(名)	dì	land	58
	弟弟	(名)	dìdi	younger brother	67
diǎn	点(鐘)	(名)	diǎn(zhōng)	o'clock	25
	点儿	(量)	diǎnr	bit (a measure word)	31
	点	(名)	diǎnr	point	65
diàn	电影	(名)	diànyǐng	film, moving picture	20
diào	掉	(动)	diào	to fall, to miss	33
dìng	訂	(动)	dìng	to make (a plan)	44

diū	丢	(动)	diū	to lose	47
dōng	东西	(名)	dōngxi	thing	26
	冬天	(名)	dōngtiān	winter	49
dǒng	懂	(动)	dǒng	to understand, to know	19
dòng	动	(动)	dòng	to move, to touch	58
	冻	(动)	dòng	to freeze	64
dōu	都	(副)	dōu	all	17
duǎn	短	(形)	duǎn	short	15
duàn	鍛鍊	(动、名)	duànliàn	to do (physical) exercise, training	43
duì	对了		duìlé	yes, that is right	17
	对	(形)	duì	right, correct	29
	对不起		duìbùqǐ	excuse me, I am sorry, I beg your pardon	40
	队伍	(名)	duìwǔ	paraders, troops	56
	对	(介、动)	duì	for, to; face; right	68
	对于	(介)	duìyú	as for, as to, to, for	68
duō	多	(形)	duō	many, much	14
	多少	(数)	duōshǎo	how many, how much	22
duó	多(么)	(副)	duó(mó)	how	69

E

è	俄文	(名)	èwén	the Russian language	15
	饿	(形)	è	hungry, to hunger	59
èr	二	(数)	èr	two	22

F

fā	發展	(动、名)	fāzhǎn	to develop, development	39
	發音	(名)	fāyīn	pronunciation	44
	發生	(动)	fāshēng	to happen, to take place	59
	發明	(动、名)	fāmíng	to invent, invention	67
fān	翻譯	(动、名)	fānyì	to translate, to interpret translation, interpretation, interpreter	28

fǎn	反对	(动)	fǎnduì	to oppose, to stand against	67
fàn	飯	(名)	fàn	food, meal, cooked rice	43
	犯	(动)	fàn	to commit (a mistake)	52
fāng	方法	(名)	fāngfǎ	way, method	29
	方面	(名)	fāngmiàn	respect, side	38
	方便	(形)	fāngbiàn	convenient	43
	方向	(名)	fāngxiàng	direction	61
fǎng	訪問	(动)	fǎngwèn	to call (on, at), to visit	64
fàng	放	(动)	fàng	to put	45
	放假	(动)	fàngjià	to take (have) a holiday	52
fēi	非常	(副)	fēicháng	uncommonly, extremely	34
	飞机	(名)	fēijī〔架〕	aeroplane	63
fēn	分	(名)	fēn	minute	25
	分	(量)	fēn	cent (a measure word)	37
	...分之...		...fēnzhī...	(the formula of fractions)	56
	分	(动)	fēn	to get a portion of, to divide, to separate	58
	分兒	(名)	fēnr	marks	62
fèn	奋斗	(动)	fèndòu	to struggle, to strive	41
fēng	封	(量)	fēng	(a measure word)	41
	風	(名)	fēng	wind	55
	風景	(名)	fēngjǐng	scenery, landscape	67
fú	服务	(动)	fúwù	to serve	41
fǔ	复杂	(形)	fǔzá	complicated, complex	51
	辅导	(动、名)	fǔdǎo	to help ... to study, help	68
fù	复习	(动)	fùxí	to review	27
	父亲	(名)	fùqīn	father	62

G

| gǎi | 改正 | (动) | gǎizhèng | to correct | 44 |

	改	(动)	gǎi	to correct, to change	50
	改善	(动)	gǎishàn	to improve,	63
gān	干淨	(形)	gānjìng	clean	15
gǎn	赶(車)	(动)	gǎn(chē)	to drive (a cart, or carriage)	61
	感到	(动)	gǎndào	to feel	64
gàn	干	(动)	gàn	to do	43
	干部	(名)	gànbù	cadre	57
gāng	鋼笔	(名)	gāngbǐ 〔枝〕	pen	17
	剛才	(副)	gāngcái	a short time ago	33
	剛	(副)	gāng	just,	50
	鋼	(名)	gāng	steel	65
gāo	高兴	(形)	gāoxìng	glad, happy	20
	高	(形)	gāo	high, tall	61
gào	告訴	(动)	gàosù	to tell, to inform	29
gē	歌兒	(名)	gēr	song	21
	哥(哥)	(名)	gē(gé)	elder brother	37
gé	革命史		gémìngshǐ	history of revolution	46
	革命	(动、名)	gémìng	to take revolution, revolution	50
gè	个	(量)	gè	(a measure word)	14
	各	(代)	gè	every, each	65
gěi	給	(动)	gěi	to give	16
	給	(介)	gěi	for	41
gēn	跟	(介)	gēn	with, after	20
	跟	(动)	gēn	to follow	64
	根据	(介、名)	gēnjù	according to, evidence, authority	71
gèng	更	(副)	gèng	more, further	51
gōng	工作	(动、名)	gōngzuò	to work, work	16
	工厂	(名)	gōngchǎng	factory	23
	工人	(名)	gōngrén	worker	43
	工业	(名)	gōngyè	industry	47

	公社	(名)	gōngshè	commune	63
	公社化	(动)	gōngshèhuà	to communize	63
	公斤	(量)	gōngjīn	kilogram	69
	公里	(量)	gōnglǐ	kilometre	69
	公尺	(量)	gōngchǐ	metre	69
	公园	(名)	gōngyuán	park	70
.gòng	共产主义	(名)	gòngchǎn-zhǔyì	communism	41
	共产党	(名)	gòngchǎndǎng	the communist party	63
	共产党員	(名)	gòngchǎn-dǎngyuán	communist	65
	貢献	(名、动)	gòngxiàn	to offer, contribution	67
gòu	夠	(形)	gòu	sufficient	46
gǔ	鼓掌	(动)	gǔzhǎng	to applaud, to clap (one's hands)	34
	古	(形)	gǔ	ancient	61
gù	故事	(名)	gùshì	story	51
guā	刮	(动)	guā	to blow (the wind blows)	55
guà	掛	(动)	guà	to hang	45
guān	关心	(动、名)	guānxīn	to concern oneself about, concern	45
	关	(动)	guān	to close, to shut	50
	观众	(名)	guānzhòng	audience	57
guāng	光荣	(形)	guāngróng	glorious, glory	69
guǎng	广場	(名)	guǎngchǎng	square	71
guó	国	(名)	guó	country	19
	国家	(名)	guójiā	country	41
guò	过	(动)	guò	to pass, past	25
	过	(尾)	guò	(a suffix)	40
	过	(动)	guò	to pass	52
	过去	(名)	guòqù	the past	71

H

hái	还	(副)	hái	also, too, still	26

	还是	(連)	háishì	or	29
	还是	(副)	háishì	still	49
	孩子	(名)	háizi	child, children	53
hǎi	海	(名)	hǎi	sea	71
hǎn	喊	(动)	hǎn	to shout, to cry	56
hàn	汉字	(名)	hànzì	Chinese character	21
	汉俄		hàn-è	Chinese-Russian	32
hǎo	好	(形)	hǎo	good, well	14
	好看	(形)	hǎokàn	good-looking	26
	好	(动)	hǎo	to recover	39
	好处	(名)	hǎochù	advantage	44
hào	号	(名)	hào	day, number	25
	号召	(动、名)	hàozhāo	to call on, summons	71
hē	喝	(动)	hē	to drink	63
hé	和	(連)	hé	and	17
	合作社	(名)	hézuòshè	co-operative store	37
	合适	(形)	héshì	suitable, proper	51
	和平	(名)	hépíng	peace	67
hēi	黑板	(名)	hēibǎn	blackboard	15
	黑	(形)	hēi	black	71
hěn	很	(副)	hěn	very	14
hóng	红	(形)	hóng	red	49
hòu	后边儿	(名)	hòubiānr	back, the following	23
	后天	(名)	hòutiān	day after tomorrow	50
hú	湖	(名)	hú	lake	61
hù	互相	(副)	hùxiāng	each other, one another, mutually	55
huā	花儿	(名)	huār	flower	45
huà	画报	(名)	huàbào 〔本〕	pictorial	17
	話	(名)	huà	words, speech	21
	話剧	(名)	huàjù	drama, stage-play	35
	画儿	(名)	huàr	picture	45
huài	坏	(形)	huài	bad	43

huān	欢迎	(动、名)	huānyíng	to welcome, welcome	38
huán	还	(动)	huán	to return, to give back	29
huáng	黃	(形)	huáng	yellow	49
huí	回	(动)	huí	to go back, to return	27
	回答	(动、名)	huídá	to answer, to reply	29
huì	会	(动)	huì	to know how to do	17
	会	(能动)	huì	can, may	26
	会	(名)	huì	meeting	38
hūn	昏迷	(动)	hūnmí	to lose consciousness	65
huó	活	(动)	huó	to live	65
huǒ	火車	(名)	huǒchē	train	71
huò	或者	(連)	huòzhě	or	31

J

jī	积極	(形)	jījí	enthusiastic, active	20
	机会	(名)	jīhuì	chance, opportunity	44
	机器	(名)	jīqì〔架〕	machine, machinery	47
	基本	(形)	jīběn	basic, fundamental	68
	基础	(名)	jīchǔ	basis, foundation	68
jí	極了		jíle	very, extremely	39
jǐ	几	(数)	jǐ	how many, several, a few	22
jì	記	(动)	jì	to remember, to take notes, to learn by heart	33
	記	(动)	jì	to take down (in the note-book)	34
	繼續	(动)	jìxù	to continue	34
	寄	(动)	jì	to post, to mail	41
	計划	(名、动)	jìhuà	plan, to plan	44
	紀念	(动、名)	jìniàn	to commemorate, commemoration	71
jiā	家	(名)	jiā	home, family	43
	家庭	(名)	jiātíng	family	62
	加入	(动)	jiārù	to join	62
jià	架	(量)	jià	(a measure word)	63

jiān	間	(量)	jiān	(a measure word)	45
	坚持	(动)	jiānchí	to insist, to maitain, to persist	67
jiǎn	簡單	(形)	jiǎndān	simple	45
	檢查	(动、名)	jiǎnchá	to examine, examination	69
jiàn	件	(量)	jiàn	(a measure word)	31
	見	(动)	jiàn	to see	32
	建設	(动、名)	jiànshè	to construct, construction	41
	健康	(形、名)	jiànkāng	healthy, health	70
jiāng	將	(副)	jiāng	shall, will, about to	49
	將来	(副)	jiānglái	in the future	68
jiǎng	講	(动)	jiǎng	to explain, to give a lecture on, to tell	27
jiāo	教	(动)	jiāo	to teach	16
	交	(动)	jiāo	to hand, to give	34
	交流	(动)	jiāoliú	to exchange	70
jiǎo	角	(量)	jiǎo	ten cents (a measure word)	37
jiào	叫	(动)	jiào	to call, to be called	19
	教室	(名)	jiàoshì	classroom	28
	叫	(动)	jiào	to call, to shout, to let	38
	叫	(介)	jiào	by, to call, to order	65
	教师	(名)	jiàoshī	teacher	70
jiē	接到	(动)	jiēdào	to receive	41
	街	(名)	jiē 〔条	street	49
	結婚	(动)	jiēhūn	to get married	58
	接受	(动)	jiēshòu	to accept, to receive	65
	阶段	(名)	jiēduàn	step, section	68
jié	节	(量)	jié	(a measure word)	28
	节目	(名)	jiémù	performance, item	53
	結果	(名)	jiéguǒ	result, effect, consequence	61
jiě	解放	(动、名)	jiěfàng	to liberate, to set free, liberation	43
	解決	(动、名)	jiějué	to solve, solution	47
	姐姐	(名)	jiějiě	elder sister	62

jiè	借	(动)	jiè	to lend, to borrow	29
	介紹	(动、名)	jièshào	to introduce, introduction	38
jīn	今天	(名)	jīntiān	today	25
	今年	(名)	jīnnián	this year	25
	斤	(量)	jīn	catty	69
jǐn	緊張	(形)	jǐnzhāng	busy, tense, energetic	47
jìn	进	(动)	jìn	to enter	27
	进步	(名、形、动)	jìnbù	progress, progressive, to progress	41
	近	(形)	jìn	near, close	57
jīng	經驗	(名)	jīngyàn	experience	38
	經过	(动、名)	jīngguò	to pass by, to undergo	59
	經常	(形)	jīngcháng	frequent, constant	69
jìng	敬爱	(动)	jìng'ài	to reverence and love	71
jiǔ	九	(数)	jiǔ	nine	72
jiù	旧	(形)	jiù	old	14
	就	(副)	jiù	then, at once	27
	救	(动)	jiù	to save	65
jǔ	举	(动)	jǔ	to hold up, to raise, to lift	56
jù	句子	(名)	jùzî	sentence	27
	剧場	(名)	jùchǎng	theatre	35
	句	(量)	jù	(a measure word)	64
	具体	(形)	jùtǐ	concrete	68
jué	觉得	(动)	juédé	to feel	26
	决定	(动)	juédìng	to decide	50
	觉悟	(名、动)	juéwù	awakening, to awake	70

K

| kāi | 开始 | (动) | kāishǐ | to start, to begin | 28 |
| | 开 | (动) | kāi | to open (a door), to drive (a car) | 33 |

	开演	(动)	kāiyǎn	to perform, to give a performance	35
	开(会)	(动)	kāi(huì)	to hold (a meeting)	38
	开(水)	(动)	kāi(shuǐ)	boiling, boiled (water)	63
kàn	看	(动)	kàn	to see, to look at	16
	看見	(动)	kànjiǎn	to see	32
kǎo	考試	(名)	kǎoshì	to examine, examination	62
kē	棵	(量)	kē	(a measure word)	55
kě	可以	(能 动)	kěyǐ	may	29
	可爱	(形)	kěài	lovable, lovely	69
kè	刻	(名)	kè	a quarter	25
	課	(名)	kè	lesson, class,	28
	課文	(名)	kèwén	text	44
	克服	(动)	kèfú	to overcome	55
	客气	(形)	kèqì	formal, polite	55
kōng	空气	(名)	kōngqì	air	45
kǒu	口号兒	(名)	kǒuhàor	watchword, slogan	56
kuài	快	(形)	kuài	quick, fast	21
	塊	(量)	kuài	(a measure word)	37
	快乐	(形)	kuàilè	happy	62
kùn	困难	(名)	kùnnǎn	difficulty	43

L

lái	来	(动)	lái	to come	16
lán	藍	(形)	lán	blue	49
láo	劳駕		láojià	excuse me, may I trouble you	33
	劳动	(名、动)	láodòng	labour, to labour	43
lǎo	老	(形)	lǎo	old	64
lē	了	(尾、助)	lē	(a suffix and a particle)	27
lèi	累	(形)	lèi	tired, weary, fatigued	58

lěng	冷	(形)	lěng	cold	49
lǐ	里边兒	(名)	lǐbiānr	inside	23
	礼堂	(名)	lǐtáng	auditorium (hall)	23
	礼物	(名)	lǐwù	present	67
	里	(量)	lǐ	lǐ	69
lì	立刻	(副)	lìkè	at once, immediately	45
	历史	(名)	lìshǐ	history	59
	力量	(名)	lìliàng	power, strength	65
	利用	(动)	lìyòng	to make use of, to utilize	67
lián	联欢	(动)	liánhuān	to hold a party, to hold a reunion	41
	連...也(都)		lián...yě (dōu)	even...(too)	64
liǎn	臉	(名)	liǎn	face	59
liàn	練習	(名、动)	liànxí	exercise, to exercise, to practise	22
liáng	凉	(形)	liáng	cool, cold	63
liǎng	两	(数)	liǎng	two	22
liàng	輛	(量)	liàng	(a measure word)	33
	亮	(形)	liàng	bright, light	47
liǎo	了解	(动)	liǎojiě	to understand	35
	了	(动)	liǎo	to complete, to finish, to settle	58
líng	零	(数)	líng	zero, naught	56
lǐng	領导	(动、名)	lǐngdǎo	to lead, leadership, guidance	59
	領袖	(名)	lǐngxiù	leader	69
	領导上	(名)	lǐngdǎoshàng	leading personnel, superiors	70
liū	溜(冰)	(动)	liū(bīng)	to skate	67
liú	流利	(形)	liúlì	fluent	51
	留学生	(名)	liúxuéshēng	student from abroad	69
liù	六	(数)	liù	six	22

lóu	楼	(名)	lóu [座]	building	50
lù	路	(名)	lù [条 tiáo]	road, way, path	61
lǚ	旅行	(动)	lǚxíng	to travel	52
lǜ	綠	(形)	lǜ	green	49

M

mā	嗎	(助)	mā	(an interrogative particle)	13
mǎ	馬	(名)	mǎ [匹]	horse	61
mǎi	买	(动)	mǎi	to buy	26
mài	卖	(动)	mài	to sell	32
mǎn	滿意	(形、动)	mǎnyì	satisfactory, satisfied, to satisfy	59
màn	慢	(形)	màn	slow	21
máng	忙	(形)	máng	busy	25
máo	毛澤东	(名)	Máozédōng	Mao Tse-tung	33
	毛	(量)	máo	(a measure word)	37
	毛衣	(名)	máoyī [件]	woolen knitted garment	49
méi	沒	(副)	méi	not	16
	沒关系		méiguānxì	never mind, it doesn't matter	26
měi	每	(代)	měi	each, every	29
	美	(形)	měi	beautiful	71
mèi	妹妹	(名)	mèiměi	younger sister	51
mén	門	(名)	mén	door	33
	門口兒	(名)	ménkǒur	door, gate, entrance	59
mí	迷信	(动、名)	míxìn	to believe superstitiously in, superstition	65
mián	棉	(形)	mián	cotton	70
mín	民主	(形、名)	mínzhǔ	democratic, democracy	70
	民族	(名)	mínzú	nation, nationality	70
míng	名字	(名)	míngzì	name	19

	明天	(名)	míngtiān	tomorrow	27
mò	默(写)	(动)	mò(xiě)	to write from dictation, to write from memory	64
mǔ	母亲	(名)	mǔqīn	mother	52

N

ná	拿.	(动)	ná	to take	33
nǎ	哪兒	(代)	nǎr	where	20
	哪里	(代)	nàlǐ	where	20
nà	那兒	(代)	nàr	there	20
	那里	(代)	nàlǐ	there	20
nán	难	(形)	nán	difficult	31
	男	(形)	nán	male	56
	南	(名)	nán	south	61
nē	呢	(助)	nē	(a particle)	27
něi	哪	(代)	něi	which	19
nèi	那	(代)	nèi, nà	that	13
nèi	內容	(名)	nèiróng	contents	67
nèn	那么	(副)	nènmò	then, thus	63
néng	能	(能动)	néng	to be able, can	26
	能力	(名)	nénglì	ability	61
nǐ	你	(代)	nǐ	you	13
	你們	(代)	nǐmén	you	15
nián	年	(名)	nián	year	22
	年級	(名)	niánjí	(year) class	37
niàn	念	(动)	niàn	to read	21
nín	您	(代)	nín	(the polite form of 你)	13
nóng	农民	(名)	nóngmín	peasant, farmer	53
	农村	(名)	nóngcūn	village, countryside	63
nǔ	努力	(形)	nǔlì	diligent, strenuous	20
nuǎn	暖和	(形)	nuǎnhé	warm	50
nǚ	女	(形)	nǚ	female	56
	女兒	(名)	nǚér	daughter	58

P

pà	怕	(动)	pà	to be afraid, to fear	57
pái	排	(名)	pái	row, rank	57
pài	派	(动)	pài	to appoint, to send	65
páng	旁边兒	(名)	pángbiānr	side, beside	23
pàng	胖	(形)	pàng	fat	69
pǎo	跑	(动)	pǎo	to run	52
péi	培养	(动)	péiyǎng	to educate, to cherish	70
péng	朋友	(名)	péngyǒu	friend	15
pī	批評	(名、动)	pīpíng	criticism, to criticize	52
piān	篇	(量)	piān	(a measure word)	57
pián	便宜	(形)	piányi	cheap	52
piào	漂亮	(形)	piàoliàng	beautiful, good-looking	53
	票	(名)	piào 〔張〕	ticket	57

Q

qī	七	(数)	qī	seven	22
qí	騎	(动)	qí	to ride, to sit astride	43
	旗(子)	(名)	qí(zi) 〔面〕	flag, banner	61
qǐ	起来	(动)	qǐlái	to get up, to rise	64
qì	汽車	(名)	qìchē 〔輛〕	motor car, automobile	33
qiāo	敲	(动)	qiāo	to knock	40
qiān	鉛笔	(名)	qiānbǐ 〔枝〕	pencil	15
	千	(数)	qiān	thousand	56
qián	前边兒	(名)	qiánbiānr	front	23
	前天	(名)	qiántiān	day before yesterday	35
	錢	(名)	qián	money	37
qiǎn	淺	(形)	qiǎn	light (in colour)	49
	淺	(形)	qiǎn	shallow, easy	57
qiáng	墙	(名)	qiáng	wall	45
qīn	亲爱	(形)	qīn'ài	dear, affectionate	68
	侵略	(动)	qīnlüè	to invade	67

qīng	清楚	(形)	qīngchǔ	clear	27
	青年	(名)	qīngnián	youth	64
	輕	(形)	qīng	light	69
qíng	情况	(名)	qíngkuàng	state, situation, case	35
	晴	(形)	qíng	fine, clear, fair (weather)	68
qǐng	請	(动)	qǐng	please, to ask	38
qiū	秋天	(名)	qiūtiān	autumn	53
qiú	球	(名)	qiú	ball	46
qù	去	(动)	qù	to go	20
	去年	(名)	qùnián	last year	56
quán	全面	(形)	quánmiàn	over-all, whole	39
	全	(形)	qúan	all	56
quàn	劝	(动)	quàn	to advise, to persuade	59
quē	缺点	(名)	quēdiǎn	defect, shortcoming	67
qún	群众	(名)	qúnzhòng	the masses	69

R

ràng	讓	(动)	ràng	to let, to cause	38
	讓	(介)	ràng	by, to let, to yield	65
rè	热	(形)	rè	hot	33
	热烈	(形)	rèliè	warm, enthusiastic	34
	热情	(形)	rèqíng	earnest, zealous	63
	热爱	(动)	rèài	to love ardently	64
rén	人	(名)	rén	man, person	13
	人民	(名)	rénmín	people	19
rèn	認識	(动、名)	rènshí	to know, to recognize	26
	任务	(名)	rènwǔ	mission, task	59
	認为	(动)	rènwéi	to consider	68
rēng	扔	(动)	rēng	to throw	71
rì	日	(名)	rì	day	25
	日記	(名)	rìjì	diary	71
róng	容易	(形)	róngyì	easy	51

S

sān	三	(数)	sān	three	14
sàn	散步	(动)	sànbù	to take a walk	46
	散(会)	(动)	sàn (huì)	to dismiss (a meeting)	67
shān	山	(名)	shān 〔座〕	hill, mountain	58
shāng	伤	(名)	shāng	wound	65
shàng	上边儿	(名)	shàngbiānr	above	23
	上(星期)		shàng(xīngqī)	last (week)	27
	上(课)		shàng(kè)	to go to class, to attend class	28
	上(月)		shàng(yuè)	last month, ultimo	28
	上午	(名)	shàngwǔ	morning, the forenoon	37
	上	(动)	shàng	to go up, to go, to take (a lesson)	46
	…上		…shàng	on, on the side of	70
	上海	(名)	Shànghǎi	Shanghai	71
shāo	烧	(动)	shāo	to burn	65
shǎo	少	(形)	shǎo	few, little	14
shào	少年先锋队	(名)	shàoniánxiānfēngduì	the young pioneers	62
	社会主义	(名)	shèhuìzhǔyì	socialism	41
shè	社员	(名)	shèyuán	member of a co-operative	64
	社长	(名)	shèzhǎng	head of a co-operative	70
shéi	谁	(代)	shéi	who	19
shēn	身体	(名)	shēntǐ	body	39
	深	(形)	shēn	deep, dark (in colour)	49
	深	(形)	shēn	profound, deep (in meaning)	51
shén	什么	(代)	shénmǒ	what	19

	什么的	(代)	shénmŏdě	etc, and others	46
shēng	生詞	(名)	shēngcí	new word	29
	生产	(动)	shēngchǎn	to produce	47
	生活	(名、动)	shēnghuó	life, to live	58
	生	(动)	shēng	to be born	72
shèng	胜利	(名、动)	shènglì	victory, to triumgh (over)	63
shí	十	(数)	shí	ten	22
	时候兒	(名)	shíhòur	time	25
	时间	(名)	shíjiān	time	43
	食堂	(名)	shítáng	dining hall, refectory	50
	石头	(名)	shítŏu 〔块〕	stone	71
shì	是	(动)	shì	to be	13
	事(情)	(名)	shì(qíng) 〔件〕	matter, business	31
	試	(动)	shì	to try	44
	世界	(名)	shìjiè	world, earth	71
shōu	收	(动)	shōu	to harvest, to gather	53
	收入	(动、名)	shōurù	to get an income, income	64
	收拾	(动)	shōushi	to put in order, to tidy up	69
shŏu	首都	(名)	shŏudū	capital	35
	手	(名)	shŏu 〔只〕	hand	64
shòu	受	(动)	shòu	to suffer	58
	瘦	(形)	shòu	lean, thin	69
shū	書	(名)	shū	book	13
	書店	(名)	shūdiàn	bookstore	31
	舒服	(形)	shūfú	comfortable	40
shú	熟	(形)	shú	well versed, well acquainted	44
shù	树	(名)	shù 〔棵〕	tree	52
	数目	(名)	shùmù	number	56
shuǐ	水菓	(名)	shuǐguŏ 〔斤〕	fruit	37

	水平	(名)	shuǐpíng	level, standard	57
	水	(名)	shuǐ	water, river	59
	水灾	(名)	shuǐzāi	calamity caused by flood	59
shuì	睡	(动)	shuì	to sleep	46
	睡觉	(动)	shuìjiào	to sleep	46
shuō	說(話)	(动)	shuō(huà)	to speak	21
sī	思想	(名)	sīxiǎng	thought, thinking, mind	65
sǐ	死	(动)	sǐ	to die	59
sì	四	(数)	sì	four	22
sòng	送	(动)	sòng	to send, to present, to see off	47
sū	苏联	(名)	Sūlián	the Soviet Union	19
sù	宿舍	(名)	sùshè	dormitory, hostel	23
suí	虽然... 但是...		suírán...dàn shì...	although... (yet)...	31
suì	岁	(量)	suì	year (a measure word)	31
suǒ	所有(的)	(形)	suǒyǒu(dé)	all	50

T

tā	他	(代)	tā	he, him	13
	他們	(代)	tāmén	they, them	15
	她	(代)	tā	she, her	15
	它	(代)	tā	it	15
tái	台	(名)	tái	platform, rostrum	34
tài	太	(副)	tài	too	21
	态度	(名)	tàidù	attitude	61
tán	談	(动)	tán	to talk, to tell	38
táng	糖	(名)	táng 〔塊、斤〕	sugar, candy	37
tǎng	躺	(动)	tǎng	to lie	45
tǎo	討論	(动、名)	tǎolùn	to discuss, discussion	38
tè	特別	(形)	tèbié	special, particular	28
	特点	(名)	tèdiǎn	characteristic, feature	51

téng	疼	(动)	téng	to ache, to feel pain	39
tí	提	(动)	tí	to raise, to express	38
	提前	(副)	tíqián	ahead of (schedule), in advance, to give precedence to	47
	提高	(动)	tígāo	to raise, to heighten	62
tì	替	(动、介)	tì	to replace, to substitute, instead of, for...	41
tiān	天	(名)	tiān	day	25
	天气	(名)	tiānqì	weather	49
	天	(名)	tiān	day	51
	天安門	(名)	Tiān'ānmén	Tien-An-Men	71
tiáo	条	(量)	tiáo	(a measure word)	61
	条件	(名)	tiáojiàn	condition	61
tiào	跳(舞)	(动)	tiào(wǔ)	to dance	21
	跳	(动)	tiào	to pulsate, to jump	71
tiě	鉄	(名)	tiě	iron	65
tīng	听	(动)	tīng	to hear, to listen to	26
	听見	(动)	tīngjiàn	to hear	32
tíng	停	(动)	tíng	to stop	40
tōng	通知	(动、名)	tōngzhī	to inform, information	38
tóng	同志	(名)	tóngzhì	comrade	15
	同屋	(名)	tóngwū	room-mate	19
	同学	(名)	tóngxué	school-mate	35
	同意	(动)	tóngyì	to agree, agreement	67
tóu	头	(名)	tóu	head	39
	头髮	(名)	tóufà	hair	58
tú	圖書館	(名)	túshūguǎn	library	23
tuán	团結	(动、名)	tuánjié	to consolidate, to unite, consolidation	55
tuī	推	(动)	tuī	to push	55

W

| wài | 外边儿 | (名) | wàibiānr | outside | 23 |

	外国	(名)	wàiguó	foreign country	53
wán	玩兒	(动)	wánr	to play, to amuse one-self	31
	完	(动)	wán	to finish	32
	完成	(动)	wánchéng	to complete, to fulfil	47
	完全	(副)	wánquán	completely	52
wǎn	晚	(形)	wǎn	late	21
	晚上	(名)	wǎnshàng	night, evening	31
	晚飯	(名)	wǎnfàn	evening meal, supper	35
	晚会	(名)	wǎnhuì	evening party	40
wàn	万	(数)	wàn	ten thousand	56
	万岁		wànsuì	long live...	56
wǎng	往	(介)	wǎng	towards, to	61
wàng	忘	(动)	wàng	to forget	34
wěi	偉大	(形)	wěidà	great, magnificent	47
wèi	为什么		wèishénmǒ	for what, why	31
	为	(介)	wèi	for	41
wén	文化	(名)	wénhuà	culture	51
	文章	(名)	wénzhāng〔篇〕	article, essay	57
	文献	(名)	wénxiàn	literature	65
wèn	問	(动)	wèn	to ask, to inquire	29
	問題	(名)	wèntí	question, problem	29
wǒ	我	(代)	wǒ	I, me	13
	我們	(代)	wǒmén	we, us	15
wū	屋子	(名)	wūzî〔間〕	room	45
wú	无綫电	(名)	wúxiàndiàn	radio	46
wǔ	五	(数)	wǔ	five	22
	五四	(名)	Wǔsì	May 4th	70
wù	勿	(副)	wù	don't	55

X

xī	希望	(动、名)	xīwàng	to hope, hope	39
	吸	(动)	xī	to smoke, to inhale	55
	牺牲	(动、名)	xīshēng	to sacrifice, sacrifice	71

xí	習慣	(名、形)	xíguàn	habit, habitual	51
xǐ	喜欢	(动)	xǐhuān	to like, to be fond of	20
	洗	(动)	xǐ	to wash	53
	喜兒	(名)	Xǐ'ér	(a proper name)	58
xì	戏	(名)	xì 〔出〕	play, opera	58
xià	下边兒	(名)	xiàbiānr	below, the following	23
	下(星期)		xià(xīngqī)	next (week)	27
	下(課)		xià(kè)	the class is over, after class	28
	下午	(名)	xiàwǔ	afternoon	34
	下兒	(量)	xiàr	(a measure word)	40
	夏天	(名)	xiàtiān	summer	53
	下(雪)	(动)	xià(xuě)	to fall, to snow	55
xiān	先生	(名)	xiānsheng	teacher, Mr., sir	13
	先...再...		xiān...zài...	first...then	41
xiàn	现在	(名)	xiànzài	now, at present	25
xiāng	箱子	(名)	xiāngzi	box, trunk	61
xiǎng	想	(动、能动)	xiǎng	to think, to want, to intend	29
xiàng	像	(动)	xiàng	to resemble	51
	像片兒	(名)	xiàngpiānr 〔張〕	photograph, snapshot	58
	向	(介)	xiàng	from, towards	71
xiǎo	小	(形)	xiǎo	little, small	14
	小說兒	(名)	xiǎoshuōr 〔本〕	novel	29
	小組	(名)	xiǎozǔ	group	43
	小时	(名)	xiǎoshí	hour	46
	小学	(名)	xiǎoxué	primary school	62
xiào	笑	(动)	xiào	to smile	45
	校园	(名)	xiàoyuán	campus	50
xiē	些	(量)	xiē	some	19
xiě	写	(动)	xiě	to write	21
xiè	謝謝		xièxiè	to thank, thanks	29

xīn	新	(形)	xīn	new	14
	新闻	(名)	xīnwén	news	46
	心	(名)	xīn	heart	71
xìn	信	(名)	xìn〔封〕	letter	41
	信心	(名)	xìnxīn	confidence	68
xīng	星期	(名)	xīngqī	week	25
	兴奋	(形)	xīngfèn	excited	56
xǐng	醒	(动)	xǐng	to wake up, to return to consciousness	65
xìng	幸福	(形)	xìngfú	happy	58
xiū	休息	(动)	xiūxi	rest, to take a rest	28
	修理	(动)	xiūlǐ	to repair	57
	修	(动)	xiū	to build, to repair	69
xū	需要	(动、名)	xūyào	to need, to require, necessity, needs	50
xuǎn	选	(动)	xuǎn	to elect, to choose, to select	65
xué	学生	(名)	xuésheng	student	13
	学习	(动)	xuéxí	to study	16
	学	(动)	xué	to learn, to study	19
	学校	(名)	xuéxiào	school	20
xuě	雪	(名)	xuě	snow	55

Y

yā	压迫	(动)	yāpò	to oppress, oppression	58
yān	烟	(名)	yān〔枝，包〕	cigarette, smoke	55
	淹	(动)	yān	to drown, to overflow	59
yán	颜色	(名)	yánsè	colour	45
	研究	(动、名)	yánjiū	to study, to research, study	53
	严格	(形)	yángé	strict	68
yǎn	演员	(名)	yǎnyuán	actor, actress	35
	演	(动)	yǎn	to perform, to play the role of...	35

yàng	样兒	(名)	yàngr	shape, sort, style	37
	样子	(名)	yàngzi	sort, kind, style	43
yāo	要求	(动、名)	yāoqiú	to ask, to demand, demand	68
yào	要	(动、能动)	yào	to want, should	26
	要是...就...		yàoshì...jiù...	if, (then)	31
	藥	(名)	yào	medicine	39
yě	也	(副)	yě	also, too	17
	也...也		yě...yě...	(compound connective)	38
	也許	(副)	yěxǔ	perhaps, probably	39
yè	叶子	(名)	yèzi	leaves (leaf)	52
	頁	(量)	yè	(a measure word)	62
yī	一	(数)	yī	a, one	14
	医院	(名)	yīyuàn	hospital	39
	衣服	(名)	yīfú 〔件〕	clothes, dress	43
	医学	(名)	yīxué	medical science	65
yí	一定	(副)	yídìng	certainly	21
	一共	(副)	yígòng	totally, altogether	37
	一样	(形)	yíyàng	the same	51
	一塊兒	(副)	yíkuàir	together	52
	一...就...		yí...jiù...	as soon as, no sooner... than	59
yǐ	椅子	(名)	yǐzi 〔把〕	chair	17
	以后	(副)	yǐhòu	afterwards	26
	已經	(副)	yǐjing	already	28
	以前	(副)	yǐqían	in the past, ago, before	34
yì	一起	(副)	yìqǐ	together	20
	意見	(名)	yìjiàn	opinion	38
	意思	(名)	yìsi	meaning	40
	一会兒		yìhuǐr	a while, a few moments	50
	义务	(名)	yìwù	voluntary (labour for public interests), duty	50

	一直		yìzhí	up to the present, straight ahead	62
	亿	(数)	yì	hundred million	56
yīn	因为...所以		yīnwèi...suǒyǐ	because (owing to) ... therefore (so)...	32
	音乐	(名)	yīnyuè	music	57
yìn	印象	(名)	yìnxiàng	impression	64
yīng	应該	(能动)	yīnggāi	should, ought	26
	英勇	(形)	yīngyǒng	heroic, brave	70
	英雄	(名)	yīngxióng	hero	71
yōng	拥护	(动)	yōnghù	to support, to uphold	68
yǒng	永远	(副)	yǒngyuǎn	forever, eternally	64
yòng	用	(动)	yòng	to use	26
yóu	遊行	(名、动)	yóuxíng	demonstration, to demonstrate, to parade	56
yǒu	有	(动)	yǒu	to have	16
	有意思		yǒuyìsi	interesting	17
	有的		yǒudè	some	39
	有名	(形)	yǒumíng	famous, noted	40
yòu	又	(副)	yòu	again, too	37
	又...又..		yòu...yòu...	(compound connective)	38
	又	(副)	yòu	again, too	52
yú	愉快	(形)	yúkuài	cheerful, happy	47
yǔ	語法	(名)	yǔfǎ	grammar	27
	語言	(名)	yǔyán	language, speech	51
	雨	(名)	yǔ	rain	55
	語音	(名)	yǔyīn	phonetics, speech sound	68
yù	遇見	(动)	yùjiàn	to meet, to come across	37
	預習	(动)	yùxí	to prepare (lessons)	46
yuán	元	(量)	yuán	dollar (a measure word)	37
	原諒	(动)	yuánliàng	to pardon, to excuse	68
yuǎn	远	(形)	yuǎn	distant, far	57
yuàn	願意	(能动)	yuànyì	will, to be willing	67

yuè	月	(名)	yuè	month	25
	越...越...		yuè...yuè...	the more ... the more	59
yùn	运动	(名、动)	yùndòng	movement, physical exercise, sport; to move, to take physical exercise	70

Z

zá	杂誌	(名)	zázhì〔本〕	magazine	17
zài	在	(动)	zài	to be, on, in, at	23
	再	(副)	zài	again, once more, any more	52
	在...下		zài...xià	under	65
	在...上		zài...shàng	on	68
zàn	赞成	(动)	zànchéng	to approve	71
zāng	髒	(形)	zāng	dirty	57
zǎo	早	(形)	zǎo	early	21
	早上	(名)	zǎoshǎng	morning	41
zěn	怎么样	(代)	zěnmǒyàng	how (is it)	19
	怎么	(代)	zěnmǒ	how	31
zèn	这么	(代)	zènmǒ	such, so	31
zēng	增加	(动)	zēngjiā	to increase	56
zhǎn	展览	(名、动)	zhǎnlǎn	exhibition, to exhibit	67
zhàn	站	(动)	zhàn	to stand	33
	占	(动)	zhàn	to amount to, to take possession of	65
	战争	(名)	zhànzhēng	war	67
zhāng	張	(量)	zhāng	(a measure word)	14
zhǎng	掌握	(动)	zhǎngwò	to master	51
	長	(动)	zhǎng	to grow	64
zhāo	着急	(动)	zhāojí	to be anxious, to be impatient	57
zháo	着	(动)	zháo	to catch, to touch, (always used as a complement)	32

zhǎo	找	(动)	zhǎo	to find, to seek, to look for	32
	找	(动)	zhǎo	to return (change), to look for	37
zhào	照(像)	(动)	zhào(xiàng)	to photograph, to take a photograph	58
zhē	着	(尾)	zhē	(a suffix)	45
zhě	(劳动)者	(尾)	(láodòng)zhě	(labour)er	70
zhè	这儿	(代)	zhèr	here	20
	这里	(代)	zhèli	here	20
zhèi	这	(代)	zhèi, zhè	this	13
zhēn	真	(形)	zhēn	real, really	50
zhèng	正	(副)	zhèng	just (a word indicating progressive aspect	44
	正确	(形)	zhèngquè	correct	44
	政府	(名)	zhèngfú	government	68
zhī	枝	(量)	zhī	(a measure word)	15
	知道	(动)	zhīdào	to know	19
	织	(动)	zhī	to knit, to weave	53
zhǐ	纸	(名)	zhǐ 〔张〕	paper	14
	只	(副)	zhǐ	only	16
	只要...就...		zhǐyào...jiù...	if only ... (then)	59
zhì	治	(动)	zhì	to cure, to heal	40
zhōng	中国	(名)	Zhōngguó	China, Chinese	13
	中文	(名)	zhōngwén	the Chinese language	16
	中间儿	(名)	zhōngjiànr	middle	23
	钟	(名)	zhōng	clock, bell	40
	钟头	(名)	zhōngtóu	hour	44
	中华人民共和国		Zhōnghuárénmin gònghéguó	The People's Republic of China	56
	终于	(副)	zhōngyú	at last, eventually	71
zhǒng	种	(量)	zhǒng	(a measure word)	34
zhòng	重要	(形)	zhòngyào	important	34

	重	(形)	zhòng	heavy	52
	种	(动)	zhòng	to sow, to plant, to cultivate	64
	重视	(动)	zhòngshì	to attach importance to, to respect highly	69
zhǔ	主席	(名)	zhǔxí	chairman	32
	主任	(名)	zhǔrèn	head (of an organization)	70
zhù	住	(动)	zhù	to live, to dwell	28
	注意	(动、名)	zhùyì	to take care, to pay attention, attention	44
	祝	(动)	zhù	to bless, to pray	68
zhuān	专业	(名)	zhuānyè	special field	31
zhuāng	庄稼	(名)	zhuāngjià	crops, grain	59
zhuī	追	(动)	zhuī	to run after, to catch up, to overtake	58
zhuō	桌子	(名)	zhuōzi〔张〕	table	17
zhǔn	准备	(动、名)	zhǔnbèi	to prepare, preparation	38
zī	资本主义	(名)	zīběnzhǔyì	capitalism	65
zì	字典	(名)	zìdiǎn	dictionary	26
	字	(名)	zì	character	28
	自己	(代)	zìjǐ	oneself, self	38
	自行车	(名)	zìxíngchē〔辆〕	bicycle	43
	自学	(动)	zìxué	to study by oneself	46
zǒu	走	(动)	zǒu	to go, to walk	34
zǔ	组织	(动、名)	zǔzhī	to organize, organization	41
	祖国	(名)	zǔguó	fatherland	47
	组长	(名)	zǔzhǎng	group-leader	68
zuì	最后	(副)	zuìhòu	finally, last	47
	最	(副)	zuì	most	51
	最近	(形)	zuìjìn	recent	53
zuó	昨天	(名)	zuótiān	yesterday	27
zuò	作	(动)	zuò	to do, to make, to work, to be	23

坐	(动)	zuò	to sit	33
座位	(名)	zuòwèi	seat	40
座	(量)	zuò	(a measure word)	50

Table of Chinese Characters and Their Combinations
(Appendix 2)

(The number in parenthesis before each word represents the number of each lesson in which the word appears.)

A

ā   啊: (63) 啊

āi   唉: (69) 唉

ài   爱: (53) 爱; (58) 爱人; (64) 热爱; (68) 亲爱; (69) 可爱; (71) 敬爱

ān   安: (55) 安静; (71) 天安門

B

bā   八: (22) 八; (58) 八 (bá) 路軍

       吧: (50) 吧

bǎ   把: (17, 47) 把

bái   白: (45) 白; (58) 白毛女

bǎi   百: (49) 百货大楼; (56) 百

bān   搬: (33) 搬

       班: (35, 71) 班

bǎn   板: (15) 黑板

bàn   半: (22) 半

       办: (32) 怎么办; (59) 办法; (65) 办

bāng   帮: (28) 帮助

bāo   包: (49, 53) 包

bǎo   饱: (62) 饱

bào   报: (13) 报; (17) 画报; (34) 报告

bēi   杯: (63) 杯; (65) 杯子

       碑: (71) 碑

běi   北: (14) 北京; (17) 北京大学; (61) 北

bèi 备: (38) 准备
倍: (56) 倍
背: (64) 背
被: (65) 被

běn 本: (14) 本; (16) 本子; (65) 資本主义; (68) 基本

bǐ 笔: (15) 鉛笔; (17) 鋼笔
比: (51) 比較; (62) 比

bì 必: (29) 必須
畢: (65) 畢业

biān 边: (23) 里边兒、外边兒、上边兒、下边兒、前边兒、后边兒、旁边兒; (70) 边兒

biàn 便: (43) 方便
遍: (52) 遍

biǎo 表: (40) 表; (46) 表演; (53) 代表

bié 别: (28) 特别; (45) 别的; (55) 别

bīng 冰: (67) 溜 (冰)、冰

bìng 病: (39) 病
并: (43) 并且

bō 播: (53) 播送

bù 不: (13) 不; (35) 差不多; (40) 对不起; (59) 不 (bú) 但; (63) 不断
步: (41) 进步; (46) 散步
部: (57) 干部; (70) 部分

C

cái 才: (33) 剛才; (44) 才

cān 参: (40) 参加; (47) 参观

cāo 操: (70) 操場

chá 查: (40) 查; (69) 檢查
茶: (55) 茶

chà 差: (25) 差; (35) 差不多

chǎn 产: (41) 共产主义; (47) 生产; (63) 共产党; (65) 共产党員

cháng 長: (15) 長
常: (21) 常常; (34) 非常; (69) 經常

chǎng 厂: (23) 工厂
場: (35) 剧場; (70) 操場; (71) 广場

chàng 唱: (21) 唱 (歌兒)

chāo 抄: (64) 抄 (写)
超: (70) 超额

chē 車: (32) 汽車; (43) 自行車; (47) 車間; (61) 車; (71) 火車
chéng 城: (27) 城; (69) 城市
　　　 成: (39) 成; (47) 完成; (71) 贊成
chī 吃: (35) 吃
chí 持: (67) 坚持
chǐ 尺: (69) 尺、公尺
chū 出: (35) 出發; (37) 出
chú 除: (61) 除了
chǔ 楚: (27) 清楚; (61) 楚国
　　　 础: (68) 基础
chù 处: (44) 好处
chuān 穿: (43) 穿
chuán 船: (63) 船
　　　 傳: (61) 傳說; (70) 傳統
chuāng 窗: (33) 窗戶
chuáng 床: (45) 床
chuàng 創: (67) 創造
chūn 春: (50) 春天; (58) 大春
cí 詞: (27) 詞彙; (29) 生詞; (49) 詞
cì 次: (40) 次
cóng 从: (20) 从; (27) 从前; (63) 从来
cūn 村: (63) 农村
cuò 錯: (33) 錯; (44) 錯誤

D

dá 答: (29) 回答
dǎ 打: (46) 打(球)
dà 大: (14) 大; (17) 北京大学; (35) 大家; (44) 大声兒; (47) 偉大;
　　　　 (49) 百货大楼; (58) 大春; (59) 大禹; (69) 大概
dài 带: (34) 带; (40) 带
　　　 大: (39) 大夫
　　　 代: (53) 代表
dān 單: (45) 簡單
dàn 但: (31) 但是; (59) 不但
dāng 当: (46) 当然; (70) 当
dǎng 党: (63) 共产党; (65) 共产党员
dǎo 倒: (55) 倒
　　　 导: (59) 領导; (68) 輔导; (70) 領导上
dào 道: (19) 知道
　　　 到: (28, 33) 到; (41) 接到; (64) 感到

	倒: (55) 倒
dē	的: (15) 的; (39) 有的; (45) 别的; (46) 什么的; (50) 所有(的)
	地: (20) 地
	得: (21) 得
dé	得: (26) 觉得; (62) 得; (63) 懂得
děng	等: (63) 等
dī	低: (57) 低
dì	地: (23) 地方; (53) 地主、地
	第: (37) 第
	弟: (67) 弟弟
diǎn	点: (25) 点(鐘); (31) 点兒; (51) 特点; (65) 点; (67) 缺点
	典: (26) 字典
diàn	电: (20) 电影; (46) 无綫电
	店: (31) 書店
diào	掉: (33) 掉
dìng	定: (21) 一定; (50) 决定
	訂: (44) 訂
diū	丢: (47) 丢
dōng	东: (26) 东西; (32) 毛澤东
	冬: (49) 冬天
dǒng	懂: (19) 懂;
dòng	动: (43) 劳动; (58) 动; (70) 运动、(劳动)者
	冻: (64) 冻
dōu	都: (17) 都
dòu	斗: (41) 奋斗
dū	都: (35) 首都
dù	度: (61) 态度
duǎn	短: (15) 短
duàn	鍛: (43) 鍛鍊
	段: (68) 阶段
duì	对: (17) 对了; (29, 68) 对; (40) 对不起; (67) 反对; (68) 对(于)
	队: (56) 队伍; (62) 少年先鋒队
duō	多: (14) 多; (22) 多少; (35) 差不多; (69) 多 (duó) (么)

E

é	额: (70) 超额
è	俄: (15) 俄文; (32) 汉俄
	餓: (59) 餓

ér　兒：(20)那兒、这兒、哪兒；(21)唱（歌兒）、歌兒；(23)里边兒、外
　　　　边兒、上边兒、下边兒、中間兒、前边兒、后边兒、旁边兒；
　　　　(25)时候兒；(29)小說兒；(31)点兒、玩兒；(37)样兒；(40)下
　　　　兒；(44)大声兒；(45)花兒、画兒；(50)一会兒；(52)一块兒；
　　　　(56)口号兒；(59)門口兒；(62)分兒；(70)边兒
　　　　(58)女兒、喜兒

　　　而：(59)而且

èr　二：(22)二

F

fā　發：(35)出發；(39)發展；(44)發音；(59)發生；(67)發明
fǎ　髮：(58)头髮
　　　法：(27)語法；(29)方法；(59)办法
fān　翻：(28)翻譯
fǎn　反：(67)反对
fàn　飯：(35)晚飯；(43)飯
　　　犯：(52)犯
fāng　方：(23)地方；(29)方法；(38)方面；(43)方便；(61)方向
fǎng　訪：(64)訪問
fàng　放：(43)解放；(45)放；(52)放假
fēi　非：(34)非常
　　　飞：(63)飞机
fēn　分：(25, 37, 58)分；(56)…分之…；(62)分兒；(70)部分
fèn　奋：(41)奋斗；(56)兴奋
fēng　封：(41)封
　　　風：(55)風；(67)風景
　　　鋒：(62)少年先鋒队
fū　夫：(39)大夫
fú　服：(40)舒服；(41)服务；(43)衣服；(55)克服
　　　福：(58)幸福
fǔ　府：(68)政府
　　　輔：(68)輔导
fù．复：(27)复习；(51)复(fú)杂
　　　父：(62)父亲

G

gāi　該：(26)应該
gǎi　改：(44)改正；(50)改；(63)改善

gài   概: (57) 大概

gān   干: (15) 干淨; (43) 干 (gàn); (57) 干 (gàn); 部

gǎn   赶: (61) 赶 (車)

      感: (64) 感到

gāng   鋼: (17) 鋼笔; (65) 鋼

      剛: (33) 剛才; (50) 剛

gāo   高: (20) 高兴; (61) 高; (62) 提高

gào   告: (29) 告訴; (34) 报告

gē   歌: (21) 唱 (歌兒)、歌兒

      哥: (37) 哥(哥)

gé   革: (46) 革命史; (50) 革命

      格: (68) 严格

gè   个: (14) 个

      各: (65) 各

gěi   給: (16, 41) 給

gēn   跟: (20, 64) 跟

      根: (71) 根据

gèng   更: (51) 更

gōng   工: (16) 工作; (23) 工厂; (37) 工人; (47) 工业

      公: (63) 公社; 公社化; (69) 公斤、公里、公尺; (70) 公园

gòng   共: (37) 一共; (41) 共产主义; (56) 中华人民共和国; (63) 共产党; (65) 共产党員

      貢: (67) 貢献

gòu   够: (46) 够

gǔ   鼓: (34) 鼓掌

      古: (61) 古

gù   故: (51) 故事

guā   刮: (55) 刮

guà   掛: (45) 掛

guān   关: (26) 沒关系; (45) 关心; (50) 关

      观: (47) 参观; (57) 观众

guǎn   館: (23) 圖書館

guàn   慣: (51) 習慣

guāng   光: (69) 光荣

guǎng   广: (71) 广场

guó   国: (13) 中国; (19) 国; (41) 国家; (47) 祖国; (53) 外国; (56) 中华人民共和国; (61) 楚国

guǒ 菓: (37) 水菓
果: (61) 結果
guò 过: (25, 40, 52) 过; (59) 經过; (71) 过去

H

hái 还: (26) 还; (29, 49) 还是
孩: (58) 孩子
hǎi 海: (71) 海、上海
hǎn 喊: (56) 喊
hàn 汉: (21) 汉字; (32) 汉俄
hǎo 好: (14) 好; (26) 好看; (39) 好; (44) 好处
hào 号: (25) 号; (56) 口号兒; (71) 号召
hē 喝: (63) 喝
hé 和: (17) 和; (50) 暖和; (56) 中华人民共和国; (67) 和平
合: (37) 合作社; (51) 合适; (63) 合作化
hēi 黑: (15) 黑板; (71) 黑
hěn 很: (14) 很
hóng 紅: (49) 紅
hòu 后: (23) 后边兒; (26) 以后; (47) 最后; (50) 后天
候: (25) 时候兒
hú 湖: (61) 湖
hù 戶: (33) 窗戶
互: (55) 互相
护: (68) 拥护
huā 花: (45) 花兒
huá 华: (56) 中华人民共和国
huà 画: (17) 画报; (45) 画兒
話: (21) 說(話)、話; (35) 話剧
划: (44) 計划
化: (51) 文化; (63) 合作化
huài 坏: (43) 坏
huān 欢: (20) 喜欢; (38) 欢迎; (41) 联欢
huán 还: (29) 还
huáng 黃: (49) 黃
huí 回: (27) 回; (29) 回答
huì 会: (17, 26, 38) 会; (38) 开(会); (40) 晚会; (41) 社会主义; (44)
机会; (50) 一会兒 (huǐr); (67) 散(会)
彙: (27) 詞彙

hūn 婚: (58) 結婚
     昏: (65) 昏迷
huó 活: (58) 生活; (65) 活
huǒ 火: (71) 火車
huò 或: (31) 或者
     貨: (49) 百貨大楼

J

jī   积: (20) 积極
     机: (44) 机会; (47) 机器; (63) 飞机
     基: (68) 基本、基础
jí   極: (20) 积極; (39) 極了
     級: (37) 年級
     急: (57) 着急
jǐ   几: (22) 几
     己: (38) 自己
jì   記: (33, 34) 記; (71) 日記
     繼: (34) 繼續
     寄: (41) 寄
     計: (44) 計划
     紀: (71) 紀念
jiā 家: (35) 大家; (41) 国家; (43) 家; (62) 家庭
     加: (40) 参加; (56) 增加; (62) 加入
jià 駕: (33) 劳駕
     假: (52) 放假
     稼: (59) 庄稼
     架: (63) 架
jiān 間: (23) 中間 (jiàn) 兒; (43) 时間; (45) 間; (47) 車間
     坚: (67) 坚持
jiǎn 簡: (45) 簡單
     檢: (69) 檢查
jiàn 件: (31) 件; (61) 条件
     見: (32) 見、看見、听見、遇見; (38) 意見
     建: (41) 建設
     健: (70) 健康
jiāng 将: (49) 将; (68) 将来

jiǎng	講:	(27) 講
jiāo	交:	(34) 交; (70) 交流
jiǎo	角:	(37) 角
	較:	(51) 比較
jiào	教:	(16) 教 (jiāo); (28) 教室; (70) 教师
	叫:	(19, 38, 65) 叫
	觉:	(46) 睡觉
jiē	接:	(41) 接到; (65) 接受
	街:	(49) 街
	阶:	(68) 阶段
jié	結:	(55) 团結; (58) 結 (jiē) 婚; (61) 結果
	节:	(28) 节; (53) 节目
jiě	解:	(35) 了解; (43) 解放; (47) 解决
	姐:	(62) 姐姐
jiè	借:	(29) 借
	介:	(38) 介紹
	界:	(63) 世界
jīn	今:	(25) 今天、今年
	斤:	(69) 斤、公斤
jǐn	紧:	(47) 紧張
jìn	进:	(27) 进; (41) 进步
	近:	(53) 最近; (57) 近
jing	京:	(14) 北京; (17) 北京大学
	經:	(28) 已經; (38) 經驗; (58) 經过; (69) 經常
jǐng	景:	(67) 風景
jìng	淨:	(15) 干淨
	靜:	(55) 安靜
	敬:	(71) 敬爱
jiū	究:	(53) 研究
jiǔ	九:	(22) 九
jiù	旧:	(14) 旧
	就:	(27) 就
	救:	(65) 救
jǔ	举:	(56) 举
jù	句:	(27) 句子; (64) 句
	剧:	(35) 話剧、剧場
	具:	(68) 具体
	据:	(71) 根据

jué 覺: (26) 覺得; (70) 覺悟

決: (47) 解決; (50) 決定

jūn 軍: (58) 八路軍

K

kāi 开: (28) 开始; (33) 开; (35) 开演; (38) 开 (会); (63) 开 (水)

kàn 看: (16) 看; (26) 好看; (32) 看見

kāng 康: (70) 健康

kǎo 考: (62) 考試

kē 棵: (55) 棵

kě 可: (29) 可以; (69) 可爱

kè 刻: (25) 刻; (45) 立刻

課: (28) 上 (課)、下 (課)、課; (44) 課文

克: (55) 克服

客: (55) 客气

kōng 空: (45) 空气

kǒu 口: (56) 口号兒; (59) 門口兒

kuài 快: (21) 快; (47) 愉快; (62) 快乐

塊: (37) 塊; (52) 一塊兒

kuàng 況: (35) 情況

kùn 困: (43) 困难

L

lái 来: (16) 来; (63) 从来; (64) 起来; (68) 将来

lán 藍: (49) 藍

lǎn 覽: (67) 展覽

láo 劳: (33) 劳駕; (43) 劳动; (70) (劳动)者

lǎo 老: (64) 老

le 了: (17) 对了; (27) 了; (39) 極了; (61) 除了

lè 乐: (62) 快乐

lèi 累: (58) 累

lěng 冷: (49) 冷

lǐ 里: (20) 那里、这里、哪里; (23) 里边兒; (69) 里、公里

礼: (23) 礼堂; (67) 礼物

理: (57) 修理

lì 立: (45) 立刻

历: (59) 历史

力: (19) 努力; (61) 能力; (65) 力量

利: (51) 流利; (63) 胜利; (67) 利用

lián 联: (19) 苏联; (41) 联欢

連: (64) 連

liǎn 脸: (59) 脸

liàn 練: (22) 練習

鍊: (43) 鍛鍊

liáng 凉: (63) 凉

liǎng 两: (22) 两

liàng 輛: (33) 輛

亮: (47) 亮; (53) 漂亮

量: (63) 产量、力量

諒: (68) 原諒

liáo 了: (35) 了解; (58) 了

liè 烈: (34) 热烈

líng 零: (56) 零

lǐng 領: (59) 領导; (69) 領袖; (70) 領导上

liū 溜: (67) 溜 (冰)

liú 留: (69) 留学生

流: (51) 流利; (70) 交流

liù 六: (22) 六

lóu 楼: (49) 百货大楼; (50) 楼

lù 路: (58) 八路軍; (61) 路

lùn 論: (38) 討論

lǚ 旅: (52) 旅行

lù 綠: (49) 綠

M

mā 嗎: (13) 嗎

mǎ 馬: (61) 馬

mǎi 买: (26) 买

mài 卖: (32) 卖

mǎn 滿: (59) 滿意

màn 慢: (21) 慢

máng 忙: (25) 忙

máo 毛: (32) 毛澤东; (37) 毛; (49) 毛衣; (58) 白毛女

méi 沒: (16) 沒; (26) 沒关系

měi 每: (29) 每

美: (71) 美

mèi	妹:	(51) 妹妹
mén	們:	(15) 我們、你們、他們
	門:	(33) 門；(59) 門口兒: (71) 天安門
mí	迷:	(65) 昏迷；迷信
mián	棉:	(70) 棉
miàn	面:	(38) 方面；(39) 全面
mín	民:	(19) 人民；(53) 农民；(56) 中华人民共和国；(70) 民主、民族
míng	名:	(19) 名字；(40) 有名
	明:	(27) 明天；(67) 發明
mìng	命:	(46) 革命史；(50) 革命
mò	么:	(19) 什么、怎么样；(31) 这么、为什么、怎么；(32) 那么、怎么办；(46) 什么的；(69) 多(么)
	默:	(64) 默(写)
mǔ	母:	(52) 母亲
mù	目:	(53) 节目；(56) 数目

N

ná	拿:	(33) 拿
nǎ	哪:	(19) 哪；(20) 哪兒、哪里
nà	那:	(13) 那；(20) 那兒、那里；(63) 那么
nán	难:	(31) 难；(43) 困难
	男:	(56) 男
	南:	(61) 南
nɛ	呢:	(27) 呢
nèi	內:	(67) 內容
néng	能:	(26) 能；(61) 能力
nǐ	你:	(13) 你；(15) 你們
nián	年:	(22) 年；(25) 今年；(37) 年級；(55) 去年；(62) 前年、少年先鋒队；(64) 青年
niàn	念:	(21) 念；(71) 紀念
nín	您:	(13) 您
nóng	农:	(53) 农民；(62) 农业；(63) 农村
nǔ	努:	(20) 努力
nuǎn	暖:	(50) 暖和
nǚ	女:	(56) 女；(58) 白毛女、女兒

P

pà	怕:	(57) 怕
pái	排:	(57) 排
pài	派:	(65) 派

páng   旁: (23) 旁边兒
pàng   胖: (69) 胖
pǎo   跑: (52) 跑
péi   培: (70) 培养
péng   朋: (15) 朋友
pī   批: (52) 批評
piān   篇: (57) 篇
pián   便: (52) 便宜
piàn   片: (58) 像片兒 (piānr)
piào   漂: (53) 漂亮
         票: (53) 票
píng   評: (52) 批評
         平: (57) 水平; (67) 和平
pò   迫: (58) 压迫

Q

qī   七: (22) 七
         期: (25) 星期; (27) 上(星期)、下(星期)
qí   騎: (43) 騎
         旗: (61) 旗(子)
qǐ   起: (20) 一起; (28) 起; (40) 对不起; (64) 起来
qì   汽: (33) 汽車
         气: (45) 空气; (49) 天气; (55) 客气
         器: (47) 机器
qiāo   敲: (40) 敲
qiān   鉛: (15) 鉛笔
         千: (56) 千
qián   前: (23) 前边兒; (27) 从前; (34) 以前; (35) 前天; (49) 提前
         錢: (37) 錢
qiǎn   淺: (49, 57) 淺
qiáng   墙: (45) 墙
qiě   且: (43) 幷且; (59) 而且
qīn   亲: (52) 母亲; (62) 父亲; (68) 亲爱
         侵: (67) 侵略
qīng   ·清: (27) 清楚
         青: (64) 青年
         輕: (69) 輕
qíng   情: (31) 事(情); (35) 情况; (62) 热情
         晴: (68) 晴

qǐng 請: (38) 請

qiū 秋: (53) 秋天

qiú 球: (46) 打 (球)、球

求: (68) 要求

qù 去: (20) 去; (56) 去年; (71) 过去

quē 缺: (67) 缺点

què 确: (44) 正确

quán 全: (39) 全面; (52) 完全; (56) 全

quàn 劝: (59) 劝

qún 群: (69) 群众

R

rán 然: (31) 虽然; (46) 当然

ràng 讓: (38, 65) 讓

rè 热: (33) 热; (34) 热烈; (63) 热情; (64) 热爱

rén 人: (13) 人; (19) 人民; (37) 工人; (56) 中华人民共和国; (58) 爱人

rèn 認: (26) 認識; (68) 認为

任: (59) 任务

rēng 扔: (71) 扔

rì 日: (25) 日; (71) 日記

róng 容: (51) 容易; (67) 內容

荣: (69) 光荣

rù 入: (62) 加入; (64) 收入

S

sān 三: (14) 三

sàn 散: (46) 散步; (67) 散 (会)

sè 色: (45) 颜色

shān 山: (58) 山

shàn 善: (63) 改善

shāng 伤: (65) 伤

shàng 上: (23) 上边兒; (27) 上 (星期); (28) 上(課)、上(月); (31) 晚上; (37) 上午; (41) 早上; (46, 68, 70) 上; (70) 領导上; (71) 上海

shāo 燒: (65) 燒

shǎo 少: (14) 少; (22) 多少; (62) 少 (shào) 少年先鋒队

shào 紹: (38) 介紹

shè 舍: (23) 宿舍

	社:	(37) 合作社; (41) 社会主义; (64) 社員;
	設:	(41) 建設
shéi	誰:	(19) 誰
shēn	身:	(39) 身体
	深:	(49, 51) 深
shén	什:	(19) 什么; (31) 为什么; (46) 什么的
shēng	生:	(13) 学生、先生; (29) 生詞; (47) 生产; (58) 生活; (59) 發生, (69) 留学生; (72) 生
	声:	(44) 大声兒
	牲:	(71) 牺牲
shèng	胜:	(63) 胜利
shī	师:	(70) 教师
shí	十:	(22) 十
	时:	(25) 时候兒; (43) 时間; (46) 小时
	識:	(26) 認識
	食:	(50) 食堂; (63) 粮食
	拾:	(69) 收拾
	石:	(71) 石头
shǐ	始:	(28) 开始
	室:	(28) 教室
	史:	(46) 革命史; (59) 历史
shì	是:	(13) 是; (29, 49) 还是; (31) 要是、但是
	事:	(31) 事 (情); (51) 故事
	試:	(44) 試; (62) 考試
	适:	(51) 合适
	世:	(71) 世界
	市:	(69) 城市
	視:	(69) 重視
shōu	收:	(53) 收; (64) 收入; (69) 收拾
shǒu	首:	(35) 首都
	手:	(64) 手
shòu	受:	(58) 受; (65) 接受
	瘦:	(69) 瘦
shū	書:	(13) 書; (23) 圖書館; (31) 書店
	舒:	(40) 舒服
shú	熟:	(44) 熟
shù	树:	(52) 树
	数:	(56) 数目

shuō   說: (21) 說 (話); (29) 小說兒

shuǐ   水: (37) 水菓; (57) 水平; (59) 水、水災; (63) 开 (水)

shuì   睡: (46) 睡、睡覺

sī   思: (17) 有意思; (40) 意思; (65) 思想

sǐ   死: (59) 死

sì   四: (22) 四; (70) 五四

sòng   送: (47) 送; (53) 播送

sū   苏: (19) 苏联

sù   宿: (23) 宿舍

        訴: (29) 告訴

sní   虽: (31) 虽然

suì   岁: (31) 岁; (56) 万岁

suǒ   所: (31) 所以; (50) 所有 (的)

T

tā   他: (13) 他; (15) 他們

        她: (15) 她

        它: (15) 它

tái   台: (34) 台

tài   太: (21) 太

        态: (61) 态度

tán   談: (38) 談

táng   堂: (23) 礼堂; (50) 食堂

        糖: (37) 糖

tǎng   躺: (45) 躺

tǎo   討: (38) 討論

tè   特: (28) 特別; (51) 特点

téng   疼: (39) 疼

tí   題: (29) 問題

        提: (38) 提; (49) 提前; (62) 提高

tǐ   体: (39) 身体; (68) 具体

tì   替: (41) 替

tiān   天: (25) 今天; (25, 51) 天; (27) 明天、昨天; (32) 前天; (49) 天气、冬天; (50) 后天、春天; (53) 夏天、秋天; (71) 天安門

tiáo   条: (61) 条、条件

tiào   跳: (21) 跳(舞); (71) 跳

tiě   鉄: (65) 鉄

tīng   听: (26) 听; (32) 听見

tíng   停: (40) 停

       庭: (62) 家庭

tōng   通: (38) 通知

tóng   同: (15) 同志; (19) 同屋; (35) 同学; (67) 同意

tǒng   統: (70) 傳統

tóu   头: (39) 头; (44) 鐘头; (58) 头髮; (71) 石头

tú   圖: (23) 圖書館

tuán   团: (55) 团結

tuī   推: (55) 推

W

wài   外: (23) 外边兒; (35) 外国; (61) 以外

wán   玩: (31) 玩兒

       完: (32) 完; (49) 完成; (52) 完全

wǎn   晚: (21) 晚; (31) 晚上; (35) 晚飯; (40) 晚会

wàn   万: (56) 万、万岁

wǎng   往: (61) 往

wàng   忘: (34) 忘

       望: (39) 希望

wěi   偉: **(47)** 偉大

wèi   为: (31) 因为、为什么; (41) 为; (68) 認为; (70) 成为

       位: (40) 座位

wén   文: (15) 俄文; (16) 中文; (44) 課文; (51) 文化; (57) 文章; (65) 文献

       聞: (46) 新聞

wèn   問: (29) 問、問題; (64) 訪問

wǒ   我: (13) 我; (15) 我們

wū   屋: (19) 同屋; (45) 屋子

       握: (51) 掌握

wú   无: (46) 无綫电

wǔ   舞: (21) 跳 (舞)

       五: (22) 五; (70) 五四

       午: (34) 下午; (37) 上午

       伍: (56) 队伍

wù   务: (41) 服务; (50) 义务; (59) 任务

       誤: (44) 錯誤

       勿: (55) 勿

       物: (67) 礼物

       悟: (70) 觉悟

X

xī	西:	(26) 东西
	希:	(39) 希望
	吸:	(55) 吸
	牺:	(71) 牺牲
xí	习:	(16) 学习; (22) 練习; (27) 复习; (46) 預习; (51) 习慣
	息:	(28) 休息
	席:	(32) 主席
xǐ	喜:	(20) 喜欢; (58) 喜兒
	洗:	(53) 洗
xì	系:	(26) 沒关系
	戏:	(58) 戏
xià	下:	(23) 下边兒; (17) 下(星期), (28) 下(課); (34) 下午; (40) 下兒; (55) 下(雪); (65) 下
	夏:	(53) 夏天
xiān	先:	(13) 先生; (41) 先; (62) 少年先鋒队
xiàn	現:	(25) 現在
	綫:	(46) 无綫电
	献:	(67) 貢献
xiāng	相:	(55) 互相
	箱:	(61) 箱子
xiǎng	想:	(29) 想; (65) 思想
xiàng	像:	(51) 像; (58) 照 (像)、像片兒
	象:	(64) 印象
	向:	(61) 方向; (71) 向
xiǎo	小:	(14) 小; (29) 小說兒; (43) 小組; (46) 小时; (62) 小学
xiào	校:	(20) 学校; (50) 校园
	笑:	(45) 笑
xiē	些:	(19) 些
xiě	写:	(21) 写; (64) 默(写)、抄(写)
xiè	謝:	(29) 謝謝
xīn	新:	(14) 新; (46) 新聞
	心:	(45) 关心; (68) 信心; (71) 心
xìn	信:	(41) 信; (68) 信心
xīng	星:	(25) 星期; (27) 上(星期)、下(星期)
xíng	行:	(43) 自行車; (52) 旅行; (56) 游行
xǐng	醒:	(65) 醒

xìng	兴:	(20) 高兴; (56) 兴 (xīng) 奋
	幸:	(58) 幸福
xióng	雄:	(71) 英雄
xiū	休:	(28) 休息
	修:	(57) 修理; (69) 修
xiù	袖:	(69) 領袖
xū	須:	(29) 必須
	需:	(50) 需要
xǔ	許:	(39) 也許
xù	續:	(34) 繼續
xuǎn	选:	(65) 选
xué	学:	(13) 学生; (16) 学習; (17) 北京大学; (19) 学; (20) 学校; (35) 同学; (46) 自学; (62) 小学; (65) 医学; (69) 留学生
xuě	雪:	(55) 下(雪)、雪

Y

yā	压:	(58) 压迫
yān	烟:	(55) 烟
	淹:	(59) 淹
yán	顏:	(45) 顏色
	研:	(53) 研究
	严:	(68) 严格
	言:	(51) 語言
yǎn	演:	(35) 开演、演員、演; (46) 表演
yàn	驗:	(38) 經驗
yǎng	养:	(70) 培养
yàng	样:	(19) 怎么样; (37) 样兒; (43) 样子; (51) 一样
yào	要:	(26) 要; (31) 要是; (34) 重要; (50) 需要; (59) 只要; (68) 要 (yāo) 求
	藥:	(39) 藥
yě	也:	(17, 38) 也; (39) 也許
yè	业:	(31) 專业; (47) 工业; (62) 农业、毕业
	叶:	(52) 叶子
	頁:	(62) 頁
yī	一:	(14) 一; (20) 一 (yì) 起; (21) 一 (yí) 定; (37) 一 (yí) 共; (50) 一 (yì) 会兒; (51) 一 (yí) 样; (52) 一 (yì) 塊兒; (62) 一 (yì) 直
	衣:	(43) 衣服; (49) 毛衣
	医:	(39) 医院; (65) 医学

yǐ 椅: (17) 椅子

    已: (28) 已經

    以: (26) 以后; (29) 可以; (31) 所以; (34) 以前; (61) 以外

yì 意: (17) 有意思; (38) 意見; (40) 意思; (44) 注意; (59) 滿意; (67) 願意、同意

    譯: (28) 翻譯

    义: (41) 共产主义、社会主义; (50) 义务; (65) 資本主义

    易: (51) 容易

    宜: (52) 便宜

    亿: (56) 亿

yīn 因: (31) 因为

    音: (44) 發音; (57) 音乐; (68) 語音

yìn 印: (64) 印象

yīng 应: (26) 应該

    英: (70) 英勇; (71) 英雄

yíng 迎: (38) 欢迎

yǐng 影: (20) 电影

yōng 拥: (68) 拥护

yǒng 永: (64) 永远

    勇: (70) 英勇

yòng 用: (26) 用; (67) 利用

yóu 遊: (56) 遊行

yǒu 有: (16) 有; (17) 有意思; (39) 有的; (40) 有名; (50) 所有 (的)

    友: (15) 朋友

yòu 又: (37, 38, 52) 又

yú 愉: (47) 愉快

    于: (68) 对于; (71) 終于

yǔ 語: (27) 語法; (51) 語言; (68) 語音

    雨: (55) 雨

    禹: (59) 大禹

yù 遇: (37) 遇見

    預: (46) 預習

yuán 員: (35) 演員; (64) 社員; (65) 共产党員

    元: (37) 元

    园: (50) 校园; (70) 公园

    原: (68) 原諒

yuǎn 远: (57) 远; (64) 永远

yuàn 院: (39) 医院

願: (67) 願意
yuè 月: (25) 月; (28) 上(月)
乐: (57) 音乐
越: (59) 越…越…
yùn 运: (70) 运动

Z

zá 杂: (17) 杂誌; (51) 复杂
zāi 災: (59) 水災
zài 在: (23) 在; (25) 现在
再: (41, 52) 再
zàn 贊: (71) 贊成
zāng 髒: (57) 髒
zǎo 早: (21) 早; (41) 早上
zào 造: (67) 創造
zé 澤: (32) 毛澤东
zěn 怎: (19) 怎么样; (31) 怎么
zēng 增: (56) 增加
zhǎn 展: (39) 發展; (67) 展覽
zhàn 站: (33) 站
占: (65) 占
战: (67) 战爭
zhāng 張: (14) 張; (47) 緊張
章: (57) 文章
zhǎng 長: (64) 長; (68) 組長; (70) 社長
掌: (34) 鼓掌; (51) 掌握
zhāo 着: (32) 着 (zháo); (45) 着 (zhě); (57) 着急
zhǎo 找: (32, 37) 找
zhào 照: (58) 照(像)
zhě 者: (31) 或者; (70) (劳动)者
zhè 这: (13) 这; (20) 这兒、这里; (31) 这(zèn)么
zhēn 眞: (50) 眞
zhēng 爭: (67) 战爭
zhèng 正: (44) 正、正确、改正
政: (68) 政府
zhī 枝: (15) 枝
知: (19) 知道; (38) 通知
織: (41) 組織; (53) 織
之: (56) …分之…

zhí   直: (53) 一直

zhǐ   紙: (14) 紙

       只: (16) 只; (59) 只要

zhì   志: (15) 同志

       誌: (17) 杂誌

       治: (40) 治

zhōng 中: (13) 中国; (16) 中文; (23) 中间儿; (56) 中华人民共和国

       鐘: (25) 点(鐘); (40) 鐘; (44) 鐘头

       終: (71) 終于

zhǒng 种: (34) 种; (64) 种 (zhòng)

zhòng 重: (34) 重要; (52) 重; (69) 重视

       众: (57) 观众; (69) 群众

zhǔ   主: (32) 主席; (41) 共产主义、社会主义; (58) 地主; (65) 資本主义; (70) 民主、主任

zhù   住: (28) 住

       助: (28) 帮助

       注: (44) 注意

       祝: (68) 祝

zhuān 專: (31) 專业

zhuāng 庄: (59) 庄稼

zhuī 追: (58) 追

zhǔn 准: (38) 准备

zhuō 桌: (17) 桌子

zī   資: (65) 資本主义

zi   子: (16) 本子; (17) 桌子、椅子; (27) 句子; (43) 样子; (45) 屋子; (52) 叶子; (53) 孩子; (61) 箱子; (63) 杯子

zì   字: (19) 名字; (21) 汉字; (26) 字典; (28) 字

       自: (38) 自己; (43) 自行车; (46) 自学

zǒu   走: (34) 走

zú   族: (70) 民族

zǔ   組: (41) 組織; (43) 小組; (68) 組长

       祖: (47) 祖国

zuì   最: (47) 最后; (51) 最; (53) 最近

zuó 昨: (27) 昨天

zuò 作: (16) 工作; (23) 作; (37) 合作社; (63) 合作化

       坐: (33) 坐

       座: (40) 座位; (50) 座

Table of Simplified Characters Placed against Their Original Complicated Forms
(Appendix 3)

(This table contains 425 characters arranged alphabetically.
Those having appeared in the new words columns
are marked with △.)

ai	△爱[愛]	chan	△产[産]	dai	△带[帶]
	碍[礙]	chang	尝[嘗]	dan	担[擔]
ao			偿[償]		胆[膽]
ba	罢[罷]		△厂[廠]	dang	△当[當噹]
bai	摆[擺襬]	chen	陈[陳]		档[檔]
ban	△办[辦]	cheng	称[稱]		△党[黨]
	板[闆]		惩[懲]	dao	△导[導]
bang	△帮[幫]	chi	迟[遲]	deng	灯[燈]
bao	宝[寶]		齿[齒]		邓[鄧]
	△报[報]	chong	冲[衝]	di	敌[敵]
bei	△备[備]		虫[蟲]	dian	淀[澱]
bi	△笔[筆]	chou	丑[醜]		△点[點]
bian	△边[邊]		筹[籌]		△电[電]
	变[變]	chu	△处[處]		垫[墊]
biao	标[標]		触[觸]	dong	冬[鼕]
	△表[錶]		△出[齣]		△东[東]
bie	别[彆]		△础[礎]		△冻[凍]
bin	宾[賓]	chuang	疮[瘡]		栋[棟]
bu	卜[蔔]	ci	辞[辭]		△动[動]
	补[補]	cong	△从[從]	dou	△斗[鬥]
cai	△才[纔]		聪[聰]	du	独[獨]
can	△参[參]		丛[叢]	duan	断[斷]
	惨[慘]	cuan	窜[竄]	dui	△对[對]
	蚕[蠶]	da	达[達]		△队[隊]

dun	吨〔噸〕	hua	△画〔畫〕		△阶〔階〕
duo	夺〔奪〕		△划〔劃〕		△节〔節〕
er	尔〔爾〕		△华〔華〕	jin	尽〔盡儘〕
fan	范〔範〕	huai	怀〔懷〕		△紧〔緊〕
	矾〔礬〕		△坏〔壞〕		仅〔僅〕
fei	△飞〔飛〕	huan	△欢〔歡〕		△进〔進〕
fen	△奋〔奮〕		环〔環〕	jing	惊〔驚〕
	粪〔糞〕		△还〔還〕		竞〔競〕
	坟〔墳〕		△会〔會〕	jiu	△旧〔舊〕
feng	丰〔豐〕	hui	秽〔穢〕	ju	△举〔舉〕
fu	妇〔婦〕	huo	伙〔夥〕		△剧〔劇〕
	△复〔復〕		获〔獲穫〕		△据〔據〕
	〔複〕	ji	△几〔幾〕		惧〔懼〕
	〔覆〕		△机〔機〕	juan	卷〔捲〕
	麸〔麩〕		击〔擊〕	jue	△觉〔覺〕
gai	盖〔蓋〕		际〔際〕	kai	△开〔開〕
gan	△干〔幹乾〕		剂〔劑〕	ke	△克〔剋〕
	△赶〔趕〕		济〔濟〕	ken	垦〔墾〕
ge	△个〔個〕		挤〔擠〕		悬〔懸〕
gong	巩〔鞏〕		△积〔積〕	kua	夸〔誇〕
gou	沟〔溝〕	jia	家〔傢〕	kuang	矿〔礦〕
	构〔構〕		价〔價〕	kui	亏〔虧〕
gu	谷〔穀〕		夹〔夾〕	kun	困〔睏〕
gua	△刮〔颳〕	jian	艰〔艱〕	kuo	扩〔擴〕
guan	△关〔關〕		荐〔薦〕	la	腊〔臘〕
	△观〔觀〕		△坚〔堅〕	lai	△来〔來〕
guang	△广〔廣〕		歼〔殲〕	lan	兰〔蘭〕
gui	归〔歸〕		监〔監〕		拦〔攔〕
	龟〔龜〕		茧〔繭〕		栏〔欄〕
guo	△过〔過〕	jiang	姜〔薑〕		烂〔爛〕
	△国〔國〕		△将〔將〕	lao	△劳〔勞〕
han	△汉〔漢〕		奖〔獎〕		痨〔癆〕
hao	△号〔號〕		浆〔漿〕	le	△乐〔樂〕
hou	△后〔後〕		桨〔槳〕	lei	类〔類〕
hu	△护〔護〕		酱〔醬〕		累〔纍〕
	壶〔壺〕	jiao	胶〔膠〕	li	△里〔裏〕
	沪〔滬〕	jie	借〔藉〕		△礼〔禮〕

	丽[麗]		麦[麥]		窍[竅]
	厉[厲]	man	蛮[蠻]	qie	窃[竊]
	励[勵]	mei	霉[黴]	qin	△亲[親]
	离[離]	meng	蒙[濛]		寝[寢]
	△历[曆歷]		[懞]	qing	庆[慶]
	隶[隸]		[矇]	qiong	穷[窮]
lia	俩[倆]		梦[夢]	qiu	秋[鞦]
lian	帘[簾]	mi	弥[彌瀰]	qu	区[區]
	△联[聯]	mian	面[麵]		趋[趨]
	恋[戀]	miao	庙[廟]	quan	权[權]
	怜[憐]	mie	灭[滅]		△劝[勸]
liang	粮[糧]		蔑[衊]	que	△确[確]
	△两[兩]	mo	么[麼]	rao	扰[擾]
liao	△了[瞭]	mu	亩[畝]	re	△热[熱]
	疗[療]	nan	△难[難]	rong	△荣[榮]
	辽[遼]	nao	恼[惱]	sa	洒[灑]
lie	猎[獵]		脑[腦]	san	伞[傘]
lin	临[臨]	ni	拟[擬]	sang	丧[喪]
	邻[鄰]	ning	宁[寧]	sao	扫[掃]
ling	灵[靈]	nong	△农[農]	se	啬[嗇]
	龄[齡]	ou	欧[歐]	sha	杀[殺]
	岭[嶺]	pan	盘[盤]	shai	晒[曬]
liu	刘[劉]	pi	辟[闢]	shang	△伤[傷]
	浏[瀏]	ping	苹[蘋]	she	舍[捨]
long	龙[龍]	pu	朴[樸]	shen	沈[瀋]
lou	△楼[樓]		扑[撲]		审[審]
lu	录[錄]	qi	齐[齊]		渗[滲]
	陆[陸]		△气[氣]	sheng	△声[聲]
	虏[虜]	qian	千[韆]		△胜[勝]
	卤[鹵滷]		迁[遷]	shi	湿[濕]
luan	乱[亂]		签[簽籤]		△适[適]
luo	罗[羅囉]		牵[牽]		△时[時]
lü	屡[屢]	qiang	△墙[墻]		实[實]
	虑[慮]		蔷[薔]		势[勢]
	滤[濾]	qiao	乔[喬]		△师[師]
mai	迈[邁]		侨[僑]	shou	寿[壽]
	△买[買]		桥[橋]		兽[獸]
	△卖[賣]		壳[殼]	shu	△数[數]

	术〔術〕		△戏〔戲〕		△亿〔億〕
	△树〔樹〕	xia	吓〔嚇〕		忆〔憶〕
shuai	帅〔帥〕		虾〔蝦〕	yin	隐〔隱〕
shuang	双〔雙〕	xian	△献〔獻〕		阴〔陰〕
sui	△虽〔雖〕		咸〔鹹〕	ying	蝇〔蠅〕
	随〔隨〕		显〔顯〕		△应〔應〕
	△岁〔歲〕		宪〔憲〕		营〔營〕
song	松〔鬆〕		县〔縣〕	yong	△拥〔擁〕
su	△苏〔蘇嗉〕	xiang	向〔嚮〕		佣〔傭〕
	肃〔肅〕		响〔響〕		踊〔踴〕
sun	孙〔孫〕		乡〔鄉〕	you	优〔優〕
tai	△态〔態〕	xie	协〔協〕		犹〔猶〕
	△台〔臺〕		△写〔寫〕		邮〔郵〕
	〔檯〕		胁〔脅〕	yu	余〔餘〕
	〔颱〕		泻〔瀉〕		御〔禦〕
tan	摊〔攤〕	xin	衅〔釁〕		吁〔籲〕
	滩〔灘〕	xing	△兴〔興〕		郁〔鬱〕
	瘫〔癱〕	xuan	△选〔選〕		与〔與〕
teng	誊〔謄〕		旋〔鏇〕		誉〔譽〕
ti	△体〔體〕		悬〔縣〕		屿〔嶼〕
tiao	△条〔條〕	xue	△学〔學〕	yuan	△远〔遠〕
tie	△鉄〔鐵〕	xun	寻〔尋〕		△园〔園〕
ting	△听〔聽〕		逊〔遜〕	yue	跃〔躍〕
	厅〔廳〕	ya	△压〔壓〕	yun	云〔雲〕
tou	△头〔頭〕	yan	艳〔艷〕		△运〔運〕
tuan	△团〔團糰〕		△严〔嚴〕	za	△杂〔雜〕
wa	袜〔襪〕		盐〔鹽〕	zao	灶〔竈〕
	洼〔窪〕	yang	△养〔養〕		枣〔棗〕
wan	△万〔萬〕		痒〔癢〕	zhai	斋〔齋〕
	弯〔彎〕		△样〔樣〕	zhan	△战〔戰〕
wei	△为〔為〕		阳〔陽〕		毡〔氈〕
	伪〔偽〕	ye	△叶〔葉〕	zhao	赵〔趙〕
wen	稳〔穩〕		爷〔爺〕	zhe	△这〔這〕
wu	△务〔務〕		△业〔業〕		折〔摺〕
	恶〔惡噁〕	yi	△医〔醫〕	zheng	征〔徵〕
	△无〔無〕		△义〔義〕		症〔癥〕
xi	△牺〔犧〕		仪〔儀〕		証〔證〕
	△系〔係繫〕		艺〔藝〕		郑〔鄭〕

zhi		zhong			
	△只〔祇隻〕	zhong	△种〔種〕		装〔裝〕
	帜〔幟〕		△众〔衆〕		妆〔妝〕
	职〔職〕	zhu	朱〔硃〕		状〔狀〕
	致〔緻〕		筑〔築〕	zhun	△准〔準〕
	制〔製〕		烛〔燭〕	zong	总〔總〕
	执〔執〕	zhuang	△庄〔莊〕	zuo	凿〔鑿〕
	滞〔滯〕		壮〔壯〕		

Rules of the Character-Combination in Writing
(Appendix 4)

(1) The syllables of a polysyllabic word are combined together. e. g.

他　喜欢　听　無綫电.

When a word is composed of four or more than four syllables, they may be written in separate sets, if possible, so
that the phonetic spelling will not be too long for the student
to recognize. e. g.

北京　大学

The name and surname of a person are written together,
but the word denoting one's title must be written separately
from the name. e. g.

毛澤东
毛　主席
毛澤东　同志

(2) The demonstrative pronoun or the numeral is written
together with the measure word. e. g.

一本　書
这張　画兒

When a demonstrative pronoun, a numeral and a measure
word happen to come together, the demonstrative pronoun
stands alone. e. g.

这　一本　書

(3) When a noun, pronoun or adjective is used as adjec-

tive modifier and if it takes a structural particle 的, they are written together. e. g.

学校的　圖書館
我們的　宿舍
很　好看的　花兒

If the adjective modifier is composed of a verb or verbal construction, the structural particle 的 stands alone. e. g.

去　的　人
教　中文　的　先生
他　買　的　東西

(4) The structural particle 地 is always written together with the adverbial modifier. e. g.

愉快地　工作
高高兴兴地　学習

(5) The structural particle 得 is always placed together with the preceding verb (or adjective). e. g.

他　走得　快.

(6) The verb and its resultative complement are placed together. e. g.

我　吃完　晚飯　來.

The directional complement is also placed together with the verb, but they must be written separately, if there is an object between them. e. g.

我　六点　回来.
他　想　回　家　去.
先生　走進來　了.
他　拿出　一本　書　来.

(7) The verb and its potential complement are placed together e. g.

你　<u>看得見</u>　<u>看不見</u>?

(8) The verb and its suffix are placed together. e. g.

他　<u>看过</u>　那个　电影.

先生　<u>問了</u>　他　又　問　我.

車上　<u>坐着</u>　两个　孩子.

(9) The modal particle stands alone at the end of a sentence. e. g.

他　走　了.

先生　上　課　呢.

(10) The monosyllabic word of locality is placed together
with the preceding element, but the polysyllabic word of locality must stand by itself. e. g.

<u>屋子里</u>　暖和.

屋子　<u>里边兒</u>　很　热.

A CATALOG OF SELECTED
DOVER BOOKS
IN ALL FIELDS OF INTEREST

A CATALOG OF SELECTED DOVER
BOOKS IN ALL FIELDS OF INTEREST

CONCERNING THE SPIRITUAL IN ART, Wassily Kandinsky. Pioneering work by father of abstract art. Thoughts on color theory, nature of art. Analysis of earlier masters. 12 illustrations. 80pp. of text. 5⅜ × 8½. 23411-8 Pa. $3.95

ANIMALS: 1,419 Copyright-Free Illustrations of Mammals, Birds, Fish, Insects, etc., Jim Harter (ed.). Clear wood engravings present, in extremely lifelike poses, over 1,000 species of animals. One of the most extensive pictorial sourcebooks of its kind. Captions. Index. 284pp. 9 × 12. 23766-4 Pa. $10.95

CELTIC ART: The Methods of Construction, George Bain. Simple geometric techniques for making Celtic interlacements, spirals, Kells-type initials, animals, humans, etc. Over 500 illustrations. 160pp. 9 × 12. (USO) 22923-8 Pa. $8.95

AN ATLAS OF ANATOMY FOR ARTISTS, Fritz Schider. Most thorough reference work on art anatomy in the world. Hundreds of illustrations, including selections from works by Vesalius, Leonardo, Goya, Ingres, Michelangelo, others. 593 illustrations. 192pp. 7⅛ × 10¼. 20241-0 Pa. $8.95

CELTIC HAND STROKE-BY-STROKE (Irish Half-Uncial from "The Book of Kells"): An Arthur Baker Calligraphy Manual, Arthur Baker. Complete guide to creating each letter of the alphabet in distinctive Celtic manner. Covers hand position, strokes, pens, inks, paper, more. Illustrated. 48pp. 8¼ × 11. 24336-2 Pa. $3.95

EASY ORIGAMI, John Montroll. Charming collection of 32 projects (hat, cup, pelican, piano, swan, many more) specially designed for the novice origami hobbyist. Clearly illustrated easy-to-follow instructions insure that even beginning papercrafters will achieve successful results. 48pp. 8¼ × 11. 27298-2 Pa. $2.95

THE COMPLETE BOOK OF BIRDHOUSE CONSTRUCTION FOR WOOD-WORKERS, Scott D. Campbell. Detailed instructions, illustrations, tables. Also data on bird habitat and instinct patterns. Bibliography. 3 tables. 63 illustrations in 15 figures. 48pp. 5¼ × 8½. 24407-5 Pa. $1.95

BLOOMINGDALE'S ILLUSTRATED 1886 CATALOG: Fashions, Dry Goods and Housewares, Bloomingdale Brothers. Famed merchants' extremely rare catalog depicting about 1,700 products: clothing, housewares, firearms, dry goods, jewelry, more. Invaluable for dating, identifying vintage items. Also, copyright-free graphics for artists, designers. Co-published with Henry Ford Museum & Greenfield Village. 160pp. 8¼ × 11. 25780-0 Pa. $8.95

HISTORIC COSTUME IN PICTURES, Braun & Schneider. Over 1,450 costumed figures in clearly detailed engravings—from dawn of civilization to end of 19th century. Captions. Many folk costumes. 256pp. 8⅜ × 11¾. 23150-X Pa. $10.95

STICKLEY CRAFTSMAN FURNITURE CATALOGS, Gustav Stickley and L. & J. G. Stickley. Beautiful, functional furniture in two authentic catalogs from 1910. 594 illustrations, including 277 photos, show settles, rockers, armchairs, reclining chairs, bookcases, desks, tables. 183pp. 6½ × 9¼. 23838-5 Pa. $8.95

AMERICAN LOCOMOTIVES IN HISTORIC PHOTOGRAPHS: 1858 to 1949, Ron Ziel (ed.). A rare collection of 126 meticulously detailed official photographs, called "builder portraits," of American locomotives that majestically chronicle the rise of steam locomotive power in America. Introduction. Detailed captions. xi + 129pp. 9 × 12. 27393-8 Pa. $12.95

AMERICA'S LIGHTHOUSES: An Illustrated History, Francis Ross Holland, Jr. Delightfully written, profusely illustrated fact-filled survey of over 200 American lighthouses since 1716. History, anecdotes, technological advances, more. 240pp. 8 × 10¾. 25576-X Pa. $10.95

TOWARDS A NEW ARCHITECTURE, Le Corbusier. Pioneering manifesto by founder of "International School." Technical and aesthetic theories, views of industry, economics, relation of form to function, "mass-production split" and much more. Profusely illustrated. 320pp. 6⅛ × 9¼. (USO) 25023-7 Pa. $8.95

HOW THE OTHER HALF LIVES, Jacob Riis. Famous journalistic record, exposing poverty and degradation of New York slums around 1900, by major social reformer. 100 striking and influential photographs. 233pp. 10 × 7⅞. 22012-5 Pa $10.95

FRUIT KEY AND TWIG KEY TO TREES AND SHRUBS, William M. Harlow. One of the handiest and most widely used identification aids. Fruit key covers 120 deciduous and evergreen species; twig key 160 deciduous species. Easily used. Over 300 photographs. 126pp. 5⅜ × 8½. 20511-8 Pa. $2.95

COMMON BIRD SONGS, Dr. Donald J. Borror. Songs of 60 most common U.S. birds: robins, sparrows, cardinals, bluejays, finches, more—arranged in order of increasing complexity. Up to 9 variations of songs of each species. Cassette and manual 99911-4 $8.95

ORCHIDS AS HOUSE PLANTS, Rebecca Tyson Northen. Grow cattleyas and many other kinds of orchids—in a window, in a case, or under artificial light. 63 illustrations. 148pp. 5⅜ × 8½. 23261-1 Pa. $3.95

MONSTER MAZES, Dave Phillips. Masterful mazes at four levels of difficulty. Avoid deadly perils and evil creatures to find magical treasures. Solutions for all 32 exciting illustrated puzzles. 48pp. 8¼ × 11. 26005-4 Pa. $2.95

MOZART'S DON GIOVANNI (DOVER OPERA LIBRETTO SERIES), Wolfgang Amadeus Mozart. Introduced and translated by Ellen H. Bleiler. Standard Italian libretto, with complete English translation. Convenient and thoroughly portable—an ideal companion for reading along with a recording or the performance itself. Introduction. List of characters. Plot summary. 121pp. 5¼ × 8½. 24944-1 Pa. $2.95

TECHNICAL MANUAL AND DICTIONARY OF CLASSICAL BALLET, Gail Grant. Defines, explains, comments on steps, movements, poses and concepts. 15-page pictorial section. Basic book for student, viewer. 127pp. 5⅜ × 8½. 21843-0 Pa. $3.95

BRASS INSTRUMENTS: Their History and Development, Anthony Baines. Authoritative, updated survey of the evolution of trumpets, trombones, bugles, cornets, French horns, tubas and other brass wind instruments. Over 140 illustrations and 48 music examples. Corrected and updated by author. New preface. Bibliography. 320pp. 5⅜ × 8½. 27574-4 Pa. $9.95

HOLLYWOOD GLAMOR PORTRAITS, John Kobal (ed.). 145 photos from 1926–49. Harlow, Gable, Bogart, Bacall; 94 stars in all. Full background on photographers, technical aspects. 160pp. 8⅜ × 11¼. 23352-9 Pa. $9.95

MAX AND MORITZ, Wilhelm Busch. Great humor classic in both German and English. Also 10 other works: "Cat and Mouse," "Plisch and Plumm," etc. 216pp. 5⅜ × 8½. 20181-3 Pa. $5.95

THE RAVEN AND OTHER FAVORITE POEMS, Edgar Allan Poe. Over 40 of the author's most memorable poems: "The Bells," "Ulalume," "Israfel," "To Helen," "The Conqueror Worm," "Eldorado," "Annabel Lee," many more. Alphabetic lists of titles and first lines. 64pp. 5³⁄₁₆ × 8¼. 26685-0 Pa. $1.00

SEVEN SCIENCE FICTION NOVELS, H. G. Wells. The standard collection of the great novels. Complete, unabridged. First Men in the Moon, Island of Dr. Moreau, War of the Worlds, Food of the Gods, Invisible Man, Time Machine, In the Days of the Comet. Total of 1,015pp. 5⅜ × 8½. (USO) 20264-X Clothbd. $29.95

AMULETS AND SUPERSTITIONS, E. A. Wallis Budge. Comprehensive discourse on origin, powers of amulets in many ancient cultures: Arab, Persian, Babylonian, Assyrian, Egyptian, Gnostic, Hebrew, Phoenician, Syriac, etc. Covers cross, swastika, crucifix, seals, rings, stones, etc. 584pp. 5⅜ × 8½. 23573-4 Pa. $10.95

RUSSIAN STORIES/PYCCKNE PACCKA3bl: A Dual-Language Book, edited by Gleb Struve. Twelve tales by such masters as Chekhov, Tolstoy, Dostoevsky, Pushkin, others. Excellent word-for-word English translations on facing pages, plus teaching and study aids, Russian/English vocabulary, biographical/critical introductions, more. 416pp. 5⅜ × 8½. 26244-8 Pa. $7.95

PHILADELPHIA THEN AND NOW: 60 Sites Photographed in the Past and Present, Kenneth Finkel and Susan Oyama. Rare photographs of City Hall, Logan Square, Independence Hall, Betsy Ross House, other landmarks juxtaposed with contemporary views. Captures changing face of historic city. Introduction. Captions. 128pp. 8¼ × 11. 25790-8 Pa. $9.95

AIA ARCHITECTURAL GUIDE TO NASSAU AND SUFFOLK COUNTIES, LONG ISLAND, The American Institute of Architects, Long Island Chapter, and the Society for the Preservation of Long Island Antiquities. Comprehensive, well-researched and generously illustrated volume brings to life over three centuries of Long Island's great architectural heritage. More than 240 photographs with authoritative, extensively detailed captions. 176pp. 8¼ × 11. 26946-9 Pa. $14.95

NORTH AMERICAN INDIAN LIFE: Customs and Traditions of 23 Tribes, Elsie Clews Parsons (ed.). 27 fictionalized essays by noted anthropologists examine religion, customs, government, additional facets of life among the Winnebago, Crow, Zuni, Eskimo, other tribes. 480pp. 6⅛ × 9¼. 27377-6 Pa. $10.95

FRANK LLOYD WRIGHT'S HOLLYHOCK HOUSE, Donald Hoffmann. Lavishly illustrated, carefully documented study of one of Wright's most controversial residential designs. Over 120 photographs, floor plans, elevations, etc. Detailed perceptive text by noted Wright scholar. Index. 128pp. 9¼ × 10¾.
27133-1 Pa. $10.95

THE MALE AND FEMALE FIGURE IN MOTION: 60 Classic Photographic Sequences, Eadweard Muybridge. 60 true-action photographs of men and women walking, running, climbing, bending, turning, etc., reproduced from rare 19th-century masterpiece. vi + 121pp. 9 × 12. 24745-7 Pa. $10.95

1001 QUESTIONS ANSWERED ABOUT THE SEASHORE, N. J. Berrill and Jacquelyn Berrill. Queries answered about dolphins, sea snails, sponges, starfish, fishes, shore birds, many others. Covers appearance, breeding, growth, feeding, much more. 305pp. 5¼ × 8¼. 23366-9 Pa. $7.95

GUIDE TO OWL WATCHING IN NORTH AMERICA, Donald S. Heintzelman. Superb guide offers complete data and descriptions of 19 species: barn owl, screech owl, snowy owl, many more. Expert coverage of owl-watching equipment, conservation, migrations and invasions, etc. Guide to observing sites. 84 illustrations. xiii + 193pp. 5⅜ × 8½. 27344-X Pa. $7.95

MEDICINAL AND OTHER USES OF NORTH AMERICAN PLANTS: A Historical Survey with Special Reference to the Eastern Indian Tribes, Charlotte Erichsen-Brown. Chronological historical citations document 500 years of usage of plants, trees, shrubs native to eastern Canada, northeastern U.S. Also complete identifying information. 343 illustrations. 544pp. 6½ × 9¼. 25951-X Pa. $12.95

STORYBOOK MAZES, Dave Phillips. 23 stories and mazes on two-page spreads: Wizard of Oz, Treasure Island, Robin Hood, etc. Solutions. 64pp. 8¼ × 11.
23628-5 Pa. $2.95

NEGRO FOLK MUSIC, U.S.A., Harold Courlander. Noted folklorist's scholarly yet readable analysis of rich and varied musical tradition. Includes authentic versions of over 40 folk songs. Valuable bibliography and discography. xi + 324pp. 5⅜ × 8½. 27350-4 Pa. $7.95

MOVIE-STAR PORTRAITS OF THE FORTIES, John Kobal (ed.). 163 glamor, studio photos of 106 stars of the 1940s: Rita Hayworth, Ava Gardner, Marlon Brando, Clark Gable, many more. 176pp. 8⅜ × 11¼. 23546-7 Pa. $10.95

BENCHLEY LOST AND FOUND, Robert Benchley. Finest humor from early 30s, about pet peeves, child psychologists, post office and others. Mostly unavailable elsewhere. 73 illustrations by Peter Arno and others. 183pp. 5⅜ × 8½.
22410-4 Pa. $4.95

YEKL and THE IMPORTED BRIDEGROOM AND OTHER STORIES OF YIDDISH NEW YORK, Abraham Cahan. Film Hester Street based on Yekl (1896). Novel, other stories among first about Jewish immigrants on N.Y.'s East Side. 240pp. 5⅜ × 8½. 22427-9 Pa. $5.95

SELECTED POEMS, Walt Whitman. Generous sampling from *Leaves of Grass*. Twenty-four poems include "I Hear America Singing," "Song of the Open Road," "I Sing the Body Electric," "When Lilacs Last in the Dooryard Bloom'd," "O Captain! My Captain!"—all reprinted from an authoritative edition. Lists of titles and first lines. 128pp. 5³⁄₁₆ × 8¼. 26878-0 Pa. $1.00

THE BEST TALES OF HOFFMANN, E. T. A. Hoffmann. 10 of Hoffmann's most important stories: "Nutcracker and the King of Mice," "The Golden Flowerpot," etc. 458pp. 5⅜ × 8½. 21793-0 Pa. $8.95

FROM FETISH TO GOD IN ANCIENT EGYPT, E. A. Wallis Budge. Rich detailed survey of Egyptian conception of "God" and gods, magic, cult of animals, Osiris, more. Also, superb English translations of hymns and legends. 240 illustrations. 545pp. 5⅜ × 8½. 25803-3 Pa. $10.95

FRENCH STORIES/CONTES FRANÇAIS: A Dual-Language Book, Wallace Fowlie. Ten stories by French masters, Voltaire to Camus: "Micromegas" by Voltaire; "The Atheist's Mass" by Balzac; "Minuet" by de Maupassant; "The Guest" by Camus, six more. Excellent English translations on facing pages. Also French-English vocabulary list, exercises, more. 352pp. 5⅜ × 8½. 26443-2 Pa. $8.95

CHICAGO AT THE TURN OF THE CENTURY IN PHOTOGRAPHS: 122 Historic Views from the Collections of the Chicago Historical Society, Larry A. Viskochil. Rare large-format prints offer detailed views of City Hall, State Street, the Loop, Hull House, Union Station, many other landmarks, circa 1904–1913. Introduction. Captions. Maps. 144pp. 9⅜ × 12¼. 24656-6 Pa. $12.95

OLD BROOKLYN IN EARLY PHOTOGRAPHS, 1865–1929, William Lee Younger. Luna Park, Gravesend race track, construction of Grand Army Plaza, moving of Hotel Brighton, etc. 157 previously unpublished photographs. 165pp. 8⅞ × 11¾. 23587-4 Pa. $12.95

THE MYTHS OF THE NORTH AMERICAN INDIANS, Lewis Spence. Rich anthology of the myths and legends of the Algonquins, Iroquois, Pawnees and Sioux, prefaced by an extensive historical and ethnological commentary. 36 illustrations. 480pp. 5⅜ × 8½. 25967-6 Pa. $8.95

AN ENCYCLOPEDIA OF BATTLES: Accounts of Over 1,560 Battles from 1479 B.C. to the Present, David Eggenberger. Essential details of every major battle in recorded history from the first battle of Megiddo in 1479 B.C. to Grenada in 1984. List of Battle Maps. New Appendix covering the years 1967–1984. Index. 99 illustrations. 544pp. 6½ × 9¼. 24913-1 Pa. $14.95

SAILING ALONE AROUND THE WORLD, Captain Joshua Slocum. First man to sail around the world, alone, in small boat. One of great feats of seamanship told in delightful manner. 67 illustrations. 294pp. 5⅜ × 8½. 20326-3 Pa. $4.95

ANARCHISM AND OTHER ESSAYS, Emma Goldman. Powerful, penetrating, prophetic essays on direct action, role of minorities, prison reform, puritan hypocrisy, violence, etc. 271pp. 5⅜ × 8½. 22484-8 Pa. $5.95

MYTHS OF THE HINDUS AND BUDDHISTS, Ananda K. Coomaraswamy and Sister Nivedita. Great stories of the epics; deeds of Krishna, Shiva, taken from puranas, Vedas, folk tales; etc. 32 illustrations. 400pp. 5⅜ × 8½. 21759-0 Pa. $8.95

BEYOND PSYCHOLOGY, Otto Rank. Fear of death, desire of immortality, nature of sexuality, social organization, creativity, according to Rankian system. 291pp. 5⅜ × 8½. 20485-5 Pa. $7.95

A THEOLOGICO-POLITICAL TREATISE, Benedict Spinoza. Also contains unfinished Political Treatise. Great classic on religious liberty, theory of government on common consent. R. Elwes translation. Total of 421pp. 5⅜ × 8½. 20249-6 Pa. $7.95

CATALOG OF DOVER BOOKS

MY BONDAGE AND MY FREEDOM, Frederick Douglass. Born a slave, Douglass became outspoken force in antislavery movement. The best of Douglass' autobiographies. Graphic description of slave life. 464pp. 5⅜ × 8½. 22457-0 Pa. $7.95

FOLLOWING THE EQUATOR: A Journey Around the World, Mark Twain. Fascinating humorous account of 1897 voyage to Hawaii, Australia, India, New Zealand, etc. Ironic, bemused reports on peoples, customs, climate, flora and fauna, politics, much more. 197 illustrations. 720pp. 5⅜ × 8½. 26113-1 Pa. $15.95

THE PEOPLE CALLED SHAKERS, Edward D. Andrews. Definitive study of Shakers: origins, beliefs, practices, dances, social organization, furniture and crafts, etc. 33 illustrations. 351pp. 5⅜ × 8½. 21081-2 Pa. $7.95

THE MYTHS OF GREECE AND ROME, H. A. Guerber. A classic of mythology, generously illustrated, long prized for its simple, graphic, accurate retelling of the principal myths of Greece and Rome, and for its commentary on their origins and significance. With 64 illustrations by Michelangelo, Raphael, Titian, Rubens, Canova, Bernini and others. 480pp. 5⅜ × 8½. 27584-1 Pa. $9.95

PSYCHOLOGY OF MUSIC, Carl E. Seashore. Classic work discusses music as a medium from psychological viewpoint. Clear treatment of physical acoustics, auditory apparatus, sound perception, development of musical skills, nature of musical feeling, host of other topics. 88 figures. 408pp. 5⅜ × 8½. 21851-1 Pa. $8.95

THE PHILOSOPHY OF HISTORY, Georg W. Hegel. Great classic of Western thought develops concept that history is not chance but rational process, the evolution of freedom. 457pp. 5⅜ × 8½. 20112-0 Pa. $8.95

THE BOOK OF TEA, Kakuzo Okakura. Minor classic of the Orient: entertaining, charming explanation, interpretation of traditional Japanese culture in terms of tea ceremony. 94pp. 5⅜ × 8½. 20070-1 Pa. $2.95

LIFE IN ANCIENT EGYPT, Adolf Erman. Fullest, most thorough, detailed older account with much not in more recent books, domestic life, religion, magic, medicine, commerce, much more. Many illustrations reproduce tomb paintings, carvings, hieroglyphs, etc. 597pp. 5⅜ × 8½. 22632-8 Pa. $9.95

SUNDIALS, Their Theory and Construction, Albert Waugh. Far and away the best, most thorough coverage of ideas, mathematics concerned, types, construction, adjusting anywhere. Simple, nontechnical treatment allows even children to build several of these dials. Over 100 illustrations. 230pp. 5⅜ × 8½. 22947-5 Pa. $5.95

DYNAMICS OF FLUIDS IN POROUS MEDIA, Jacob Bear. For advanced students of ground water hydrology, soil mechanics and physics, drainage and irrigation engineering, and more. 335 illustrations. Exercises, with answers. 784pp. 6⅛ × 9¼. 65675-6 Pa. $19.95

SONGS OF EXPERIENCE: Facsimile Reproduction with 26 Plates in Full Color, William Blake. 26 full-color plates from a rare 1826 edition. Includes "The Tyger," "London," "Holy Thursday," and other poems. Printed text of poems. 48pp. 5¼ × 7. 24636-1 Pa. $3.95

OLD-TIME VIGNETTES IN FULL COLOR, Carol Belanger Grafton (ed.). Over 390 charming, often sentimental illustrations, selected from archives of Victorian graphics—pretty women posing, children playing, food, flowers, kittens and puppies, smiling cherubs, birds and butterflies, much more. All copyright-free. 48pp. 9¼ × 12¼. 27269-9 Pa. $5.95

PERSPECTIVE FOR ARTISTS, Rex Vicat Cole. Depth, perspective of sky and sea, shadows, much more, not usually covered. 391 diagrams, 81 reproductions of drawings and paintings. 279pp. 5⅜ × 8½. 22487-2 Pa. $6.95

DRAWING THE LIVING FIGURE, Joseph Sheppard. Innovative approach to artistic anatomy focuses on specifics of surface anatomy, rather than muscles and bones. Over 170 drawings of live models in front, back and side views, and in widely varying poses. Accompanying diagrams. 177 illustrations. Introduction. Index. 144pp. 8⅜ × 11¼. 26723-7 Pa. $7.95

GOTHIC AND OLD ENGLISH ALPHABETS: 100 Complete Fonts, Dan X. Solo. Add power, elegance to posters, signs, other graphics with 100 stunning copyright-free alphabets: Blackstone, Dolbey, Germania, 97 more—including many lower-case, numerals, punctuation marks. 104pp. 8⅛ × 11. 24695-7 Pa. $6.95

HOW TO DO BEADWORK, Mary White. Fundamental book on craft from simple projects to five-bead chains and woven works. 106 illustrations. 142pp. 5⅜ × 8. 20697-1 Pa. $4.95

THE BOOK OF WOOD CARVING, Charles Marshall Sayers. Finest book for beginners discusses fundamentals and offers 34 designs. "Absolutely first rate . . . well thought out and well executed."—E. J. Tangerman. 118pp. 7¾ × 10⅝. 23654-4 Pa. $5.95

ILLUSTRATED CATALOG OF CIVIL WAR MILITARY GOODS: Union Army Weapons, Insignia, Uniform Accessories, and Other Equipment, Schuyler, Hartley, and Graham. Rare, profusely illustrated 1846 catalog includes Union Army uniform and dress regulations, arms and ammunition, coats, insignia, flags, swords, rifles, etc. 226 illustrations. 160pp. 9 × 12. 24939-5 Pa. $10.95

WOMEN'S FASHIONS OF THE EARLY 1900s: An Unabridged Republication of "New York Fashions, 1909," National Cloak & Suit Co. Rare catalog of mail-order fashions documents women's and children's clothing styles shortly after the turn of the century. Captions offer full descriptions, prices. Invaluable resource for fashion, costume historians. Approximately 725 illustrations. 128pp. 8⅜ × 11¼. 27276-1 Pa. $10.95

THE 1912 AND 1915 GUSTAV STICKLEY FURNITURE CATALOGS, Gustav Stickley. With over 200 detailed illustrations and descriptions, these two catalogs are essential reading and reference materials and identification guides for Stickley furniture. Captions cite materials, dimensions and prices. 112pp. 6½ × 9¼. 26676-1 Pa. $9.95

EARLY AMERICAN LOCOMOTIVES, John H. White, Jr. Finest locomotive engravings from early 19th century: historical (1804–74), main-line (after 1870), special, foreign, etc. 147 plates. 142pp. 11⅜ × 8¼. 22772-3 Pa. $8.95

THE TALL SHIPS OF TODAY IN PHOTOGRAPHS, Frank O. Braynard. Lavishly illustrated tribute to nearly 100 majestic contemporary sailing vessels: Amerigo Vespucci, Clearwater, Constitution, Eagle, Mayflower, Sea Cloud, Victory, many more. Authoritative captions provide statistics, background on each ship. 190 black-and-white photographs and illustrations. Introduction. 128pp. 8⅞ × 11¾. 27163-3 Pa. $12.95

EARLY NINETEENTH-CENTURY CRAFTS AND TRADES, Peter Stockham (ed.). Extremely rare 1807 volume describes to youngsters the crafts and trades of the day: brickmaker, weaver, dressmaker, bookbinder, ropemaker, saddler, many more. Quaint prose, charming illustrations for each craft. 20 black-and-white line illustrations. 192pp. 4⅝ × 6. 27293-1 Pa. $4.95

VICTORIAN FASHIONS AND COSTUMES FROM HARPER'S BAZAR, 1867–1898, Stella Blum (ed.). Day costumes, evening wear, sports clothes, shoes, hats, other accessories in over 1,000 detailed engravings. 320pp. 9⅜ × 12¼.
22990-4 Pa. $12.95

GUSTAV STICKLEY, THE CRAFTSMAN, Mary Ann Smith. Superb study surveys broad scope of Stickley's achievement, especially in architecture. Design philosophy, rise and fall of the Craftsman empire, descriptions and floor plans for many Craftsman houses, more. 86 black-and-white halftones. 31 line illustrations. Introduction. 208pp. 6½ × 9¼. 27210-9 Pa. $9.95

THE LONG ISLAND RAIL ROAD IN EARLY PHOTOGRAPHS, Ron Ziel. Over 220 rare photos, informative text document origin (1844) and development of rail service on Long Island. Vintage views of early trains, locomotives, stations, passengers, crews, much more. Captions. 8⅞ × 11¾. 26301-0 Pa. $13.95

THE BOOK OF OLD SHIPS: From Egyptian Galleys to Clipper Ships, Henry B. Culver. Superb, authoritative history of sailing vessels, with 80 magnificent line illustrations. Galley, bark, caravel, longship, whaler, many more. Detailed, informative text on each vessel by noted naval historian. Introduction. 256pp. 5⅜ × 8½. 27332-6 Pa. $6.95

TEN BOOKS ON ARCHITECTURE, Vitruvius. The most important book ever written on architecture. Early Roman aesthetics, technology, classical orders, site selection, all other aspects. Morgan translation. 331pp. 5⅜ × 8½. 20645-9 Pa. $8.95

THE HUMAN FIGURE IN MOTION, Eadweard Muybridge. More than 4,500 stopped-action photos, in action series, showing undraped men, women, children jumping, lying down, throwing, sitting, wrestling, carrying, etc. 390pp. 7⅞ × 10⅝. 20204-6 Clothbd. $24.95

TREES OF THE EASTERN AND CENTRAL UNITED STATES AND CANADA, William M. Harlow. Best one-volume guide to 140 trees. Full descriptions, woodlore, range, etc. Over 600 illustrations. Handy size. 288pp. 4½ × 6⅜. 20395-6 Pa. $4.95

SONGS OF WESTERN BIRDS, Dr. Donald J. Borror. Complete song and call repertoire of 60 western species, including flycatchers, juncoes, cactus wrens, many more—includes fully illustrated booklet. Cassette and manual 99913-0 $8.95

GROWING AND USING HERBS AND SPICES, Milo Miloradovich. Versatile handbook provides all the information needed for cultivation and use of all the herbs and spices available in North America. 4 illustrations. Index. Glossary. 236pp. 5⅜ × 8½. 25058-X Pa. $5.95

BIG BOOK OF MAZES AND LABYRINTHS, Walter Shepherd. 50 mazes and labyrinths in all—classical, solid, ripple, and more—in one great volume. Perfect inexpensive puzzler for clever youngsters. Full solutions. 112pp. 8⅛ × 11.
22951-3 Pa. $3.95

PIANO TUNING, J. Cree Fischer. Clearest, best book for beginner, amateur. Simple repairs, raising dropped notes, tuning by easy method of flattened fifths. No previous skills needed. 4 illustrations. 201pp. 5⅜ × 8½.   23267-0 Pa. $4.95

A SOURCE BOOK IN THEATRICAL HISTORY, A. M. Nagler. Contemporary observers on acting, directing, make-up, costuming, stage props, machinery, scene design, from Ancient Greece to Chekhov. 611pp. 5⅜ × 8½.   20515-0 Pa. $10.95

THE COMPLETE NONSENSE OF EDWARD LEAR, Edward Lear. All nonsense limericks, zany alphabets, Owl and Pussycat, songs, nonsense botany, etc., illustrated by Lear. Total of 320pp. 5⅜ × 8½. (USO)   20167-8 Pa. $5.95

VICTORIAN PARLOUR POETRY: An Annotated Anthology, Michael R. Turner. 117 gems by Longfellow, Tennyson, Browning, many lesser-known poets. "The Village Blacksmith," "Curfew Must Not Ring Tonight," "Only a Baby Small," dozens more, often difficult to find elsewhere. Index of poets, titles, first lines. xxiii + 325pp. 5⅜ × 8¼.   27044-0 Pa. $7.95

DUBLINERS, James Joyce. Fifteen stories offer vivid, tightly focused observations of the lives of Dublin's poorer classes. At least one, "The Dead," is considered a masterpiece. Reprinted complete and unabridged from standard edition. 160pp. 5³⁄₁₆ × 8¼.   26870-5 Pa. $1.00

THE HAUNTED MONASTERY and THE CHINESE MAZE MURDERS, Robert van Gulik. Two full novels by van Gulik, set in 7th-century China, continue adventures of Judge Dee and his companions. An evil Taoist monastery, seemingly supernatural events; overgrown topiary maze hides strange crimes. 27 illustrations. 328pp. 5⅜ × 8½.   23502-5 Pa. $7.95

THE BOOK OF THE SACRED MAGIC OF ABRAMELIN THE MAGE, translated by S. MacGregor Mathers. Medieval manuscript of ceremonial magic. Basic document in Aleister Crowley, Golden Dawn groups. 268pp. 5⅜ × 8½.   23211-5 Pa. $7.95

NEW RUSSIAN-ENGLISH AND ENGLISH-RUSSIAN DICTIONARY, M. A. O'Brien. This is a remarkably handy Russian dictionary, containing a surprising amount of information, including over 70,000 entries. 366pp. 4½ × 6⅛.   20208-9 Pa. $8.95

HISTORIC HOMES OF THE AMERICAN PRESIDENTS, Second, Revised Edition, Irvin Haas. A traveler's guide to American Presidential homes, most open to the public, depicting and describing homes occupied by every American President from George Washington to George Bush. With visiting hours, admission charges, travel routes. 175 photographs. Index. 160pp. 8¼ × 11. 26751-2 Pa. $10.95

NEW YORK IN THE FORTIES, Andreas Feininger. 162 brilliant photographs by the well-known photographer, formerly with *Life* magazine. Commuters, shoppers, Times Square at night, much else from city at its peak. Captions by John von Hartz. 181pp. 9¼ × 10¾.   23585-8 Pa. $12.95

INDIAN SIGN LANGUAGE, William Tomkins. Over 525 signs developed by Sioux and other tribes. Written instructions and diagrams. Also 290 pictographs. 111pp. 6⅛ × 9¼.   22029-X Pa. $3.50

ANATOMY: A Complete Guide for Artists, Joseph Sheppard. A master of figure drawing shows artists how to render human anatomy convincingly. Over 460 illustrations. 224pp. 8⅜ × 11¼. 27279-6 Pa. $9.95

MEDIEVAL CALLIGRAPHY: Its History and Technique, Marc Drogin. Spirited history, comprehensive instruction manual covers 13 styles (ca. 4th century thru 15th). Excellent photographs; directions for duplicating medieval techniques with modern tools. 224pp. 8⅜ × 11¼. 26142-5 Pa. $11.95

DRIED FLOWERS: How to Prepare Them, Sarah Whitlock and Martha Rankin. Complete instructions on how to use silica gel, meal and borax, perlite aggregate, sand and borax, glycerine and water to create attractive permanent flower arrangements. 12 illustrations. 32pp. 5⅜ × 8½. 21802-3 Pa. $1.00

EASY-TO-MAKE BIRD FEEDERS FOR WOODWORKERS, Scott D. Campbell. Detailed, simple-to-use guide for designing, constructing, caring for and using feeders. Text, illustrations for 12 classic and contemporary designs. 96pp. 5⅜ × 8½. 25847-5 Pa. $2.95

OLD-TIME CRAFTS AND TRADES, Peter Stockham. An 1807 book created to teach children about crafts and trades open to them as future careers. It describes in detailed, nontechnical terms 24 different occupations, among them coachmaker, gardener, hairdresser, lacemaker, shoemaker, wheelwright, copper-plate printer, milliner, trunkmaker, merchant and brewer. Finely detailed engravings illustrate each occupation. 192pp. 4⅝ × 6. 27398-9 Pa. $4.95

THE HISTORY OF UNDERCLOTHES, C. Willett Cunnington and Phyllis Cunnington. Fascinating, well-documented survey covering six centuries of English undergarments, enhanced with over 100 illustrations: 12th-century laced-up bodice, footed long drawers (1795), 19th-century bustles, 19th-century corsets for men, Victorian "bust improvers," much more. 272pp. 5⅜ × 8¼. 27124-2 Pa. $9.95

ARTS AND CRAFTS FURNITURE: The Complete Brooks Catalog of 1912, Brooks Manufacturing Co. Photos and detailed descriptions of more than 150 now very collectible furniture designs from the Arts and Crafts movement depict davenports, settees, buffets, desks, tables, chairs, bedsteads, dressers and more, all built of solid, quarter-sawed oak. Invaluable for students and enthusiasts of antiques, Americana and the decorative arts. 80pp. 6½ × 9¼. 27471-3 Pa. $7.95

HOW WE INVENTED THE AIRPLANE: An Illustrated History, Orville Wright. Fascinating firsthand account covers early experiments, construction of planes and motors, first flights, much more. Introduction and commentary by Fred C. Kelly. 76 photographs. 96pp. 8¼ × 11. 25662-6 Pa. $7.95

THE ARTS OF THE SAILOR: Knotting, Splicing and Ropework, Hervey Garrett Smith. Indispensable shipboard reference covers tools, basic knots and useful hitches; handsewing and canvas work, more. Over 100 illustrations. Delightful reading for sea lovers. 256pp. 5⅜ × 8½. 26440-8 Pa. $6.95

FRANK LLOYD WRIGHT'S FALLINGWATER: The House and Its History, Second, Revised Edition, Donald Hoffmann. A total revision—both in text and illustrations—of the standard document on Fallingwater, the boldest, most personal architectural statement of Wright's mature years, updated with valuable new material from the recently opened Frank Lloyd Wright Archives. "Fascinating"—*The New York Times*. 116 illustrations. 128pp. 9¼ × 10¾. 27430-6 Pa. $10.95

PHOTOGRAPHIC SKETCHBOOK OF THE CIVIL WAR, Alexander Gardner. 100 photos taken on field during the Civil War. Famous shots of Manassas, Harper's Ferry, Lincoln, Richmond, slave pens, etc. 244pp. 10⅝ × 8¼.
22731-6 Pa. $9.95

FIVE ACRES AND INDEPENDENCE, Maurice G. Kains. Great back-to-the-land classic explains basics of self-sufficient farming. The one book to get. 95 illustrations. 397pp. 5⅜ × 8½.
20974-1 Pa. $6.95

SONGS OF EASTERN BIRDS, Dr. Donald J. Borror. Songs and calls of 60 species most common to eastern U.S.: warblers, woodpeckers, flycatchers, thrushes, larks, many more in high-quality recording.
Cassette and manual 99912-2 $8.95

A MODERN HERBAL, Margaret Grieve. Much the fullest, most exact, most useful compilation of herbal material. Gigantic alphabetical encyclopedia, from aconite to zedoary, gives botanical information, medical properties, folklore, economic uses, much else. Indispensable to serious reader. 161 illustrations. 888pp. 6½ × 9¼.
2-vol. set. (USO)
Vol. I: 22798-7 Pa. $9.95
Vol. II: 22799-5 Pa. $9.95

HIDDEN TREASURE MAZE BOOK, Dave Phillips. Solve 34 challenging mazes accompanied by heroic tales of adventure. Evil dragons, people-eating plants, bloodthirsty giants, many more dangerous adversaries lurk at every twist and turn. 34 mazes, stories, solutions. 48pp. 8¼ × 11.
24566-7 Pa. $2.95

LETTERS OF W. A. MOZART, Wolfgang A. Mozart. Remarkable letters show bawdy wit, humor, imagination, musical insights, contemporary musical world; includes some letters from Leopold Mozart. 276pp. 5⅜ × 8½.
22859-2 Pa. $6.95

BASIC PRINCIPLES OF CLASSICAL BALLET, Agrippina Vaganova. Great Russian theoretician, teacher explains methods for teaching classical ballet. 118 illustrations. 175pp. 5⅜ × 8½.
22036-2 Pa. $3.95

THE JUMPING FROG, Mark Twain. Revenge edition. The original story of The Celebrated Jumping Frog of Calaveras County, a hapless French translation, and Twain's hilarious "retranslation" from the French. 12 illustrations. 66pp. 5⅜ × 8½.
22686-7 Pa. $3.50

BEST REMEMBERED POEMS, Martin Gardner (ed.). The 126 poems in this superb collection of 19th- and 20th-century British and American verse range from Shelley's "To a Skylark" to the impassioned "Renascence" of Edna St. Vincent Millay and to Edward Lear's whimsical "The Owl and the Pussycat." 224pp. 5⅜ × 8½.
27165-X Pa. $3.95

COMPLETE SONNETS, William Shakespeare. Over 150 exquisite poems deal with love, friendship, the tyranny of time, beauty's evanescence, death and other themes in language of remarkable power, precision and beauty. Glossary of archaic terms. 80pp. 5³⁄₁₆ × 8¼.
26686-9 Pa. $1.00

BODIES IN A BOOKSHOP, R. T. Campbell. Challenging mystery of blackmail and murder with ingenious plot and superbly drawn characters. In the best tradition of British suspense fiction. 192pp. 5⅜ × 8½.
24720-1 Pa. $5.95

THE WIT AND HUMOR OF OSCAR WILDE, Alvin Redman (ed.). More than 1,000 ripostes, paradoxes, wisecracks: Work is the curse of the drinking classes; I can resist everything except temptation; etc. 258pp. 5⅜ × 8½. 20602-5 Pa. $4.95

SHAKESPEARE LEXICON AND QUOTATION DICTIONARY, Alexander Schmidt. Full definitions, locations, shades of meaning in every word in plays and poems. More than 50,000 exact quotations. 1,485pp. 6½ × 9¼. 2-vol. set.
Vol. 1: 22726-X Pa. $15.95
Vol. 2: 22727-8 Pa. $15.95

SELECTED POEMS, Emily Dickinson. Over 100 best-known, best-loved poems by one of America's foremost poets, reprinted from authoritative early editions. No comparable edition at this price. Index of first lines. 64pp. 5³⁄₁₆ × 8¼.
26466-1 Pa. $1.00

CELEBRATED CASES OF JUDGE DEE (DEE GOONG AN), translated by Robert van Gulik. Authentic 18th-century Chinese detective novel; Dee and associates solve three interlocked cases. Led to van Gulik's own stories with same characters. Extensive introduction. 9 illustrations. 237pp. 5⅜ × 8½.
23337-5 Pa. $5.95

THE MALLEUS MALEFICARUM OF KRAMER AND SPRENGER, translated by Montague Summers. Full text of most important witchhunter's "bible," used by both Catholics and Protestants. 278pp. 6⅝ × 10. 22802-9 Pa. $10.95

SPANISH STORIES/CUENTOS ESPAÑOLES: A Dual-Language Book, Angel Flores (ed.). Unique format offers 13 great stories in Spanish by Cervantes, Borges, others. Faithful English translations on facing pages. 352pp. 5⅜ × 8½.
25399-6 Pa. $7.95

THE CHICAGO WORLD'S FAIR OF 1893: A Photographic Record, Stanley Appelbaum (ed.). 128 rare photos show 200 buildings, Beaux-Arts architecture, Midway, original Ferris Wheel, Edison's kinetoscope, more. Architectural emphasis; full text. 116pp. 8¼ × 11. 23990-X Pa. $9.95

OLD QUEENS, N.Y., IN EARLY PHOTOGRAPHS, Vincent F. Seyfried and William Asadorian. Over 160 rare photographs of Maspeth, Jamaica, Jackson Heights, and other areas. Vintage views of DeWitt Clinton mansion, 1939 World's Fair and more. Captions. 192pp. 8⅞ × 11. 26358-4 Pa. $12.95

CAPTURED BY THE INDIANS: 15 Firsthand Accounts, 1750–1870, Frederick Drimmer. Astounding true historical accounts of grisly torture, bloody conflicts, relentless pursuits, miraculous escapes and more, by people who lived to tell the tale. 384pp. 5⅜ × 8½. 24901-8 Pa. $7.95

THE WORLD'S GREAT SPEECHES, Lewis Copeland and Lawrence W. Lamm (eds.). Vast collection of 278 speeches of Greeks to 1970. Powerful and effective models; unique look at history. 842pp. 5⅜ × 8½. 20468-5 Pa. $12.95

THE BOOK OF THE SWORD, Sir Richard F. Burton. Great Victorian scholar/adventurer's eloquent, erudite history of the "queen of weapons"—from prehistory to early Roman Empire. Evolution and development of early swords, variations (sabre, broadsword, cutlass, scimitar, etc.), much more. 336pp. 6⅛ × 9¼. 25434-8 Pa. $8.95

AUTOBIOGRAPHY: The Story of My Experiments with Truth, Mohandas K. Gandhi. Boyhood, legal studies, purification, the growth of the Satyagraha (nonviolent protest) movement. Critical, inspiring work of the man responsible for the freedom of India. 480pp. 5⅜ × 8½. (USO) 24593-4 Pa. $6.95

CELTIC MYTHS AND LEGENDS, T. W. Rolleston. Masterful retelling of Irish and Welsh stories and tales. Cuchulain, King Arthur, Deirdre, the Grail, many more. First paperback edition. 58 full-page illustrations. 512pp. 5⅜ × 8½. 26507-2 Pa. $9.95

THE PRINCIPLES OF PSYCHOLOGY, William James. Famous long course complete, unabridged. Stream of thought, time perception, memory, experimental methods; great work decades ahead of its time. 94 figures. 1,391pp. 5⅜ × 8½. 2-vol. set.
Vol. I: 20381-6 Pa. $12.95
Vol. II: 20382-4 Pa. $12.95

THE WORLD AS WILL AND REPRESENTATION, Arthur Schopenhauer. Definitive English translation of Schopenhauer's life work, correcting more than 1,000 errors, omissions in earlier translations. Translated by E. F. J. Payne. Total of 1,269pp. 5⅜ × 8½. 2-vol. set.
Vol. 1: 21761-2 Pa. $10.95
Vol. 2: 21762-0 Pa. $11.95

MAGIC AND MYSTERY IN TIBET, Madame Alexandra David-Neel. Experiences among lamas, magicians, sages, sorcerers, Bonpa wizards. A true psychic discovery. 32 illustrations. 321pp. 5⅜ × 8½. (USO) 22682-4 Pa. $7.95

THE EGYPTIAN BOOK OF THE DEAD, E. A. Wallis Budge. Complete reproduction of Ani's papyrus, finest ever found. Full hieroglyphic text, interlinear transliteration, word-for-word translation, smooth translation. 533pp. 6½ × 9¼. 21866-X Pa. $9.95

MATHEMATICS FOR THE NONMATHEMATICIAN, Morris Kline. Detailed, college-level treatment of mathematics in cultural and historical context, with numerous exercises. Recommended Reading Lists. Tables. Numerous figures. 641pp. 5⅜ × 8½. 24823-2 Pa. $11.95

THEORY OF WING SECTIONS: Including a Summary of Airfoil Data, Ira H. Abbott and A. E. von Doenhoff. Concise compilation of subsonic aerodynamic characteristics of NACA wing sections, plus description of theory. 350pp. of tables. 693pp. 5⅜ × 8½. 60586-8 Pa. $13.95

THE RIME OF THE ANCIENT MARINER, Gustave Doré, S. T. Coleridge. Doré's finest work; 34 plates capture moods, subtleties of poem. Flawless full-size reproductions printed on facing pages with authoritative text of poem. "Beautiful. Simply beautiful."—*Publisher's Weekly*. 77pp. 9¼ × 12. 22305-1 Pa. $5.95

NORTH AMERICAN INDIAN DESIGNS FOR ARTISTS AND CRAFTSPEOPLE, Eva Wilson. Over 360 authentic copyright-free designs adapted from Navajo blankets, Hopi pottery, Sioux buffalo hides, more. Geometrics, symbolic figures, plant and animal motifs, etc. 128pp. 8⅜ × 11. (EUK) 25341-4 Pa. $6.95

SCULPTURE: Principles and Practice, Louis Slobodkin. Step-by-step approach to clay, plaster, metals, stone; classical and modern. 253 drawings, photos. 255pp. 8⅛ × 11. 22960-2 Pa. $9.95

THE INFLUENCE OF SEA POWER UPON HISTORY, 1660–1783, A. T. Mahan. Influential classic of naval history and tactics still used as text in war colleges. First paperback edition. 4 maps. 24 battle plans. 640pp. 5⅜ × 8½.
25509-3 Pa. $12.95

THE STORY OF THE TITANIC AS TOLD BY ITS SURVIVORS, Jack Winocour (ed.). What it was really like. Panic, despair, shocking inefficiency, and a little heroism. More thrilling than any fictional account. 26 illustrations. 320pp. 5⅜ × 8½.
20610-6 Pa. $7.95

FAIRY AND FOLK TALES OF THE IRISH PEASANTRY, William Butler Yeats (ed.). Treasury of 64 tales from the twilight world of Celtic myth and legend: "The Soul Cages," "The Kildare Pooka," "King O'Toole and his Goose," many more. Introduction and Notes by W. B. Yeats. 352pp. 5⅜ × 8½.
26941-8 Pa. $7.95

BUDDHIST MAHAYANA TEXTS, E. B. Cowell and Others (eds.). Superb, accurate translations of basic documents in Mahayana Buddhism, highly important in history of religions. The Buddha-karita of Asvaghosha, Larger Sukhavativyuha, more. 448pp. 5⅜ × 8½.
25552-2 Pa. $9.95

ONE TWO THREE . . . INFINITY: Facts and Speculations of Science, George Gamow. Great physicist's fascinating, readable overview of contemporary science: number theory, relativity, fourth dimension, entropy, genes, atomic structure, much more. 128 illustrations. Index. 352pp. 5⅜ × 8½.
25664-2 Pa. $7.95

ENGINEERING IN HISTORY, Richard Shelton Kirby, et al. Broad, nontechnical survey of history's major technological advances: birth of Greek science, industrial revolution, electricity and applied science, 20th-century automation, much more. 181 illustrations. ". . . excellent . . ."—Isis. Bibliography. vii + 530pp. 5⅜ × 8¼.
26412-2 Pa. $13.95

Prices subject to change without notice.

Available at your book dealer or write for free catalog to Dept. GI, Dover Publications, Inc., 31 East 2nd St., Mineola, N.Y. 11501. Dover publishes more than 500 books each year on science, elementary and advanced mathematics, biology, music, art, literary history, social sciences and other areas.